Growing Teen Disciples

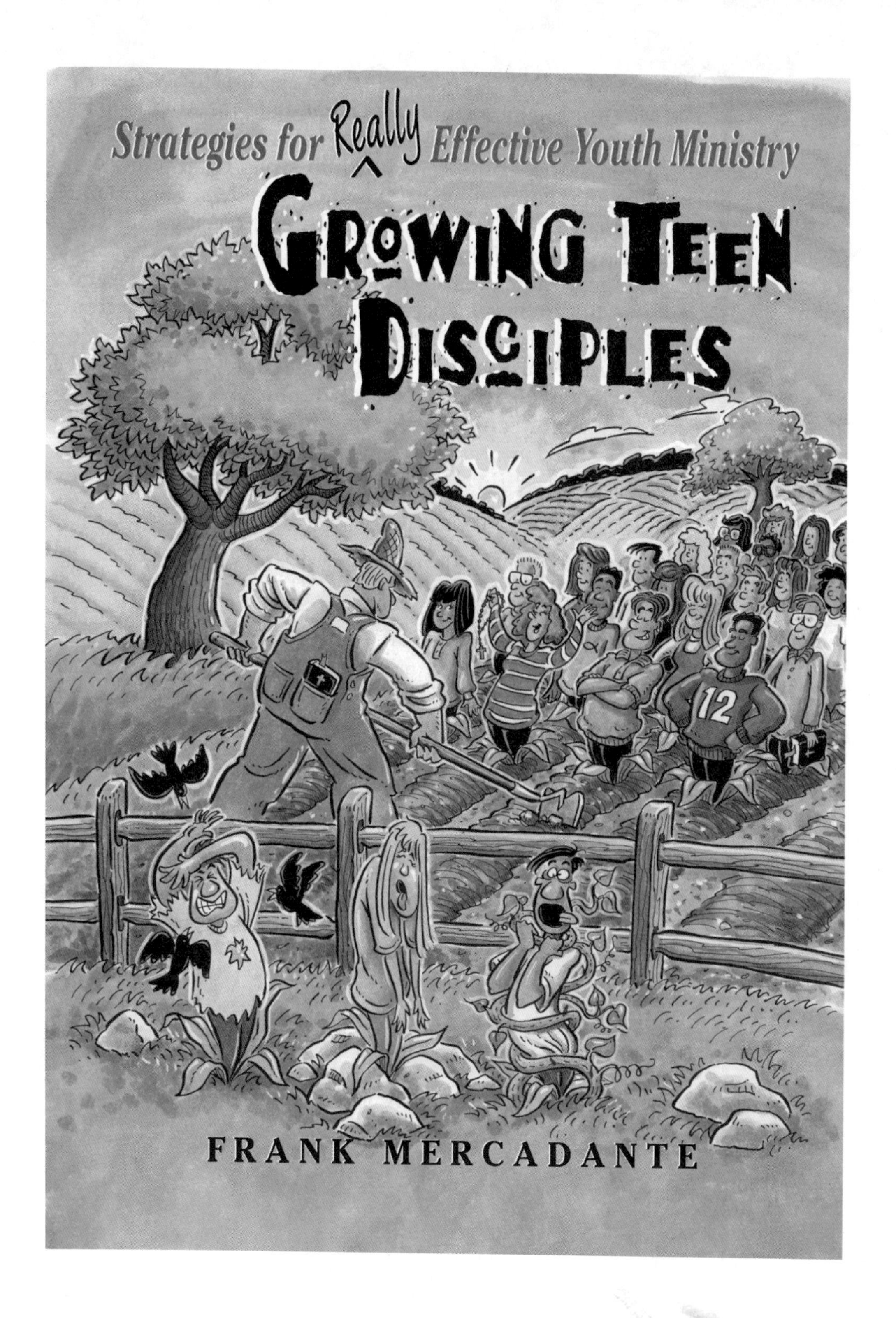

AVE MARIA PRESS Notre Dame, Indiana 46556

FRANK C. MERCADANTE is the director of *Cultivation Ministries,* a not-for-profit corporation founded in 1990 for the purpose of cultivating team-based, comprehensive, and disciple-making Catholic youth ministries by training, resourcing, and supporting adult and teen leaders. Mercadante is a graduate of Wheaton College, where he received a bachelor of arts degree in Christian Education. In addition, he has a master's in pastoral studies from Loyola University, Chicago, and a certificate in advanced studies in youth ministry from the Center for Ministry Development. Mercadante was Director of Youth Ministry at St. John Neumann in St. Charles, Illinois, for ten years, recognized at that time as one of the most successful youth ministry programs in the Chicago area. Mercadante's work in youth evangelization was featured in the book *Parishes That Excel* by Patrick Brennan.

Nihil Obstat: Reverend Monsignor Charles W. McNamee, S.T.L., J.C.L.

Imprimatur: Most Reverend Thomas G. Doran, D.D., J.C.D.

Given at Rockford, IL on 6 February 1998

The *Nihil Obstat* and *Imprimatur* are official declarations that a book or pamphlet is free of doctrinal or moral error. No implication is contained therein that those who have granted the *Nihil Obstat* and *Imprimatur* agree with its contents, opinions, or statements expressed.

International Standard Book Number: 0-87793-652-8

Project Editor: Michael Amodei

Text design by Katherine Robinson Coleman

Cover Illustration by Rex Bohn, Bohn Illustration, St. Charles, IL 60174

Printed and bound in the United States of America.

IN MEMORY

In loving memory of Robert A. Kolschowsky
May God use this book
to make a difference in the lives
of young people like Bobby.

I want to express my gratitude to:
Gerald A. and Karen A. Kolschowsky
Timothy J. and Lucy L. Kolschowsky
Michael J. Kolschowsky

for their generous support
that made this book a reality.

ACKNOWLEDGMENTS

This book would not be possible without the
faithful love and support of
my wife, Diane,
and the support and generosity of
my children,
Sarah, Michael, Rebekah, Angela, Deborah, and Daniel.

I want also to express my gratitude
to all those who have faithfully
and generously supported the
work of Cultivation Ministries,
the "Epaphrus Team" who
faithfully prayed for me while I wrote,
the many parishes that allowed me
to learn from their faith communities,
the many teens who have
taught me so much over the years,
and those whose thoughts and suggestions
increased the quality of this book.

Thank you: Jeff Andrini, Eric Groth, Diane Honeyman,
Jennifer Kuhn, Clover Loos, and Jay Payleitner.

CONTENTS

Section Two: Sowing the Seed 115

Section Three: Growing Mature Disciples 187

PREFACE

During adolescence I ventured as close to church-sponsored events as one does to a person suffering from the effects of the stomach flu. I kept a *safe* distance. Even though I considered church programming as enjoyable as a good toothache, I was, however, thinking about spiritual things. I was interested in God, but not the church. I was asking some of the classic life questions, such as: What is life all about? What is the purpose of it all? Where am I going in my life? If the church had the answers, I wasn't convinced they could communicate them in a way I would understand.

During my senior year in high school some of my friends kept pestering me about attending this retreat. I couldn't imagine its being worth my time. Besides, I didn't want to take a chance on jeopardizing my reputation by getting involved in something that could be labeled as "uncool." Finally, I broke down, gave in, and went.

The retreat weekend was supported by adults, but primarily led by teens. Several people my own age gave what they called "witness" talks, speaking of a Jesus who was actively involved in their lives. It sounded as if they knew Jesus well enough to go out to lunch with him. I had no idea until that weekend that God could be that personal. For the first time that I could name, I felt Christ's love and presence in a deeply profound manner. What I experienced that weekend seemed to address and satisfy the hungers of my heart.

It's been twenty years since that retreat weekend and its effects have not worn off. For starters, I married the girl who gave the first witness talk that weekend. Second, my experience was not a fleeting emotional high. It was the beginning of a relationship with Jesus Christ, which has steadily grown. He continues to touch and transform my life in ways that amaze me. Third, my love for the church of my youth was reignited, and I began to appreciate and value my Catholic heritage again. Finally, I felt called to proclaim the love of God, embodied in the person of Jesus Christ, and wanted to equip others to do the same. Since it was during the rocky times of my own adolescence that God so powerfully impacted my life, I have made teens the focus of my own ministry.

This book is written with teens like I was in mind. It is written for teens who find the church and God boring, outdated, and irrelevant.

There are many spiritually hungry teens who may not find the church's menu very appetizing. In this book I describe a youth ministry approach that is teen-friendly, culturally-relevant, and that creatively expresses the gospel. Often youth ministry is introverted, primarily addressing teens who either want to or have to come to our programs, while forgetting those teens who need to come. This book is intended to help expand our vision in light of Christ's call to minister to "all" people.

Fruitful youth ministry, however, goes beyond such evangelization. Fruitful evangelization is about the whole process of disciple-making. As the USCC statement *Renewing the Vision: A Framework for Catholic Youth Ministry* states, the first goal of youth ministry is "To empower young people to live as disciples of Jesus Christ in our world today." *Growing Teen Disciples* is written with the hope that it will shed further light on what it means to be a teenage disciple of Jesus Christ, and to provide practical strategies for adolescent disciple-making. The process I have outlined in this book—Preparing the Soil, Sowing the Seed, Growing Mature Disciples, and Reaping the Fruit—is proven and practical and will help take us to that goal.

I am forever grateful for the teenage disciples who risked inviting me to the retreat that opened my guarded heart to God's transforming love. My prayer is that God would use this work to encourage and equip youth workers in their continuing efforts to "make disciples of all nations" (Matthew 28:19).

—Frank Mercadante
St. Charles, Illinois
January, 1998

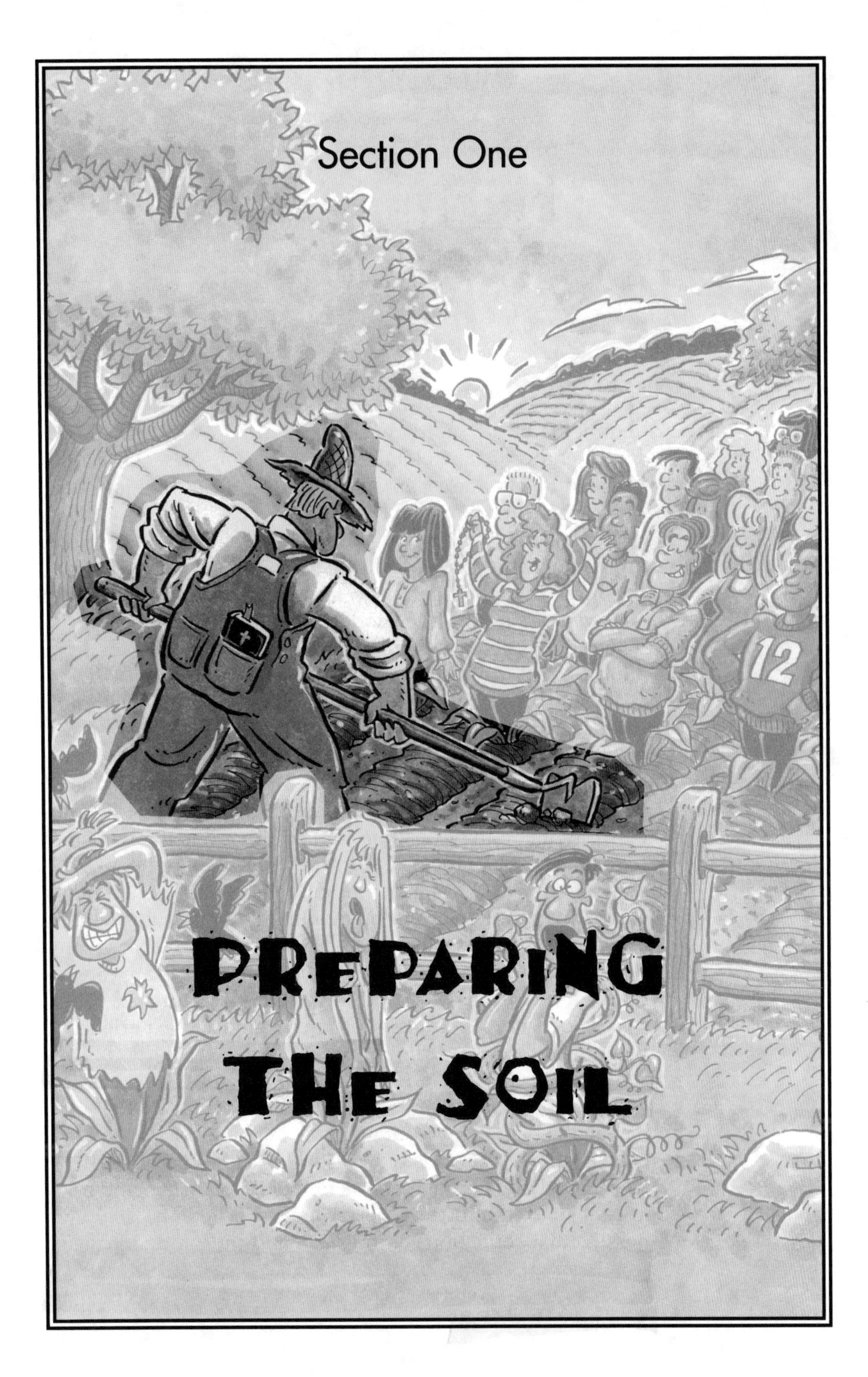
Section One
12
PREPARING
THE SOIL

1

DISCIPLE-MAKING YOUTH MINISTRY

Immediately after his encounter with Jesus, the apostle Philip enthusiastically shared his messianic discovery with his friend Nathaniel. Nathaniel's response was nothing short of a verbal bucket of cold water. Familiar with the reputation of Jesus' hometown, he responded by asking whether or not anything good could come from Nazareth (see John 1:43-46).

Similarly, when someone speaks enthusiastically about *youth ministry*, we, like modern day Nathaniels, might be tempted to reply by asking, "could anything good come from adolescence?"

Just ask your typical adult if he or she would like to go through adolescence again. Among the sane there are few takers. Most are simply thankful they survived the first time! To be honest, youth have been trouble for literally thousands of years. Throughout history a sure-fire marker that one has successfully made the transition into adulthood is the tendency to see the youth of the day as much worse than previous generations, especially one's own! Of course, each generation's elders thought the same of them. But, like a gift fruitcake, this attitude gets successively passed down the line. That is why for many adults the words "teenage discipleship" are categorized with terms like "jumbo shrimp," as oxymorons.

After over fifteen years of youth ministry experience, I would readily concede that adolescence is one of the most difficult periods of life, and that youth ministry is one of the most challenging areas of service in the church today. Yet, I have witnessed many young people over the years who have been exemplary models of Christian discipleship. Historically, our Catholic heritage boasts of childhood saints and adolescent martyrs. Today's youth are no different. They still possess that contagious enthusiasm and refreshing idealism. They are capable of serving Christ in a heroic manner when these natural, developmental characteristics are applied to living out the gospel.

Defining Youth

We must first ask the question, what do we mean by youth? The time span of adolescence has stretched as our techno-society requires more preparation to function fully as an adult. In recent years, adolescence has been stratified into three distinct categories: early adolescence: 12- to 15-year-olds; middle adolescence: 15- to 18-year-olds; late adolescence: 18- to 21-year-olds. Discipleship takes on a different appearance in each of these time frames.[1] This book, unless otherwise noted, will generally focus on the ages of 14- to 18-years-old, or roughly, the senior high years. The general principles, however, are applicable to each of the three categories.

The Need for a New Term

Do you remember when a "mouse" was simply a small, gray rodent that caused you to leap onto kitchen counters? Do you remember when "gay" was a word for happy? Or, "pot" was something you cooked a roast in? Well, sometimes, the meaning of words change. For example, an "enabler" once meant someone who helped others to channel their gifts in a positive way. Redefined by AA and the 12-step movement, the word has come to mean assisting someone in irresponsible behavior. The last thing you want to be today is an "enabler."

Similarly, our culture seems to have redefined the words "Catholic" and "Christian." These wonderful words have lost their powerful, positive impact. To some, a Catholic is someone who is born to Catholic parents. Or, maybe it means a married person with lots of kids. A "Christian" may be thought of as a preachy person who always totes a bible.

We cannot steer the culture toward more accurate definitions. But for the sake of our young people, we do need to find and use words that capture the essence of what it means to follow Jesus. We need to provide for youth a handle on who they can be as Catholics and Christians. They need a worthy, uplifting, and scripturally-sound term that describes the exciting and challenging adventure of serving Christ, without any ambiguous or negative connotations. That very designation could be *disciple*.

It has been only in recent times that the word disciple has made a comeback in Catholic vocabulary. The Second Vatican Council officially reintroduced the term of discipleship into Roman Catholic consciousness.[2]

What Is a Disciple?

Disciples are certainly not unique to Christianity. Discipleship was a common form of training employed in Hellenistic, Roman, and Jewish cultures. The word disciple comes from the Greek term *mathletes*, which means "learner, apprentice, or pupil." A disciple was a person who studied under a great teacher.[3] Each of these great masters would apply their own unique conditions for discipleship. Jesus was no exception.

Discipleship is indeed normal Christianity.

A *disciple of Christ* is a committed follower of the person, teachings, values, and lifestyle of Jesus. This kind of "learner" goes beyond theory and book knowledge. A disciple of Christ can be thought of as a practitioner in the kingdom of God. Jesus' "mathletes" learn through action in the context of everyday living. The goal of this apprenticeship of life is to become like the teacher himself (see Luke 6:40). The disciple is not, however, a special or elite type of Christian. The Second Vatican Council documents use the term as a virtual synonym for any Christian.[4] Discipleship is indeed normal Christianity.

Qualities of Discipleship

1. Discipleship is a process

As the New Testament describes what it means to be a disciple of Christ, we cannot help but be disturbed by some confusing and contradictory facts. On one hand, the disciple is described as one who puts Jesus before all relationships (Luke 14:26), possessions and property (Luke 14:33), personal ambition (Mark 10:42-45), and even life itself (Luke 9:24). On the other hand, we see disciples behaving in ways that are not all that worthy of emulation. They are contentious (Mark 9:34), violent (Luke 9:52-55), spiritually dull (Matthew 16:5-12), and even mean to children (Luke 18:15)!

So who is the real disciple? Is it the saintly spiritual superhero? Or is it the bungling religious oaf? The answer is: both are. By definition, the disciple is a learner—not an ecclesial-board-certified expert. A disciple is someone who has yet to arrive. Discipleship is not a destination, but a process of stretching, falling, growing, questioning, and advancing in the lifelong pursuit of becoming like Jesus. Like the kingdom of God, the disciple's journey resides within the constant tension between the "here and now" and the "not yet." I am a disciple, but not yet fully a disciple. The apostle Paul states this clearly when he writes in Philippians 3:12-15:

> It is not that I have already taken hold of it or have already attained perfect maturity, but I continue my pursuit in hope that I may possess it, since I have indeed been taken possession of by Christ Jesus. Brothers, I for my part do not consider myself to have taken possession. Just one thing: forgetting what lies behind but straining forward to what lies ahead, I continue my pursuit toward the goal, the prize of God's upward

calling, in Christ Jesus. Let us, then, who are "perfectly mature" adopt this attitude.

Appreciating discipleship as a process or journey is critical to understanding the adolescent disciple. To avoid unrealistic expectations, discipleship needs to be placed in the context of human development.

2. Discipleship is lived in the context of community

The word "disciple," in its singular form, is used very little in the New Testament.[5] When it is used, it is primarily in the context of Jesus describing the conditions of being a disciple. The vast majority of citations is the plural form: "disciples." This suggests that discipleship is normally carried on in the context of community.

Beyond this, the New Testament makes it clear that the disciples of Jesus spent a considerable amount of time together. Jesus' disciples were called to live in relationship with one another. Jesus went as far as to say that a distinguishing characteristic that would help identify his disciples in the world would be their love for one another (see John 13:35). Their interaction with one another was a critical aspect of their discipleship formation.

Naturally, youth discipleship is carried out in the environment of the teen's participation in the peer and larger faith community. Youth need to experience a sense of belonging, feel like valuable members of their groups and be challenged by their peers. There is no Christian discipleship apart from the faith community.

3. Discipleship is lived while in relationship with Christ

During my son Michael's preschool years, I spent countless hours pitching plastic baseballs to him. It was a tedious process, but after some time I saw considerable improvement in his ability to hit the ball. Steadily, his coordination increased, his concentration became better focused, and his strength grew. He was becoming a consistent hitter.

One day, during a picnic with numerous preschoolers, a parent-child Whiffle ball game began. We gave each of the kids a chance to hit the ball five times. For the first time, I watched Michael play ball with kids his own age. I was amazed at how he hit the ball more consistently than the others. His coordination and ability to connect with the ball was outstanding.

Instantly, as only a father can, I came to the conclusion that my son was athletically gifted and headed for the major leagues. I thought to myself, "This kid is a baseball prodigy! He must have inherited it from his dad."

Needless to say, it didn't take long for me to re-enter the atmosphere of reality. With time, further experience, and observation, I came to some very different conclusions concerning my son's athletic ability. When Michael played better than his peers as a preschooler, it was not because he was uniquely gifted or divinely destined to enter the baseball Hall of Fame. The difference that made Michael stand out was really very simple: *Michael spent focused time with his daddy.*

It works that way in discipleship. Effective living, loving, and ministering are by-products of spending time with the Lord Jesus Christ. A disciple of Jesus Christ is not a person who simply ascribes to Jesus' philosophy of life. Jesus calls the disciple to be in intimate union with him (see John 15:1-8). Discipleship is lived in relationship with Jesus. Our true effectiveness as a disciple is directly related to the quality of the relationship we have with Jesus. The result of abiding in him is fruitfulness for our own lives.

Effective living, loving, and ministering are by-products of spending time with the Lord Jesus Christ.

4. Discipleship is lived in every aspect of life

Discipleship is a part of what we do each day. It is not like being a member of a club where we only take on a designated role during meeting times. Being a disciple is who we are; it is central to our identity. It encompasses everything we do. It affects our view of life, our values, and our actions. It cannot be separated from the whole of our existence. The disciple of Jesus Christ is called to be a disciple every minute of the day and in every area of life. Discipleship involves interacting with all of human life as a follower of Jesus Christ, including the physical, mental, social, emotional, and spiritual dimensions. Additionally, a disciple impacts his world by extending the values and priorities of Jesus into every larger area of life, such as the political, economical, and cultural.

5. Discipleship is fruit-bearing

Jesus clearly intended for his disciples to be fruitful (see John 15:5-8). A functioning disciple is a fruitful disciple. There are several types of spiritual fruit of which the scriptures speak. The first is the fruit of the Spirit (see Galatians 5:22-23). As the disciple matures, and he or she surrenders more deeply to the work of the Holy Spirit, his or her life is characterized by love, joy, peace, patient endurance, kindness, generosity, faith, mildness, and chastity. These internal attributes become a gift to all those around the disciple. The second type of fruit is the fruit of the harvest (see Matthew 9:36-38). The fruit of the harvest involves the proclamation of the kingdom of God through evangelization, teaching, healing, delivering, and serving. A third type of fruit is produced as a result of living and obeying

God's commandments through a lifestyle of justice, love, and service to others (see Isaiah 5:7; Luke 6:43ff.).

Stages of Discipleship

In the final chapter and verses of Matthew's gospel, Jesus mandated making "disciples of all nations." What did this mean? Some have understood it as the call to evangelization. Others have seen it as the initial follow-up process of catechesis after a person had been baptized. Another understanding is that Jesus' mandate is the call to full-time Christian service.

Actually Jesus meant the *whole process* of leading a person to conversion, establishing the person in their faith through catechesis, and training her or him to make an impact on the world. Discipleship includes this complete cycle of Christian development.

Making disciples can be likened to the cultivation process in farming. It begins with the preparing of the soil. We till the ground, remove the rocks, fertilize the plot, and irrigate the land. After the soil is worked, we can gently scatter the seed, water it each night, chase the menacing crows, and hope for germination. In time, a tiny bud bursts forth, and we find ourselves with the task of nurturing it towards maturity and fruitfulness. Our focus and tasks change so that we occupy ourselves with weeding, further fertilization, watering, staking, and protecting the young shoot. As the plant gradually matures, it begins to yield the anticipated fruit. Fruit is not only a gift to others, but within it are the seeds that bring the entire process to life again.

Using cultivation imagery, we can identify three distinct stages in the discipleship process for teens. The first is the **sowing of the seed.** This stage is characterized by pre-evangelistic and evangelistic activities. The process includes preparing teens to consider the gospel by demonstrating Christ's love, and the actual proclamation of the good news. The goal is germination, or conversion of hearts. The potential target groups are the inactive unconverted, the active unevangelized, active teens in need of renewal, and the secular unchurched.

The second stage is the **nurturing for growth**. This stage is devoted to securely rooting, firmly establishing, and building up the believer in faith (see Colossians 2:7). The goal of this stage is Christian maturity. It targets those who have been initially evangelized and need to bring that experience to greater depth and maturity.

The third stage is the **fruitfulness phase** in which the fruit of the labors are reaped and shared. This stage involves training, equipping, and sending forth the disciple to build up the church and serve the world. This period is characterized by the process of becoming like Jesus in an "other-focused" lifestyle. This phase targets those who have been evangelized, are growing in faith, and are now ready to become workers in the kingdom. This is the "give it away" phase.

All three stages form a continuous cyclical loop, building from the previous stage and ideally leading to the next. It is important to note, however, that each stage is never fully achieved, but once begun, is ongoing in the life of the disciple. For instance, a teen might regularly share his or her faith on a peer ministry team (stage three activity), but still be in need of deeper personal renewal (stage one), and greater spiritual maturity (stage two). On the other hand, a teen who has yet to be evangelized (stage one) might participate in a service-oriented work camp (stage three) and experience an initial faith-awakening experience. In theory, the stages might appear to have a linear motion, but in reality could be best described as having a spiral movement.

In addition to the three stages for cultivating teen disciples there is a stage that mainly involves the adult leaders who will be working with the teens. This "pre-stage" can be known as "soil preparation." It allows for many techniques for selecting and training adults to work with teens. This soil preparation stage is a primary focus of the text that follows in Section 1 of this book.

Principles for the Harvest

A fruitful crop does not just happen. Producing fruit is an *intentional* effort. Without the careful planning and persistent effort on the part of the farmer there is no harvest. In a similar manner, disciples of Christ will not just spring up spontaneously in our youth ministries. If they do appear, it will be because they were purposed by the leadership. Youth ministries produce disciples because they begin with that end in mind. All programs, events, structures, and activities can be traced back to this central mission.

If [teen disciples] do appear, it will be because they were purposed by the leadership.

Secondly, germination and growth are beyond the natural abilities of the farmer. *Growth is a work of God* (see 1 Corinthians 3:6-7). The sower cannot cause a seed to germinate, grow, or bear fruit. The role of the farmer is to cooperate and partner with God by providing the right conditions to produce growth. Creating fertile conditions requires great effort and hard work on the part of the leadership. Youth ministry leaders do not play the role of God attempting to force growth.

Thirdly, *fruitfulness comes in due season*. Crops may have differing time tables, but none are instantaneous. The discipling process takes time. We must be patient. Expecting a bumper crop within the first year is unrealistic. Forced growth is most certainly a recipe for failure.

Programming Based on the Discipling Process

Each distinct stage of growth requires a particular focus, specific tools, and offers a set of unique challenges. If a youth ministry is to be effective in making disciples, the leadership must intentionally address the whole process. Young people need to be evangelized, established in the faith, and equipped for service. All the stages need to be *philosophically* reflected in a youth ministry mission, and *practically* addressed in its structures, programs, and events. Programs need to be linked and built upon each other in a purposeful manner, meeting a variety of spiritual dispositions, yet moving teens progressively towards developing greater Christian maturity. If our desire is to produce mature disciples, our structures need to lead us successively to this end.

Too often, however, youth ministry programs have no clear destination or focus. When helping plan any event, I always ask what the purpose of the activity is. Before I can plan I need to know what we are hoping to achieve. More than once event organizers have responded to my question with, "I really don't know." Without clear initial objectives it becomes impossible to evaluate outcomes.

Often, success is measured solely by how many teens attend an event, or by how much fun they have. Instead, we need to ask: In what way is this event, approach, or program contributing to the development of committed disciples of Jesus Christ? In what way do our various programs work together to facilitate progressive growth in discipleship?

It is not enough to address or emphasize only one aspect of discipleship. For instance, a perennial vulnerability for Catholics has been the absence of effective youth evangelization. We have been busy providing kids with information *about* God. Somehow, we presumed young people had already experienced a personal encounter with Christ. We scratched our heads in bewilderment by their lack of interest in our catechetically-based programs. Our problem lay in the fact that we did not prepare them spiritually for catechesis.

Effective discipling of teens is based on our ability to build a youth ministry that follows this natural step-by-step sequence of development. Normal growth and development follows a sequential progression. Infants begin life with liquids, moves to pureed solids, and finally, after they grow some teeth and further develop their digestive systems, they consume solids.

Summary

"Christian" was a term coined in Antioch during the first century and was used to refer to those who followed the teaching and way of Jesus of Nazareth. To be called and known as a Christian in this era carried with it serious ramifications. One's life was literally at risk because of such an association.

Today, it is not unusual and even very culturally acceptable to be considered a Christian; and while its significance has certainly not lessened, true devotion to this title has. It is often misunderstood, taken for granted, and misused. The term "Catholic" can complicate things further. Teens who describe themselves as Catholic today may do so only because their parents are or were Catholics. Perhaps the use of the word "disciple" will more accurately define the Catholic Christian who is committed to following the person, teachings, values, and lifestyle of Jesus Christ.

True discipleship is a lifelong process that typically begins with baptism. The disciple or learner has yet to "arrive" but must continually work out his salvation with fear and trembling (see Philippians 2:12). Discipleship is lived in relationship with Christ within a community context. The disciple does more than subscribe to a philosophy, but, rather, strives to commit all that he or she has and does to the Lord; no aspect of life can be left unaffected (or infected). Proof of one's discipleship is living a fruitful existence.

Teen discipleship occurs in three cyclical stages: the sowing stage, the nurturing for growth stage, and the fruitfulness stage. In simple terminology, we want to "bring em' in, get em' ready, and send em' out!" When seeking to call God's children to discipleship, we must be intentional in our efforts, we must recognize that any growth that takes place is the work of God, and we must understand that fruitfulness comes in due season. Patience—but also persistence—is a definite requirement. All youth ministry programming must keep in mind and correspond to the discipling process. Programs must genuinely lead teens to Jesus and not only be designed as fun, large-scale events.

A pre-stage to the discipleship process involves training adult leaders and can be thought of as "soil preparation." The chapters in Section One deal primarily with the "preparation of the sowers," that is, the recruitment and training of adults who will lead and work with youth.

Application

The resource on page 23, "Youth Program Assessment," is designed to aid in the assessment of current youth programs, activities, or events according to the three stages of "growing teen disciples" described in this chapter. This resource may be used as a tool for initial assessment by all who work with youth.

Youth Program Assessment

In the first column, list your parish's regular youth programs, activities, and events. In the second column, write what you see as the primary purpose of each. In the third column, enter which discipling stage (sowing, nuturing, or fruitfulness) best defines the program. In the fourth column, describe the role this program plays in the overall discipling process. That is, how does it relate to the other programs, activities, and events?

Program/Activity/Event	Primary Purpose	Discipling Stage	Role in Overall Discipling Process

2

Disciples Make Disciples

One Friday night a group of teenage peer ministers made a spontaneous visit to our home. My then six-year-old son Michael joined them in our lower-level family room. While still upstairs, I could hear their loud chatter and cackling. Feeling a bit envious of their fun, I made my way downstairs. I found, to my immediate dismay, my innocent first-grade son sitting on a couch with a puzzled and troubled look on his face. He was surrounded by a group of astonished teenagers who were pointing and laughing at him. My facial expression must have given me away, as they nervously tried to explain the situation. Ray, the only teen with enough composure to communicate, said, "Frank, we aren't laughing at him. Really. We just can't get over how he looks, talks, and acts like you! He even has all your weird mannerisms. He's a little Frank!"

I glanced over to Michael, and it became quite obvious to me why they were laughing. There he sat, sporting a posture and expression typical of me. I guess they were right. He was a "little Frank."

Over the years my wife and I have heard similar comments about all our children. They all have that "Mercadante look." No great mystery: they share the same parents.

Developing Adult Leadership

The offspring of pigs are pigs. Cattle beget cattle. And disciples make disciples. To spiritually reproduce disciples of Jesus Christ, we, ourselves, must first become disciples.

Youth ministries that make a real difference in the lives of teens invest a significant amount of time and energy into developing their adult leadership. Our leaders must live and model the lives we want our teens to grow towards.

The apostle Paul understood this principle well when he challenged the Corinthian church to be imitators of himself (see 1 Corinthians 4:16; 11:1). The Corinthian "youth group" was a youth minister's worst nightmare. They fought with each other, winked at immorality, tended toward spiritual conceit, and sued one another, to name just a few of their infractions. Because they were spiritually immature, Paul had to provide for them a tangible and practical expression of what it meant to follow Christ. Likewise, today's teens need concrete models to demonstrate vividly what it means to follow Jesus. Leaders must be genuine models whose lives serve as fully illustrated instruction manuals on how to live genuinely as a disciple.

When Paul guided the Philippian church he said, "Be imitators of me. Observe those who conduct themselves according to the *model* (italics mine) you have in us" (see Philippians 3:17). Additionally, Paul challenges the young leader Timothy to be a continuing *example* in speech, conduct, love, faith, and purity to those he is called to lead (see 1 Timothy 4:12). The Greek word *tupos* is used for "model" and "example" in both citations. In other words Paul, is saying that we need to be a representation or standard which other believers can emulate.

The fact is our lives are advertisements for Jesus Christ and the church. The more significant question is: Are we the kind of advertisements that continuously compel teens single-heartedly to follow Christ? Or, do our unexamined lives provide a ready-made and convenient excuse to dismiss the gospel as a hypocritical sham?

Are we the kind of advertisements that continuously compel teens single-heartedly to follow Christ?

Mahatma Gandhi considered becoming a Christian when he was a young man. He was not, however, all that impressed with too many Christians. In his autobiography Gandhi tells of a time when he fell asleep during a church service. Initially he felt bad, but was comforted by the fact that many of the believers in Christ were also sleeping—and they did not seem to feel bad at all! (Why should they? They probably left refreshed!) Gandhi was left with the impression that Christians didn't take their faith seriously. He was later quoted as saying, "I would become a Christian if it were not for the Christians."

This, unfortunately, represents a common impression teens receive of many adult Christians. The root meaning of *example* carries the very idea of leaving an impression. As adults pass through teens' lives, we leave our impressions or marks on them in one way or another. In the positive sense they could be indelible reminders of what it means truly to follow Jesus. In the negative sense, a mark can be a lasting scar that provides a stockpile of ammunition for one to reject the faith.

Becoming a visible example to others by embodying the gospel message is a very Catholic concept. Jesus is the first model of this approach. The incarnation brought God to flesh. Jesus' words, deeds, and life embody all that it means to love and serve God. He provides the ultimate example. In addition, we have many other heroes of our faith whose lives echo Paul's words: "Imitate me as I imitate Christ." As Catholics, we have the lasting gift of those exemplary brothers and sisters who walked before us in the faith. The lives of the saints serve as a living art museum, vividly displaying in many different colors and styles how the spiritual masters served Christ. At the very heart of our Catholic tradition, we deeply value and understand the need for flesh-and-blood heroes and heroines to guide and inspire us in our faith journey.

Beyond the canonized saint, our church has always taught the importance of every believer living in a manner worthy of the gospel. When the saints seem beyond our capabilities, or unrelatable to the present day, teens still have Mr. Lawlor the salesman, Georgia the mom, and Antonio the grandfather to provide relevant and tangible examples of following Christ. The first key to fruitful youth ministry is the development of leaders whose lives give our message credibility.

People-Centered Youth Ministry

Disciples are not made through clever programs, activities, or events. Structures and meetings can be helpful, but they have no life in and of themselves. The life they give comes from the people involved. *Fruitful youth ministry is not program-centered, but people-centered.*

The impact of a people-centered ministry became crystal-clear to me through an experience of one of my stellar teens. As often happens, one particular senior class had a handful of "standout kids." Jessica was one of them. She had an attractive, even contagious spirituality that profoundly touched those around her. She was known for her warmth, kindness, and love towards all. She was one of those people who could make anyone feel special.

I hoped to spiritually clone Jessica. I said, "Jessica, you've barely missed a meeting in four years. Your commitment to Jesus and those around you has served as a model for all of us. What's your motivation? What sold you?"

Jessica's response was immediate and without a hint of hesitation. "That's easy," she said. "It was my first meeting."

"What was so special about that first meeting?" I inquired, secretly hoping I gave a dynamic, life-changing talk that night.

No such luck. She was unable to even recall the topic of the meeting, let alone the speaker. Something of greater significance left an indelible mark on her life. She related the following experience to me:

Jessica was already nervous when her grandparents dropped her off and drove away that first night. When she walked in the door she was startled by the large number of kids—not one of whom she recognized. And on top of that, she soon realized that these were all high schoolers and someone had made a huge mistake—she was a mere eighth grader!

Think back, if you will, to your junior high days. What would you do? Well, young Jessica retreated to the bathroom and began to cry. Becky, a senior peer minister with just the right compassion and leadership abilities, was in the restroom at the time. She asked, "Hey, are you okay?" And Jessica let go another flood of tears. The two girls talked a while, and Becky empathetically shared how she attended a different high school than almost all the other kids at these meetings and she, too, had once felt like a nervous, uncomfortable outsider.

To make a long story short, Becky took Jessica by the hand, sat next to her all night, introduced her to all her senior friends (including boys!), and genuinely cared for her. She even walked Jessica to her grandfather's car door when the meeting ended.

Jessica concluded the story by adding, "I kept coming because Becky and the others were nice. Through them I really saw what it was like to follow Christ."

Clearly, in direct response to Becky's gentle witness, Jessica would reproduce in dozens (maybe hundreds) of other kids the experience of feeling welcomed and loved at youth meetings over her years in high school.

Disciples make disciples. We reproduce in others what we ourselves are. Jessica had no recollection of the program, but only of a person who concretely demonstrated Christ's love. Too often, however, we fail to recognize the importance of developing people and spend more time on a relentless treadmill, frantically searching for a magical program or a fresh-off-the-press ministry fad that will finally be the spiritual panacea for which we've been waiting. I have yet to see a program that can take teens beyond the spiritual maturity of those administering it. The depth of our impact will be proportionate to the spiritual maturity of our leaders. There are no magical programs. We need to stop building programs and begin to build people. It is flesh-and-blood people who touch people.

The depth of our impact will be proportionate to the spiritual maturity of our leaders.

The culture in which we live is characterized by the superficial over-emphasis on appearance. Its influence can creep unnoticeably into the church. As a result we can major on the minors and minor on the majors. For example, while serving as a parish youth minister, our large-group evangelization outreach attracted as many as three hundred teens on a typical evening. Because of the large numbers, several local youth ministers would visit our gatherings in an effort to find the "secret" of the program. When asked what I felt was the reason for success, I consistently pointed to the prayerfulness and spirituality of both my adult and teen leaders. Almost without exception, I would get a polite acknowledgment of what I said, but no further interest or questioning in that area. By the look on some of their faces, I got the impression they felt I was holding back on them, jealously guarding the *real* secret of success. In an effort to get to the heart of the matter, the conversation would be redirected with questions like, "Where do you get those games from? Who are some good speakers? Do you know of any great skits?"

I would never be so extreme as to say that program resources are unimportant and matter little, yet I would say they are virtually insignificant in comparison to the internal development of our leadership. I know this because a year or so later, some of these youth ministers would be promoting similar programs, events, and activities, sometimes down to the same name! Regretfully, I must report, they failed to achieve the level of success for which they hoped. But in all honesty, I was never surprised.

We can never program or package spiritual impact. It's like the person who copies his neighbor's wiring and lighting blueprints in the hope of duplicating the warmth and hospitality of her home. He may have all the hardware in place, but no "people power" to light it. Likewise, programming can only serve as a conduit for God's Spirit to work. We often mistake the form for the substance. The electricity is in the power of God's Spirit working through us. Maybe that's what Paul meant when he said "my message and my proclamation were not with persuasive words of wisdom, but with a demonstration of Spirit and power so that your faith might rest not on human wisdom but on the power of God" (1 Corinthians 2:4-5).

To impact young people spiritually we need to be plugged in to the outlet. That power source is not the latest trend in programming or youth ministry activities. It is God's Spirit. God's Spirit works through those who are filled by him.

We are our ministry. Who we are spiritually will be the most significant factor in our effectiveness as youth workers.

Youth Leader Profile

What does the disciple-making leader look like? Stereotypically, we might envision Ted Tosterone, a young man in his twenties with movie star looks and a Schwarzenegger physique, who plays guitar and sings better than most rock stars and can communicate in a manner that emotionally bounces teens from doubled over laughter to streaming tears in a single opening story. Or maybe Lauren Looks, Ted's female counterpart. She coaches the local high school's state champion cheerleading squad, has super model looks and clothes, inspires all the girls with spiritual lessons from her beauty pageant tales, and embodies the success every teen longs after.

Ted and Lauren may feature in Fox Network's latest teen drama series, but they are not likely to star in any parish youth ministry program. In reality, the disciple-making leader comes in many shapes and sizes. There is no single look, personality, or profile of the effective youth worker.

Unlike the stereotypical Ted and Lauren, most youth workers don't feel all that spectacular—and maybe that's good. Instead of placing their confidence in their own natural abilities, they are forced to rely on the power of God. Ralph was one such leader. He was a simple, quiet, and unassuming plumber, who with his wife, Donna, led one of our discipleship groups. During one of our youth gatherings, I asked teens to name a person who was an example of faith for them. Ralph's name topped the list (surpassing my own!). There was nothing about Ralph's personality that would draw attention to him, but there was an inner quality of character that young people saw as an example of what it meant to be a follower of Jesus.

Ralph taught me the importance of focusing on the internals, rather than the externals. It's not an outside flash, but an inside fire that ignites the flame of faith in others. When the prophet Samuel journeyed to the house of Jesse to anoint the next king of Israel, he was overcome by the appearance of Eliab and thought surely this is the Lord's anointed one. But the Lord said to Samuel: "Do not judge from his appearance or from his lofty stature, because I have rejected him. Not as man sees does God see, because man sees the appearance but the Lord looks into the heart" (1 Samuel 16:7). Spiritual leadership and ministry impact is an inside work.

What Are the Internal Qualities of a Youth Leader?

The development of internal qualities is far more important for a youth leader than majoring in external characteristics. Let me suggest three internal qualities that distinguish the disciple-making youth worker.

1. Contagious Faith

I don't know all the physiological aspects of the influenza virus. I don't know exactly how it is spread from one person to another and another. I do, however, have an excellent understanding of the word "contagious." That understanding comes from experience. On more than one occasion, one of my six children has unsuspectingly smuggled some microscopic mischief into our home. And, by the way, I apologize in advance for this story.

The details are foggy, but I will never forget the overall impact of the autumn night when the stomach flu hit the Mercadante home. The kids were young—not old enough to realize the vital importance of getting to the commode in time.

I don't remember who was first, but in a two-hour span, six out of eight of us were struck by the almost lethal virus. My wife De and I scurried from bedroom to laundry room to bedroom, but we were always just one step too late. Of course, we, too, were making our own stops at the bathroom between cleanups. (I'm getting queasy just thinking about it!)

Well, in the end, we survived. So, you may ask, besides demonstrating the fact that you are a true youth minister by sharing a gross story, what's the point?

The point is this: Faith—like the flu—is contagious. We can't pass the stomach flu on to others without being infected with it ourselves. Leaders who have a one-hour-a-week faith cannot expect their teens to exhibit anything greater than that. It simply isn't enough to be deemed "dangerous" to others.

The Indian missionary Gordon Maxwell might be described as one "dangerous" person of faith—the kind an unbeliever might prefer quarantined. Those around him were well aware of his deep commitment to Christ. On one occasion, he asked a Hindu man to teach him the local language. The Hindu man replied, "No, sahib, for you will convert me to Christianity."

Maxwell tried to clarify: "You don't understand; all I want you to do is teach me the language." But the Hindu man replied, "I will not, for no one can live with you and not become a Christian." [6]

Now that is a "dangerous" form of faith!

We become contagious with the love of Christ when we are consistently exposed to Jesus' loving presence through a rich prayer and sacramental life. A contagious faith is a natural by-product of a living, active, intimate, and personal relationship with God. As we lovingly interact with God, he lovingly interacts through us. Ministry is not about doing good things for God. It is about God doing good things through us as we simply walk with him.

A contagious faith is not a personality trait. Often, we can erroneously associate it with someone with an outgoing and extroverted personality who also happens to have faith. Reserved individuals as well as bubbly people can exhibit a contagious faith. Contagious faith is measured not by volume of verbal expression, but by the quality of experiential knowledge of Christ, both illustrated in one's words and actions.

Ministry is not about doing good things for God. It is about God doing good things through us as we simply walk with him.

Contagious faith does not come overnight. It differs from human enthusiasm and zeal. It is not excitement. Instead, contagious faith is cultivated through consistent practice of spiritual disciplines. Our ability to respond to others as Jesus would respond does not depend on the intensity of our desire, but on how well we have spiritually prepared for the event. We cannot make large withdrawals of love and invest in others if we have not made any deposits. Those deposits are made as we regularly take time for solitude, prayer, scripture study, reconciliation, meditation, and eucharist.

I may get excited about an advertisement of an upcoming triathlon. I would be foolish, however, if I entered the competition in my present physical condition—unless, of course, I didn't mind drowning in the first event!

Embracing the message and values of the kingdom of God and effectively passing them on to others requires a daily spiritual conditioning. Contagious faith is a fruit of ongoing spiritual training.

Each day we must ask ourselves whether or not we are so infected with Jesus that those around us are at serious risk of catching our faith.

Is our faith contagious enough to cause a spiritual epidemic?

2. Christian Integrity

A few years back, I took a group of teens to a summer conference. I also had the joy of bringing along my pastor, who is a wonderful and godly man. We were sitting on a hard concrete floor in a large auditorium in the blistering heat of the early afternoon. I huddled the teens and my pastor around me just prior to the afternoon speaker.

I said, "Guys, I know what it is like after lunch. I feel it, too. We are tired and would like nothing more than to take a nap. It's a challenge to listen to another speaker; however, please try to sit up in a respectful position, make eye contact with the presenter, and listen to the best of your ability. Now, if your mind can't hold on to the content, I understand, but at least maintain a respectful posture. No speaker likes to look out at a comatose-like audience, blissfully snoring through his heart-felt message!"

Our speaker came on and sure enough his style was reminiscent of the most skilled anesthesiologist. A spirit of narcolepsy invaded the room as he droned on in a monotonous way.

My own teens were getting a little restless, but they were all holding to an attentive posture. The pastor, however, slipped into a more comfortable position with his back flat to the floor and his knees raised. At least his eyes were open, I assured myself, as I observed his glazed, blank stare at the ceiling. All of my teens looked at me and smirked.

A few minutes later, my pastor's knees collapsed to the floor while my entire group carefully observed him, and then me. He was now lying flat on the floor, with his eyes half open. It was then that an interesting dynamic took place. It was obvious that my teens wanted to be as comfortable and carefree as their pastor, but were wrestling with the weight of my earlier words. They were torn because I said to pay attention, but he was not, and he was the pastor!

Five more minutes passed by, and our "sleeping beauty" was now flat on his back, eyes tightly closed, and breathing very heavy. By the end of the talk, guess what position my teens were in? If you guessed the attentive one described by my earlier words to them, you are wrong. They followed what was modeled.

Although a humorous and light-hearted illustration, the fact is that what we do by way of our conduct will always weigh heavier than our words. Living with integrity means we are who we are no matter whom we are with, or what we are doing. It means being true to the good news we represent, even when others are not looking.

Once there was an unemployed young man who was applying for a new position. As he was filling out the application he came across a question asking whether he had ever been arrested for a crime. Without much thought he wrote "no." Below that question was a second, related to the first. It read: "Please explain why."

Not realizing it was a follow-up question for those who answered "yes" to the first question, the young man naively wrote: "Well, I guess I never got caught." Needless to mention, he was not hired.

Integrity means never having to worry about getting caught. We have no need to cover up anything because there is nothing to hide. What you see is what you get.

In the wake of recent scandals rocking governments, corporations, and the church, we have a greater awareness than ever of the importance of a leader operating with integrity. Hypocrisy is a huge stumbling block that cheapens the message of the most costly sacrifice of love this world has ever known. The message of the gospel must be accompanied by a life lived with the utmost dignity. Jesus warns us about our lives detouring a young person from the kingdom when he says, "Woe to the world because of things that cause sin! Such things must come, but woe to the one through whom they come" (Matthew 18:7).

Integrity means never having to worry about getting caught.

Integrity lends credibility to our message. It adds value to what we say. When my financial advisor suggests a particular investment, I first ask whether he has put his own money in the same fund. If he hasn't, I ignore his advice. If he places his money where his mouth is, then I will gladly follow his lead. Only when he lives his own financial advice am I willing to risk my own hard-earned cash.

Young people operate in a similar manner. When they see us speaking, living, and making decisions consistent with the principles of the good news we proclaim, only then will they consider investing their own lives. Integrity builds trust, and trust leads to confidence in our message. It is that very confidence that influences a young person towards commitment. The disciple-making leader impacts teens by living a life of Christian integrity.

3. A Servant's Heart

Servanthood has never enjoyed mass popularity in practice. (It remains to be seen if the latest national effort in volunteerism is a breakthrough in servanthood.) Rather, in an age highly influenced by both consumerism and hedonism, we are even less attracted to servanthood's demands. Instead, we are encouraged to grab for it all. We are reminded daily to look out for ol' number one. Jesus' teaching and example could not be more opposite of this contemporary approach to life. But what, we might ask, was the final reward of this selfless man? In light of his "final prize"—death on a cross—was his lifestyle of servanthood worth emulating?

To answer that question we have to reflect on the fifth chapter of the book of Revelation. The scene is of heaven during the end of the age. Jesus is declared by heavenly multitudes to be the only One who is worthy to open the scroll in which begins the consummation of the world. John describes the scene:

> I looked again and heard the voices of many angels who surrounded the throne and the living creatures and the elders. They were countless in number, and they cried out in a loud voice:
>
> "Worthy is the Lamb that was slain
> to receive power and riches,
> wisdom and strength, honor and
> glory and blessing!" (Revelation 5:11, 12)

Consider Jesus' prize: power, riches, wisdom, strength, honor, glory, and blessing. These seven items comprise the most sought-after things in this world. History is soiled with stories of individuals, tribes, and nations who stopped at nothing to possess riches, power, or honor. Countless people have been killed and destroyed and ruthlessly stepped on in the savage, self-seeking pursuit of strength, wisdom, glory, and blessing.

It is paradoxical when we consider that all seven of the most sought-after prizes in the history of our planet were awarded to the one person who lived his life seeking absolutely nothing for himself. Jesus' whole existence was synonymous with sacrificial love. His life demonstrates that when we focus our love upon others, instead of on our own selfish desires, we truly receive. Jesus' road to servanthood is certainly not easy, but it is well worth the investment.

The most miserable people I know are those who invest all their energy serving their own needs and wants. Seeking one's own interests never satisfies one's heart. It is like trying to quench your thirst by drinking salt water; it leaves you thirstier than before. We were created to love. When we love others in a truly healthy manner, we truly live.

St. Paul, recognizing Jesus' ultimate model of servanthood, calls us to follow Jesus' example:

> Do nothing out of selfishness or out of vainglory; rather, humbly regard others as more important than yourselves, each looking out not for his own interests, but also everyone for those of others.
>
> Have among yourselves the same attitude that is also yours in Christ Jesus,
>
> Who, though he was in the form of
> God,
> did not regard equality with God
> something to be grasped.

Rather, he emptied himself,
taking the form of a slave,
coming in human likeness;
and found human in appearance,
he humbled himself,
becoming obedient to death,
even death on a cross.
Because of this, God greatly exalted
him
and bestowed on him the name
that is above every name,
that at the name of Jesus
every knee should bend,
of those in heaven and on earth and
under the earth,
and every tongue confess that
Jesus Christ is Lord,
to the glory of God the Father. (Philippians 2:3-11)

The servant leaders place the interests of God and those of others above their own. Likewise, our spiritual maturity advances in proportion to our own willingness to sacrifice our personal desires for the sake of the kingdom of God or those around us.

Rob was a young man who went through our senior high ministry and later came back to serve as an adult leader. He quickly became my right-hand man. As a meeting ended, before I was even aware of what happened, he would organize a group of teens to clean up the room. He was always willing to do anything that was useful, no matter how menial.

My own children watched Rob's example in action. They observed serving him in our home and at the church. One evening my son Michael, then six, looked at me inquisitively and asked, "Dad, is Rob your slave?"

In reality there are no *volunteers* in the kingdom of God.

At first I chuckled at the question, but when I looked at Michael, his facial expression was one of dead-seriousness. I then explained to him that Rob was not my slave, but he was a young man who took to heart Jesus' call to be a servant to others. He demonstrated the true meaning of servanthood.

The servant leader does not approach ministry with an attitude of: "I am doing you a favor by *volunteering* my time. You're lucky to have me. I could be doing a lot of other things right now." In reality there are no *volunteers* in the kingdom of God. We are members of God's Family. We have calls, and with those calls come responsibilities to our Father and one another.

After dinner in the Mercadante household, we aren't looking for volunteers to clean the table and do the dishes. An outsider might volunteer, but the dishes are one of many basic responsibilities of being a member of the Mercadante family. Our attitudes should be the same as we serve teens in our own parish families. The disciple-making leader has a servant's heart.

Begin Where Your Parish Is

Not all parish youth ministries start on the same ground. We may have the same destination in mind, but the place where we begin working towards that goal may differ drastically from parish to parish.

The organization in which I serve, *Cultivation Ministries*, was founded for the purpose of aiding parishes in developing fruitful, disciple-making youth ministries. The call originated from my own ten-year experience as a parish youth minister. With the support of my pastor, fellow staff, and parish volunteer youth workers, we grew a youth ministry from fourteen reluctant teens to over five hundred active high schoolers. We experienced great success with over seventy-five adult volunteers, fifty peer ministers, and youth programming extending to almost every day of the week. Our parish youth ministry enjoyed a felicitous "feast" with almost twice the number of registered teens involved in some aspect of our ministry. I was deeply concerned, however, by the youth ministry "famine" in parishes a few miles from our door. Through prayerful discernment, I left my parish youth ministry position at St. John Neumann, co-founded *Cultivation Ministries*, and began to address this famine that gnawed at my heart.

During my first year I began training and consulting for eight local parishes. I modestly estimated that in the first two years I would heroically escort these parishes (whose histories were riddled with youth ministry failures) to a spiritual "about-face," and gloriously lead them in building model, mega-youth ministries.

In retrospect, I was either incredibly naive or suffering from delusions of grandeur. Maybe both. I was shocked to find that these parishes did not immediately respond to my "messianic" program and become clones of the St. John Neumann youth ministry. I had to ask myself why this worked so well in one place and not in another.

I eventually awoke to the realization that each parish has a culture, history, and spiritual heritage that impacts every aspect of parish life. In other words, faith communities share certain values, practices, experiences, and backgrounds. For some parishes, its culture, history, and heritage positively contribute to the effectiveness of any ministry effort. For instance, a parish that sponsors opportunities for spiritual renewal and fruitfully evangelizes its adult membership will fill its volunteer positions with renewed leaders. Because these parishioners have a personal experience of being evangelized, they are better able to reproduce this experience in others. These leaders are spiritually equipped for ministry.

On the other hand, some parishes have little history of lay involvement and few opportunities for spiritual renewal. Weekend liturgies may be celebrated with the same enthusiasm one might have about facing a root canal procedure at the dentist's office. I have found that parishes that are anemic in their adult evangelistic efforts and overall spiritual renewal need to begin with these types of efforts in order to begin a renewal of parish leadership.

The process of building a disciple-making youth ministry must begin at the place in which the parish presently finds itself. The following steps are helpful:

Step One: Assess Your Present Condition. First, ask the question: To what degree is our parish making disciples of our adult members? What kind of evangelistic and spiritual renewal opportunities do we presently have? Who are the adults with a contagious faith, Christian integrity, and a servant's heart at our parish?

As we address each of these questions, we will begin to get an idea of where we must begin. Because it takes a disciple to make a disciple, we will have to start with the assessment of potential leaders.

Step Two: Develop and Implement a Plan. The next step involves designing a plan that either builds upon the parish's present abilities to make disciples of its potential leaders or offers a new plan. If we find that our parish offers little in the way of renewal, we may consider hosting an annual retreat that has as its focus the spiritual renewal of adults active in parish ministry. To economize time and effort, renewal efforts may be combined among parish ministries or even more than one parish.

Also, during regular leadership meetings, time should be built in for ongoing faith-building and spiritual formation opportunities. Some parishes offer many renewal opportunities for professional and volunteer ministries. In places such as these, youth ministers should work under the model established by their parish to address the needs of the leaders on their core teams.

Step Three: Monitor and Evaluate. Whether we offer spiritual renewal to adults working with teens initiated under the umbrella of the youth ministry program or by the parish at large, we should always monitor the efforts to see if the renewal is helping to make disciples of the adult leaders. If one type of retreat or form of renewal works better than another, stay with what works, always adapting it so that it aids the leaders in ministry.

Remember, the overall objective is to encourage and develop adult *and* teen leaders who will model discipleship in their words and, more importantly, in their actions.

Summary

Disciples make disciples. The extent to which our leaders embrace discipleship in their own lives is proportionate to the extent to which we will reproduce disciples in our teens. Like Paul, we must grow to say, "Imitate me as I imitate Christ."

Instead of investing all of our energy in building programs, we would do better to focus our efforts in forming the people who will serve as our leaders. In turn, these leaders will provide powerful visual models to teens that will serve as examples of what it means to be followers of Christ.

Disciples minister from the inside out. They are characterized by a contagious faith that infects others with the love of God. Additionally, they live their faith with integrity. Their words, actions, decisions, and lifestyle are consistent with the principles of God's kingdom. The disciple-maker is a servant. Those who make disciples are not volunteers, but members of God's family, serving God and others with sacrificial love.

Finally, every parish has a culture that affects their ability to produce disciples. We first must assess our present situation. Next, we build and implement a plan that addresses our assets and deficits. Finally, we continually evaluate our plans, making revisions and changes when necessary.

Application

The resource "Steps for Evangelistic and Spiritual Renewal of Parish Leaders" (page 39) provides a format for overviewing the disciple-making process described in this chapter as related to your parish and ministry.

Steps for Evangelistic and Spiritual Renewal of Parish Leaders

Directions: Answer the questions under each step as you analyze what is needed for renewal of adults who lead or have the potential to lead teens.

Step One: Assess Your Present Condition	Step Two: Develop and Implement a Plan	Step Three: Monitor and Evaluate
Who are parish leaders?	What opportunities are available at the parish for spiritual renewal?	What are some objectives you feel should be the basis of any spiritual renewal effort?
Who are potential adults who can lead youth?		
What qualities of discipleship do these adults have?	How can the opportunity for spiritual renewal among youth leaders be incorporated in current parish offerings?	What methods will you employ to monitor and evaluate evangelistic and spiritual renewal opportunities?
How are the leaders being renewed spiritually?	What is an opportunity that we, as a youth ministry, could sponsor for adult renewal?	

3

Cultivating a Team of Disciple-Makers

During my early teen years, I became more conscious of my body and my looks, as is typical for most adolescents. Not much liking what my mirror reported back, I assembled a little gym in my basement and began working out five days a week. Among my numerous training goals was the transformation of my quarter barrel belly into a more fashionably attractive abdominal six pack.

One day after scarfing down one of my mother's spaghetti dinners, I felt particularly strong and invincible. I swaggered downstairs alone, and confidently loaded a bar with more weight than I had ever benched before. Slipping under the weight, I hoisted it up and carefully lowered it to my chest. With a sudden burst of strength, I immediately raised it six inches. The following six inches progressed slowly until a foot away from my chest it became an immovable wall of weight. My strength gave out as the crushing mass arrived full-force upon my chest. As I struggled beneath it, the cold iron bar began to sinisterly slide toward my throat. A sense of panic began to overwhelm me when, to my good fortune, my sister's boyfriend arrived downstairs. He rushed towards the bench with an expression that declared "Are you nuts?" He pulled the bar off my chest and yelled, "You *never* lift alone!"

He was right. Weightlifting should be done with others. There are some things we should never do alone, and weightlifting is one of them. Swimming is another, and youth ministry is a third.

Choosing the Right Leaders

Doing youth ministry alone is not safe, smart, efficient, or effective. And, bottom line, Jesus didn't do it that way. Consider who Jesus is: the omnipotent King of kings, the omniscient Lord of lords! If there was any one person who could have done it on his own, it was Jesus. But he chose to surround himself with a team to share his work. How much more do we need the support of others?

You may be thinking, "Okay, I get the point. I shouldn't do this alone. But, that's not really the dilemma. The problem isn't so much me wanting to do it alone, as it is trying to find someone—anyone—to join with me!"

There are a few factors when building an effective youth ministry that are absolutely critical to its success. The most immediate and important is the choice of the leadership. Good leadership can transform a mediocre ministry into a phenomenal program. On the other hand, a great or potentially great youth ministry program can be sabotaged by poor leadership, rendering it ineffective and spreading a cloud of disillusionment throughout the parish community. The importance of choosing the right leaders in the beginning cannot be underestimated.

Good leadership can transform a mediocre ministry into a phenomenal program.

The "any warm body will do" approach to youth ministry recruitment has a proven track record for trouble. Having a pulse and brain wave activity does not adequately qualify a person to work with teens! Too many of us, motivated by desperation, have defaulted into this approach, only to painfully regret it later. The emotional, spiritual, and team energy required to "de-volunteer" someone has the potential to exhaust, exasperate, and even execute a young team.

The first principle for effective youth ministry recruitment is: *Choose our leaders wisely and carefully because they will be the foundation on which our ministry rests.* We must be proactive in our approach to recruitment. We need to make recruiting decisions based on what we determine as best. We cannot simply resign ourselves as victims of circumstances and conditions. Additionally, when it comes to leadership, we cannot be passive, accepting whatever comes as "God's providence." This may seem "spiritual," but it is not very scriptural. Jesus made a very prayerful and proactive choice of his leaders (see Luke 6:12-13).

To reiterate, effective recruitment of adult youth workers is critical to the future success of the ministry. We cannot afford to take it lightly or surrender it to circumstances. To make a significant impact on young people in the future, we need to make a significant investment in time and thought when recruiting and selecting leaders in this initial stage of development.

The Importance of Prayer in Attracting Good Leaders

Some things never change. Close to 2000 years ago, Jesus said, "the harvest is abundant, but the laborers are few"

(Matthew 9:37). So often, especially in a ministry to teenagers, we find ourselves short on adult leadership. Most adults, while genuinely concerned about the welfare of teens in their parish, would just as soon repair the church roof as work with adolescents. It is like asking for volunteers to clean the shark tank.

So we humble ourselves and grovel before the parish begging, pleading, and weepingly imploring the congregation for help. After coming up empty-handed we resort to the "tried and true" plan B: threats about the closing down of youth programs and other guilt-inducing manipulation tactics.

When experiencing a shortage of youth workers, begging is admittedly scriptural. Jesus referred to it as the solution to a scarcity of workers in the harvest. He actually exhorts us to beg. And beg we have. The problem is that we have been begging the wrong people. We are not called to beg the potential workers. Jesus said, "Beg the *Lord of the harvest* to send forth laborers" (Matthew 9:38).

We easily can become overwhelmed in light of our lack of youth workers, especially when we consider the enormous needs of our present-day teens. It is precisely at this time we should direct our attention to God in prayer.

Prayer has been an overlooked resource in recruiting leaders in the church today. We have often put all our energy and thought into cleverly and creatively designed recruitment plans. Unfortunately, this approach is not biblical. Jesus made it clear that our first priority and response for the need of more workers is prayer. He taught this (see Matthew 9:37-38) and modeled it (see Luke 6:12-13). Prior to his choosing the twelve apostles, Jesus spent the night in prayer.

Application

Page 56 lists "Practical Options for Incorporating Prayer." This resource may be duplicated as a reference for youth leaders.

Our recruitment needs to begin and end with prayer. God knows our need more than we do. He loves our young people more than we do. God can stir hearts toward action better than we can. Ministry is a matter of call. We cannot attempt to play the Holy Spirit in people's lives, seeking to cleverly persuade them towards action. Our job is to prayerfully present our need to God, and to invite the parishioners to prayerfully discern whether this is God's call in their life, and their charism to the community.

Seeking to follow Jesus' example and exhortation, the second principle for effective recruiting is: *When there is a need for more workers, prayer is our first response and greatest resource.*

Who Works Best With Youth?

Many people presume the best age group to work with youth is young adults, reasoning that people in their twenties are not so distant from their own adolescent experience, high on energy, and low on responsibilities. They are developmentally designed and destined to work with teens!

Another opinion is that parents of teenagers are best positioned to work with adolescents. Because youth programming most affects their own children, they are naturally concerned with and deeply invested in developing a worthwhile youth ministry. Additionally, who better understands teenagers' peculiarities than one who is being sanctified and made holy through them!

A third assumption is that senior citizens offer a viable option as youth leaders. Their wisdom, experience, and greater amount of free time are advantages often named. (Oppositely, some may believe that older adults are too distant developmentally and lack the vital energy to work with teens.)

Admittedly, each of these opinions have some validity, yet, none of them taken alone paint the entire picture of an effective leadership team. A best-case scenario for a leadership team would include a variety of people, male and female, old and young, single and married, parents and grandparents.

With little experience of an extended family, the breakdown of the nuclear family, and a more transient society, today's youth need a greater variety of role models in their lives. They need to see what it means to follow Christ from many different ages and states in life.

Additionally, a youth ministry team benefits by the experiences of many different age groups and vocations. For example, where a senior citizen might not be able (or want) to lead a game of volleyball, he or she might have an advantage in time, experience, and wisdom. A young adult might be just the opposite—bubbling with energy and developmentally and culturally relevant, but possibly lacking in experience. A parent of an adolescent might lack time, but offer great insight into what teens are like to live with. An ideal team would be comprised of a variety of different age groups, vocations, gifts, and perspectives, making a balanced mix.

A third principle for youth ministry recruitment is: *There is no single ideal age or description of a youth ministry team, except one that includes balance and variety.*

Not only do we often have misconceptions about the *age* of effective youth leaders, we might also carry a distorted picture of the *character qualities* of those who minister with youth. One extreme might be, "If you are still breathing and crazy enough to do it, then you're in!" The opposite extreme contends, "You had best be canonized, or at least in the beatification process. Don't apply unless your salutation is 'Saint'."

I want to offer a more realistic perspective. The following are some important characteristics of the potential youth leader:

Availability

We need adults who either have the time or are willing to make the time to be involved. The person who is too busy and over-committed will be unable to devote the needed energy to do effective ministry. Availability, however, is more than just having the time to schedule for meetings. It is a disposition or attitude that says to teens, "I am here for you. You are important to me. When you need me, I will be here."

We can never advocate the neglect of one's own family for the sake of ministry.

Availability, however, must be appropriate, healthy, and balanced. We can never advocate the neglect of one's own family for the sake of ministry. A person who is married with six kids, has a sixty-hour-a-week job, coaches soccer, baseball, and wrestling, leads the Boy Scout troop, and is pastoral council chairperson and a choir member need not apply! A good general rule of thumb is that volunteers be involved in only one parish ministry at a time. This approach helps prevent burn out, and allows people to devote enough time in one area, creating greater potential for success.

Authenticity

Let's face it, for most teens we are cultural relics of the prehistoric past. At best, we are one cultural step behind. If we're wearing it, it's out. If we're saying it, it was last year's colloquialism. If we're listening to it, it's now being played instrumentally on elevators. *And that's the way it's supposed to be.*

Adolescents seek to distinguish themselves from mainstream, adult society by being different in dress, music, and language. We had our turn and it is over. We are now adults. Teens do not want us to be like them. In actuality, when we start to look, talk, and act like adolescents they know something is not quite right. It is like spotting someone sporting a toupee. We may not notice it at first glance. But, the funny thing about toupees is that there is always a second glance. We know there is something not quite right and we strain our necks a second time to figure it out. It is not the toupee; most toupees are quite a slick, thick, and well-groomed plot of hair. The problem is that it isn't *their* plot of hair, and we know it. Likewise, teens can spot a phony with relative ease. They are not seeking a pseudo-adult in teen clothing. We will relate best to young people when we are authentically ourselves. Authenticity means being who we are, being real. It means being an adult if we happen to be one.

Healthy Love for Teens

When I was a small child I always made sure I was near those adults who I sensed loved me. Somehow, I was just an arm's length away from them. That was not by chance. On the contrary, it was quite intentional. I always seemed to feel better around those people. They laughed at my jokes, poked and wrestled with me, and took an interest in what I was doing.

Now, on the other hand, I remember a woman who I sensed did not like me. She preferred my cousin over me and made no bones about it. Being in the same county with her was too close for me. She seemed ugly to me. I remember her as having an angry, contorted expression on her face even when she was happy. She had thick horn-rimmed glasses with small beady eyes behind them. On her gigantic nose she had a large wart with three protruding black hairs growing from its creviced tip. It was amazing how much she resembled the sinister features of those animated villains I watched on Saturday mornings.

Now, in reality, she did not really look that way (at least that is what my parents tell me), but she did to me. It is a funny thing, no matter how old we get, we like to be around people who genuinely love us, and we do not like being around those we perceive not to like us. Teens are no different. The face of one who loves us is always more attractive than the face of one who does not. Teens need to be surrounded by faces of people who love them.

It is essential that the volunteer youth worker have an altruistic love for the adolescent. Our motivation should be rooted in a sincere care and other-centered concern for teens, not a co-dependency-inspired need to be needed. Sadly, youth ministry has a track record for attracting adults who need teens' approval, loyalty, and love more than they are able to give it. Youth ministry is not the place to work out old wounds and hurts. That can be better done through counseling.

Our love cannot be co-dependent, or coerced. It is important that young people do not think that we view them as a pain, or a necessary source of suffering for time off in purgatory. Likewise, when we are with them, we do not want to leave them with the impression that we are there only to work off our community service hour sentence. The Apostle Peter wrote, "Tend the flock of God in your midst, not by constraint but willingly, as God would have it, not for shameful profit but eagerly" (1 Peter 5:2). Teens, like anyone else, are naturally attracted to those who they perceive genuinely love them. It means that we respect and appreciate them for who they are individually and developmentally.

Ability to Communicate With Youth

Youth ministry may not be our call if we break out in hives when we are around teens. A youth worker should feel comfortable talking with teens and open to expanding on communication skills he or she already possesses. Our ability to communicate to young people will be the vehicle in which we express our love and concern. Being comfortable talking with adolescents, however, does not imply we are polished, professional communicators, or ready to open an adolescent counseling center. We may not be all that confident, but we are open to learn. We may not always know what to say, but we are willing to be present. It simply means that we are at home with teenagers and we are comfortable with talking and listening to them.

Growing Faith

While considering the purchase of a computer I encountered a new salesman who knew very little about his product. Within a few minutes of conversation I realized I knew far more about the model he was trying to sell than he did. That left me a bit insecure because I did not know all that much. Consequently, I did not buy the computer from him. Likewise, to give away our faith we have to have some personal knowledge and experience with it. We cannot speak of Jesus as some remote, historical figure. Ministry implies that we have a growing relationship with Christ and live a Christian lifestyle. Our faith is the substance of what we communicate. We cannot take a young person where we have never journeyed ourselves. Again, this does not imply that we have a "St." before our name; it means that we are spiritually healthy, open, and growing.

Sense of Calling

Youth ministry is not a matter of volunteering time as much as it is a matter of discerning and obeying God's call. We need to be called by the Lord for our ministry to be truly authentic. Very few of us receive a lightening bolt and an audible voice directing us in what to do. Most of us operate out of a sense of conviction, rooted in a prayerful relationship with Christ. The potential youth worker must sense God's calling to serve the church in this manner. This call should not only be prayerfully discerned by each potential youth worker, but also confirmed by the pastoral leadership.

Skills for Recruiting Youth Workers

Finding potential youth workers with the above characteristics requires both positive attitudes and practical effort on our part. We need to be enthusiastic, realize that recruiting is an ongoing task, and appeal to different motivations. Let's look at these important recruiting skills in greater detail.

Be Enthusiastic

Enthusiasm! Without it there is little chance others will want to join us in our work. Think about it. We are combining the two scariest things known to the average adult Catholic—working with teenagers (technically known as adolesceaphobia) and sharing our faith (technically known as evangelphobia). If we are not excited about it, we cannot expect others to be.

The word *enthusiasm* literally means "in God or possessed by God." If there are any people who ought to be enthusiastic, it ought to be us, the followers of Christ. We should convey a deep sense of excitement about who we are and what we are all about. Like individuals, every group has an image of itself. People with a poor self-image are sometimes very difficult to be around. And likewise, if a group has a really negative image of itself, it will not be very attractive to others. People will say, "I don't want to be a part of this group; they don't seem to like being with each other or enjoy what they are doing."

If there are any people who ought to be enthusiastic, it ought to be us, the followers of Christ.

We do not want to possess or convey a poor group image by being negative or pessimistic. We don't want to start the year saying, "It's September and we've been hit with heavy attrition again." Or, "Working with teenagers is a bear." Or, "Sure, it's a thankless job, but somebody has to make the sacrifice and minister to those rebellious adolescents."

We do not want to approach recruiting from a negative standpoint. People will walk away feeling guilty—and I mean walk away; they won't be interested in joining our sinking ship. A youth ministry will never soar to the heights of eagles if it is being promoted by a flock of turkeys.

Instead, we need to be enthusiastic as we go about recruiting. Enthusiasm does not mean we are in denial over the difficulties that we are surrounded by, but, rather, we are focusing on the grace of God to provide the wisdom, resources, and strength to bring about great things. Enthusiasm is knowing that the omnipotent God who created the universe with a single thought is on our side. As someone once said, "if one tenth of what we believe is true, then we ought to be ten times more excited than what we are." If we are still struggling with being enthusiastic, then take to heart the inspirational words of football coach Vince Lombardi, who said, "If you aren't fired by enthusiasm, you will be fired with enthusiasm." So be enthusiastic!

Recognize Recruiting Is an Ongoing Task

The football team that excels during their season is one who prepares in the off-season. Throughout the year players continue to lift weights and train for endurance. A team loses unrecoverable ground when players sluggishly meander into the season overweight and out of shape. Likewise, recruitment cannot be just an annual autumn activity. We need to keep in good shape by approaching potential youth workers throughout the year. When we observe in others qualities that are assets in youth work, we may want to say, "You have the kind of faith and disposition that would really make an impact on teens. Have you ever considered working with youth?" Recruiting is an all-year task.

With the birth of our fourth child my family outgrew our car. So, we began to consider the purchase of a mini-van. While researching the different models, I looked for mini-vans on the road as I traveled. I was astounded at what I observed. It seemed like every other car out there was a mini-van! I never noticed them before, primarily because I was never looking for them. Similarly, there are plenty of potential youth workers all around us, and we will never notice them if we aren't actively looking.

Effective recruiting is a team effort. Each youth worker must share the responsibility of growing the ministry by enthusiastically inviting others to join us in our vision. We must recognize there are people all around us who have the charism, faith, and personalities that could make a difference in the life of a teen.

Appeal to Different Motivations

People have different motivations for involving themselves in ministry. Most individuals are primarily motivated by one of three social needs: achievement, affiliation, or influence. A good recruiting approach will highlight the benefits of participating from each of these perspectives. Here are some ways to do that:

Achievement-oriented people derive great satisfaction in setting and reaching goals. They tend to be very practical and detailed in their approach to life. They are no-nonsense and business-like. They do not want to be bored with theory; they want to get to the bottom line: "What are we going to do?"

When appealing to the achiever, it is important to communicate the practical activities in your ministry and how they relate to the overall objectives of the program. We need to offer these individuals roles that have specific tasks attached to them.

Affiliation-oriented people get involved with and enjoy ministry because they like interacting with others; they value human companionship. These individuals find it very satisfying to be affiliated with and belong to the youth ministry team. They enjoy the relational aspect of ministry.

For potential youth workers with this motivation, stress how the youth ministry team operates as a small-base Christian community, or how it is able to foster relationships with teens. Affiliation-oriented people will be more motivated by roles that place them in the middle of human interaction and relationships.

Impact-oriented people are primarily motivated by the desire to make an impact. "We want to make a difference" is their motto. They do not want to waste time on insignificant or trivial matters. Their bottom line is: Are lives being touched through our efforts?

When appealing to the impactors, we must help them see how their contribution can affect the lives of teens. Sharing stories of how teens' lives were changed through the influence of adult leaders would catch their interest. Impact-oriented people need to be offered roles that provide opportunities for them to effect change in their lives and the lives of others.

It is natural to think that everyone will want to join the youth ministry team for the same reasons as we did. We tend to recruit from the need that essentially motivates us. For instance, an impactor may emphasize to others the eternal difference the ministry is making in teens' lives. An affiliator may yawn through such an appeal until he hears about the wonderful, caring community of which the other is a part. A fruitful recruitment campaign will therefore, give voice to all three of these approaches. Most people who join groups will be primarily motivated by one, or in some cases two, of these needs. When we explain the ministry in light of these social needs, potential leaders will hear what we do in their own "language."

Be careful, however, to be truthful in your presentation. It can be easy to get carried away in appealing to the different motivations and lose sight of reality. We cannot passionately persuade the affiliator with dramatic stories of Christian community when we know our team is riddled with unreconcilable conflict and dissent. We must be truthful in what we can offer.

Basic Recruiting Approaches

There are two basic approaches to recruiting that are applicable to potential youth workers of each kind of motivation: *selective recruiting* and *general recruiting*. To understand these approaches it might be best to describe them in fishing terms.

Selective recruiting is the angler's approach. We target the species of fish we hope to catch by the kind of rod, bait, and presentation we employ. On the other hand, general recruiting can be likened to commercial fishing. Send your boat out to the deep water and drag your nets. Let's look at each of these approaches in greater detail.

Selective Recruiting

Selective recruiting is a targeted approach. It is the process of identifying known individuals who possess the necessary gifts, faith, and energies for youth ministry. In other words, we surface the names of potential leaders and initiate contact.

Selective recruitment begins by producing a list of individuals in the parish who are potentially qualified to serve as youth workers. This is done by consulting with parish staff, past youth workers, parents, teenagers, and other key members of the parish. Once an exhaustive list is created, each person is individually contacted. This can be done by phone, letter, in person, or any combination of the three.

Listed below are five sources for securing names based on the selective approach:

1. *Parish staff*—Communication among staff members is key. Arrange to speak at a parish staff meeting to share the vision of youth ministry. Approaching the staff will help ensure we do not recruit people from high involvement roles in other ministries within the parish, and in the process damage relationships.

Prior to a scheduled meeting, distribute directories to each staff member. Include with it a written request to review the directory and highlight those individuals they think might have the necessary skills to work with youth. At the staff meeting, discuss possible candidates and compile a list of potential people. A round-table discussion with parish staff members is an essential part of increasing ownership and support for youth ministry.

2. *Youth workers or catechists*—The adult leaders involved in ongoing youth ministry or religious education may be able to identify other adults who have previously assisted in their programs who might be ready to expand their leadership roles. They may also be able to recommend former students who are now adults.

3. *Parents of adolescents*—Getting feedback from parents of teens (individually or through listening sessions) can serve three functions. First, the feedback can be used as a vehicle for assessing the needs of parents in regards to youth programming. Second, parents can be invited to become involved in

youth ministry. Third, parents may be able to identify other adults who might be capable and willing to work with teens.

4. *Long-time parishioners*—Every parish has a group of "pillar leaders." These are individuals with a long history of parish leadership and commitment. Long-time parishioners have a unique perspective that may be very helpful in understanding the past history and present needs of the parish. Furthermore, because of their vast experience and relationships with people in the community, they may be able to identify a number of prospective youth workers. This group can be extremely helpful when a parish has a new pastor and staff members. If nothing else, they will appreciate the fact that we value their experience, wisdom, and longtime membership in the parish.

5. *Youth*—Teens should be asked for their input on youth leaders. In many ways, who knows better? Compile a list of names the teens suggest and make contact with those adults by phone or mail. Without exception, adults who are recommended by teens feel quite honored and have difficulty refusing a request to take a role in youth ministry. We may even consider having teens contact these individuals themselves.

In a selective approach, the individuals identified are, for the most part, known quantities. They have been identified because they have leadership experience, potential, or possess the needed abilities. Most likely, they are "proven" people. Therefore, the risk factor is lowered and there is less concern over the possibility of de-volunteering or "firing" them.

Dealing with a person who has slipped into leadership who is not emotionally or spiritually healthy can be like dealing with a "team tapeworm" who devours all the group's energy and resources. Selective recruiting reduces the possibility of this occurring.

However, not every qualified person in the parish can be identified by another. In most parishes, it is likely that only twenty percent of the registered parishioners are involved beyond Sunday liturgy. A selective approach usually identifies only the names of this minority. Subsequently, all parish ministries are pooling from this same group. The total selective yield might be slim. The "Achilles heel" of the selective approach is that gifted individuals can be overlooked and new parishioners skipped over entirely.

Another drawback is that this approach could be perceived as an effort to gather only an elite, specially chosen group. Good people may feel they have been snubbed and considered not good enough to be part of the youth ministry "clique." This can cause resentment on the part of those who were not invited.

General Recruitment

General recruiting is more of a shotgun approach. It is the process of making known to the entire parish the need for adult youth workers. This approach does not distinguish between who receives an invitation and who does not. Every adult in the parish is considered a potential youth worker.

The purpose is to make a broad appeal, reaching as many people as possible. The following methods are common to a general approach:

- ✔ A newsletter sent to all families in the parish
- ✔ A homily devoted to adolescent ministry and recruitment
- ✔ Flyers posted around the church
- ✔ Mass and bulletin announcements
- ✔ General "Time and Talent" forms as part of a stewardship campaign

With general recruiting, it is also wise to interview potential candidates. Though this process can demand a considerable amount of time, the value of it cannot be underestimated. A one-to-one interview provides an opportunity to ensure that the interested person understands and is ready for the position.

Additionally, interviewing could be used when the pastor or parish leadership has some potential concerns or hesitations regarding an interested person. It is always best to deal with these kinds of issues directly and immediately. As uncomfortable as this task is, we must resist the temptation to close our eyes and hope for the best when we suspect difficulty.

The following situations and characteristics should warrant concern with regard to being involved in the youth ministry:

- ✔ Having present marriage and family difficulties
- ✔ Emotionally or spiritually unhealthy
- ✔ Overextended and over-committed
- ✔ Emotionally immature
- ✔ Having an immoral lifestyle
- ✔ Possessing hidden agendas (e.g., "I will teach these kids what the church is *really* about.")

Like selective recruiting, general recruiting has both its positive and negative sides. The benefits of general recruiting are usually the deficits of the selective approach, and vice-versa.

On the plus side, general recruitment reaches a greater number of possible volunteers than selective recruitment. Those gifted "unknowns" are on equal footing with the "knowns." There is less chance of missing qualified potential youth workers. Also, general recruitment builds a strong parish awareness and ownership of the youth ministry by all. Visibility is a key to both teen and adult involvement.

However, like drag netting, the haul may bring forth both desirable and undesirable results. It is not uncommon to attract people who lack the necessary gifts, lifestyle, or disposition for youth ministry. There is the greater probability of finding ourselves stuck with the unpleasant task of de-volunteering someone later. This procedure is typically messy and distracting for a youth ministry team.

Finally, the general approach is broad, somewhat generic, and impersonal. Because it lacks a personal touch, it is easier to ignore or not seriously consider.

I would not recommend doing an exclusively general approach. I would suggest either an exclusively selective appeal, or a combination of the two approaches. If any case, you should possess the gumption to "fire" volunteers if they are not suited for youth ministry.

Job Description of a Youth Leader

Normal people (technically speaking, there aren't any normal people in youth ministry) are more inclined to commit to a role when expectations are clearly stated. Most of us are wary of positions that seem ambiguous or vague. We want to know what we are getting ourselves into before we sign the dotted line. A practical way to provide this clarity is through the development of specific job descriptions.

Job descriptions outline the objective, tasks, and responsibilities of key roles such as "Peer Ministry Team Director" or "Director of Communications." It is best to design a job description that is realistic in today's busy world. Most people are not interested in a second full-time, volunteer job. So, instead of listing one position with ten tasks, have two positions under the same job description that evenly divide the tasks. Also, I think an important key to attracting potential leaders is to offer short-term rather than open-ended commitments. We are more apt to step in and think, "Well, this I can manage."

The following are helpful components of a job description:

Position Title—The name or title of the role (e.g., Peer Ministry Director, Social Director, Discipleship Leader).

Desired Characteristics—A listing of gifts and skills that are needed to perform the role well. Examples might be organizational skills, discussion-leading skills, ability to share your faith.

Purpose—A brief statement or general summary of what is to be accomplished through the position.

General Responsibilities—Details the specific duties and functions of the role.

The job description might also describe the specific *training* one receives to prepare for and function completely in the position. Also, a clear indication of the *time commitment* required to fill the role is suggested. For example, answers to the questions: What is the duration of the commitment? How many hours per week or month might it involve?

Application

Examples of job descriptions for various youth ministry positions are listed on pages 57-61.

Summary

Like swimming and weightlifting, youth ministry was never meant to be done alone. Good youth ministry is team-based. Our effectiveness is multiplied when we utilize the gifts and skills of many leaders as opposed to relying on one charismatic individual or couple.

Assembling a team of adult leaders should not be left to chance. It is essential that we be proactive in our approach to recruitment. We must choose our leaders wisely and carefully because they will be the foundation on which our ministry rests.

When experiencing a shortage of leaders in light of an overwhelming need, Jesus instructed us to pray that God will send forth workers into the harvest. Our first response to recruitment should always be prayer.

A team of youth workers is not necessarily a homogenized group. When recruiting, we should seek to attract people from different age groups, cultures, genders, and backgrounds. What they should have in common is a disposition of availability, a sense of authenticity, a healthy love for teens, a comfort communicating with youth, a growing faith, and a sense of calling.

Recruiting is an ongoing task that should be carried on with great enthusiasm. People are attracted to winning teams and not attracted to losing teams. Additionally, people hear God's call in light of their personal gifts and dispositions. We should appeal to potential leaders in light of three social drives: achievement, affiliation, and influence.

There are two different approaches to recruiting leaders. The first is the *selective* approach, which identifies potential leaders and personally invites them to be a part of the youth ministry team. The second is the *general* approach, which makes no distinction in potential candidates. In the general approach, everyone is invited. Many people combine the approaches, but to do so we must be willing to say no to those who are not suited for youth ministry.

Finally, most people like to know exactly what they are getting themselves into when they commit to a job. Designing job descriptions that detail what a person does in a role is a helpful way to accomplish this.

Practical Options for Incorporating Prayer

The following options are some practical ways prayer can be incorporated into efforts at recruiting adult leaders.

1. Ask all pastoral leaders to schedule personal prayer to "beg the Lord of the harvest to send laborers," especially mentioning the needs for youth ministry.

2. Hold an evening prayer service with a group of parents to pray for the entire recruitment process.

3. Contact a few known "prayer warriors" (individuals who are committed to regular prayer). Ask them to organize a group of ten or more volunteers to pray for the recruitment process. Request they individually spend ten minutes a day praying for this need for the next thirty days.

4. Incorporate the intentions for the youth ministry and recruitment process into the daily and weekend Mass/bulletin announcements and the prayers of the faithful.

5. Acquire a list of homebound parishioners' names. By phone or letter make contact with them, requesting their daily prayer for the youth ministry recruiting process.

6. Contact leaders of parish Bible studies, prayer groups, and the like. Request that they add this intention during their meetings.

Director of Communications Job Description

PURPOSE

To ensure that consistent and pertinent information regarding the youth ministry is effectively communicated to the youth, their parents, potential youth workers, the parish family, and the outside community.

DESIRED CHARACTERISTICS

- ✔ Organizational skills
- ✔ Writing skills

Helpful, but not necessary:

- ✔ Layout knowledge
- ✔ Computer skills (Desktop publishing, word processing, graphics)

GENERAL RESPONSIBILITIES

- ✔ To coordinate and oversee all communication efforts (from design to execution) of the youth ministry to the youth, parents, potential youth workers, parish, and outside community.
- ✔ To develop effective plans to publicize and promote programs, meetings, events, and activities through the use of various available mediums.
- ✔ To create a positive image awareness of the youth ministry to young people, parents, the parish, and the larger community.
- ✔ To inform the parish of the direction, plans, the reason behind the plans, and progress of the youth ministry.
- ✔ To educate and inform the parish on relevant youth-related issues, statistics, trends, etc.
- ✔ To motivate and organize the involvement of both students and adults in the communication efforts of the youth ministry.
- ✔ To ensure that all communication is done in sincerity and truthfulness, and with high quality.
- ✔ To be an active member of the youth ministry planning team.
- ✔ To plan and oversee the communications budget.
- ✔ To maintain a current database of all eligible teens.

Peer Ministry Team Director Job Description

PURPOSE

To direct the Peer Ministry Team through community building, spiritual formation, leadership development, and the organization of ministry opportunities.

DESIRED CHARACTERISTICS

- ✔ Organizational skills
- ✔ Ability to motivate young people
- ✔ Healthy spirituality
- ✔ Comfortable in sharing one's own faith

GENERAL RESPONSIBILITIES

- ✔ To foster the growth of community and effective team work.
- ✔ To foster the spiritual growth of the peer ministers.
- ✔ To help develop the leadership potential and giftedness of the peer ministers.
- ✔ To help foster creativity, responsibility, ownership, and investment in the peer ministers.
- ✔ To help organize the Peer Ministry Team outreach, evangelistic, and service opportunities.
- ✔ To ensure that the peer ministers receive the necessary training for ministry.
- ✔ To enforce the covenant agreement or lifestyle contract.
- ✔ To facilitate meetings.
- ✔ To work together with the Director of Large Group Evangelization in planning and organizing the outreach meetings.
- ✔ To collaborate and communicate with the youth ministry planning team concerning the direction and plans for the peer ministry (Member of Planning Team).
- ✔ To plan and oversee Peer Ministry Team scheduling and budgeting.

Director of Large Group Evangelization Job Description

PURPOSE

To plan, direct, and oversee Large Group Outreach programming.

DESIRED CHARACTERISTICS

- ✔ Organizational skills
- ✔ An appreciation and love for evangelization
- ✔ Creativity
- ✔ Ability to work well with others

GENERAL RESPONSIBILITIES

- ✔ To effectively assess, plan, design, organize, execute, and evaluate Large Group Outreach programming.
- ✔ To work together with the Peer Ministry Team in planning and organizing the meetings.
- ✔ To recruit, train, organize, and supervise Large Group Outreach adult team leaders, the planning team, and the Competition Coordinator.
- ✔ To collaborate and communicate with the youth ministry planning team concerning the direction and plans for the upcoming meetings (Member of Planning Team).
- ✔ To work together with the Director of Communication for effective promotion, publicity, etc. of the Large Group Outreach.
- ✔ To resource the planning team with speakers, skits, activities, videos, etc.
- ✔ To ensure that the meetings are rooted in the mission of the youth ministry, based on the needs of young people, and in sync with the vision and objectives of Large Group Outreach programming.
- ✔ To ensure the development of a warm climate and effective content for the meetings.
- ✔ To plan and oversee Large Group Outreach scheduling and budgeting.

Large Group Evangelization Team Leader Job Description

PURPOSE

To facilitate discussion, organize game and activity participation, motivate attendance and enthusiasm, and evangelize young people through large group outreach.

DESIRED CHARACTERISTICS

- ✔ Discussion leading skills
- ✔ Ability to motivate students
- ✔ Personable/comfortable with youth
- ✔ Desire to share faith
- ✔ Like to have fun

GENERAL RESPONSIBILITIES

- ✔ Facilitate discussions.
- ✔ Build a warm, accepting, and enthusiastic climate.
- ✔ Share your faith with students before, during, and after meetings.
- ✔ Build morale, ownership, and a sense of excitement in the group.
- ✔ Organize the team for games and activities.
- ✔ Call and/or send postcards reminding students of meetings.
- ✔ Motivate students to bring friends to the meetings.

Large Group Evangelization Games/Competition Leader Job Description

PURPOSE

To provide quality community-building, team-oriented games and activities at all outreaches.

DESIRED CHARACTERISTICS

- ✔ Organizational skills
- ✔ Ability to relate, motivate, and mobilize teens
- ✔ Like to have fun
- ✔ Creative

GENERAL RESPONSIBILITIES

- ✔ Foster a sense of ownership among the teens regarding outreach.
- ✔ Plan, organize, and present game activities for the community-building activities of outreach.
- ✔ Foster and aid in the growth of team development.
- ✔ Choose appropriate games, mixers, and crowd-breakers for the large group evangelization meetings.
- ✔ Motivate student and team involvement; build enthusiasm, team investment, and growth.
- ✔ Keep accurate scores and team points for each game.
- ✔ To work in conjunction with the Director of Large Group Evangelization.

4

Envisioning a Verdant Horizon

A few years ago I attended a diocesan youth rally planning meeting with several youth ministers. "So," the director began, "what should we do this year?" A long pause followed. My peers then responded enthusiastically with rapid-fire suggestions of new speakers, workshops, topics, music, themes, and activities. The flurry of exchange was dazzling, and my head was spinning. To make matters worse, I felt self-conscious because I had yet to contribute one measly idea to the discussion.

But then it dawned on me why I had not been caught up in the planning. I had no idea what we were aiming to achieve with the event. I did not know the goals. So, I asked, "What are we trying to achieve through this rally? What is its purpose?" The room grew ghostly silent. My question served as a verbal fire extinguisher. I put out every spark of creativity in the room. After what seemed like an eternity, the diocesan director responded to my question. With a confused and puzzled look on his face, he replied, "Well, I guess I never thought about that."

It is foolish to organize any youth ministry event without a clear focus of its purpose and its final destination. How could we ever evaluate an event if we have no idea of what we want to accomplish in the first place? Every single activity we plan must be guided by the rudder of an overriding purpose. It is that very purpose that serves as the energy behind all our efforts. If we have no idea of where we are going, it is a sure bet we will arrive there. Nowhere, that is.

The Driving Forces of Youth Ministry

All youth ministries have some driving force. The driving force may not be clear or even articulated. It may be set in motion by decision or even by default, but something drives it. There are always some underlying assumptions, guiding factors, and bottom-line results that factor in to a youth ministry program. What is the driving force of your youth ministry?

Driven by Numbers

Too often we evaluate our success by the number of people involved. Big numbers equal big success. Small numbers equal big failure. Our first question about an event, activity, or program can give away what really drives us. How often do we ask, "How many kids came?"

Full-time youth ministers may feel pressure to justify their jobs by the number of teens involved. We can feel that our pastors, parents, or the parish council are simply playing the numbers game, and if we want to be successful in their eyes we had better produce. The "ministry by accounting" approach to youth ministry is understandable. Numbers are tangible, concrete, and measurable. They do not lie. But, do they tell the whole truth? If they do, then we must concede that Jesus was somewhat of a failure at this game.

Jesus' own ministry numbers seemed to fluctuate. His miracles and healings seemed to draw huge crowds. But when he taught "hard" things like "eating his flesh and drinking his blood" his popularity waned. In the end everyone abandoned him, including his closest followers.

The Apostle Peter smelled trouble early on. After Peter heard Jesus' mission—one that included death on a cross—Peter knew he had to take things into his own hands. A suffering Messiah did not appeal to Peter, let alone the masses. When Peter attempted to steer Jesus to a more sane and popular approach, Jesus' response was not mild. He called Peter "Satan" and told him to go the rear.

Numbers were never Jesus' bottom line. That is not to say that Jesus did not want to reach as many people as possible. Jesus' love was such that he wanted to draw all people to himself. But, Jesus never compromised the truth and power of his message by diluting it in a manner that made it more appealing to the crowds.

Numbers were never Jesus' bottom line.

A youth ministry driven by numbers can easily lose focus on what is really important. If our activities are designed only to draw a crowd, we will major on events such as ski trips, amusement parks, dances, and professional sporting events. The message of the gospel and the meaning of ministry can be compromised or even completely ignored as we steadfastly pursue packing the house. In the end, we may gather a lot of teens for no lasting purpose.

Driven by "Fun"

Some youth ministries are primarily driven by fun. Success is measured by whether or not the teens are having a good time. This emphasis is not difficult to understand. We live in a society where entertainment is one of our highest values. We seem to live by the rule that teens will not attend an event if it is not "fun" (unless their parents make them, of course). Surveys reveal that one of the highest motivating factors to a teen's involvement in a youth ministry is whether it is "fun" or not.

So, we design and evaluate programming and events through the filter of fun. A typical youth ministry activity might begin by leaving our spouses and own children behind on Friday evening to help lead an all-night marathon or amusement. The night is energetically launched by non-stop gaming in the church gym. Next, we are rushed by bus to the local skating rink. After hours of endless orbiting, we charge to a nearby bowling alley. Finally, fifty frames later, the bus grinds to a screeching halt in the church parking lot. After seeing the last sleep-deprived teen to his or her parent's car, we clean up and head home. Exhausted and in a semi-stuporous state, we hoarsely greet our own rising family. After sleeping the day away, we awake only to ask ourselves, "What did we accomplish by that triathlon of fatigue? Was it worth losing a Saturday with my own family?" We try to assure ourselves, "The kids had fun, and therefore, it was worthwhile." Deep down inside, however, we know something is wrong; a steady diet of youth ministry junk food can only lead to spiritual malnutrition.

"Fun" may really be a dietary necessity for teens, but what do young people really mean when they use the word? We tend to think they are primarily looking for good times, laughter, and entertainment. Really, that's only part of it. The kind of fun that leads to a sustaining involvement for a teen essentially includes meaningful experiences, depth of relationships, appealing challenges, touching worship, and engaging content. Youth are looking for far more than roller coaster rides. They are searching for causes to which they can apply their natural idealism. They are seeking a worthy endeavor in which to invest their enthusiasm. Young people want to be challenged beyond the superficiality of the present-day culture. Entertainment may keep us light-hearted, but it lacks the ability to transform one's heart. Entertainment may help us forget our troubles, but it rarely provides us with the resources with which to address those difficulties. Youth ministry solely based on "fun" is, frankly, not worth the time and energy expended. Our vision and purpose for youth ministry must go well beyond entertainment.

Driven by Activities

Some parish youth programs are driven by activity. Success is measured by the sheer volume of programs, activities, or events. For every need and night there is something happening. More is always better when we are caught in the activity trap. The youth ministry driven by activities, however, usually looks better on paper than in reality. The calendar is filled in, but are teens really benefiting by what is offered, or even attending?

The church can easily become like the world around us. In our day and age, we can equate busy-ness with importance. A busy ministry is thought to be an important ministry. This may or may not have some truth to it. However, a busy ministry definitely does not mean an impacting ministry. We can indeed be very, very busy doing ministry yet not produce any real fruit. Our wheels might be spinning, and we might even cover a lot of ground, but in the end we industriously rambled in the wrong direction.

Driven by the "Latest Fads"

Did your parish begin a new youth ministry last year? And the year before? And the year before? And the year before? Some parish youth ministries begin anew each year. They tend to change a lot—depending on the latest youth ministry resource, fad, or program. Sega Genesis evangelization two years ago, theological-sensitivity groups last year, mystic-therapeutic mentoring this year, Internet chat room catechesis next year. The newer, the better. "We have to stay on top of the current trends" is the motto of the fad-driven youth ministry.

Did your parish begin a new youth ministry last year? And the year before? And the year before?

Fad-driven ministries have little long-term direction or focus. Usually, the means are mistaken for the ends. How things are done becomes more important than what is done. Substance is second to style. We feel good about what we are doing if some expert (someone who lives over fifty miles away) says it is the spiritual breakthrough for which youth ministry professionals have been searching since the beginning of time.

Time has proven, however, there are no youth ministry panaceas. Something in us craves easy or simple answers. I guess that is why there will always be a market for new diet books. The lettuce, cantaloupe, and chocolate diets have come (made a fortune) and gone, making little sustaining impact in the lives of overweight people. The same is true with ministry fads. Youth ministry that is effective over the long term, like dieting, requires a lot of hard work, discipline, and a healthy all-around approach. Just like effective dieting, building an effective youth ministry involves organizing all we do around an overriding purpose.

Driven by Spiritual Highs

Some youth ministries are centered around activities or events that have a tradition of high-powered spiritual impact. It may be an annual retreat, conference, mission trip, or rally. You can usually tell if a youth ministry functions this way by the manner in which leaders talk about the event. After listening, one might get the impression that this event has replaced Jesus as the Way, the Truth, and the Life; no one comes to the Father but through this experience! Instead of teens witnessing about an encounter with the person of Jesus, they will more affectionately speak of the name of the retreat movement or conference experience. "You must go on the 'Blast Retreat.' *It* will change your life!"

There is always the temptation to build a youth ministry around the experience of spiritual highs. Leading a teen to a significant personal encounter with Jesus Christ and a meaningful experience of Christian community are very important aspects of an effective youth ministry. These kinds of experiences can be wonderful starting points to a growing, maturing Christian faith. However, they are not the only essential components. These kinds of experiences should be followed up with solid catechetical and spiritual formation. If teens are ever to reach any kind of faith maturity, they must learn how to follow Christ in the mundane routines of everyday life. Essential to growing is the development of regular spiritual disciplines and practices that help bring Christ's presence and word into our daily lives. Solid youth ministries offer a balance of opportunities that include evangelization, formation, and ministry activities—not just one or two big events.

Youth ministries centered around events that tend to produce spiritual highs eventually produce "retreat or conference junkies." These teens live from retreat high to retreat high. Unfortunately, their growth as disciples may ultimately be stifled by their dependence on these experiences.

Driven by Confirmation

Too many parish youth ministries are primarily driven by confirmation. "Receiving" the sacrament can be used as a carrot or bottom-line motivation for attendance. Instead of drawing teens by our own creative efforts and quality ministry, we can easily be tempted to rely on having a "captive" audience who is required to be present. The problem with captives is that they may really feel and act like prisoners, as they are forced to be present at meetings they really do not want to attend. Most prisoners are not happy campers and, therefore, do not make the best learners. Anytime we perceive our freedom is being denied we tend defiantly to fold our arms in a closed disposition. Ministry of this type already begins behind the eight ball.

Because the sacrament tends to be the focus and destination, few teens stay involved once confirmation is celebrated. Instead of understanding the sacrament as a beginning or strengthening for a more committed Christian lifestyle, most teens walk away with a sense of relief that it is all over. Realistically, it is viewed more as a rite of graduation from the inconvenience of religious education. It is rather ironic that confirmation celebrates an initiation into a church from which many immediately drop out. With relatively few post-confirmandi investing their time, energy, and gifts into the church, we have to question, "What did we accomplish in the first place?"

Defining Mission and Purpose

Youth ministers and youth ministry teams are often influenced by the "just do it" mentality. Team member Preston Needs reminds us, "The need is pressing and we have got to do something NOW!" Pat Shintzlacking enthusiastically adds, "We don't have time for elaborate planning. Besides, by the time we get something going we will lose this year's senior class." "Let's just get at it," pipes in Justin Dewit.

Imagine if we employed this kind of approach to construct a new home. We might reason that winter is coming and so we had better get building. Forget the blueprints or plans—let's just start pounding away! In the haste to raise our dwelling, we might find at its completion that we failed to construct some important foundational beams. On top of that, the house leaks and the kids hate it! To remedy the problem we must quadruple our costs. So, instead, we bulldoze it under and start over. Sound too much like parish youth ministry?

In reality, a new home begins in the mind of the builder before a stone is ever cleared for construction. The builder works through a myriad of mental details even before the blueprints are drafted. A visual picture of the house is first constructed. Those ideas are then drawn on paper. Finally, the physical creation is completed and lived in.

Before a new youth ministry planning team lifts a hand to begin any programming or activities, they should together share a clearly defined purpose or mission. Defining our purpose is the starting point for every youth ministry. If we are involved in an existing youth ministry that has lost its focus or seems like it is just spinning its wheels, then we need to take a step back and redefine or recapture our mission. In both cases, we must begin with the questions:

✔ For what purpose do we exist?

✔ What end do we hope to achieve?

Benefits of a Clearly Defined Mission

A youth ministry team that shares a clearly defined mission enjoys numerous benefits that not only contribute towards fruitful ministry with teens, but also serve positively to enhance the leader's experience in youth ministry, thus leading to long-term commitment. The benefits of establishing an overriding purpose far outweigh the cost invested toward achieving it. Some of the benefits are:

1. Unity—The tedious process of arriving at a common purpose, as difficult as it is, helps forge the kind of unity needed to achieve this very purpose. When a group is unified in its mission, the members experience a oneness of mind that shelters them from being strangled by strenuous circumstances and challenges that might essentially suffocate teams that do not share a common vision. A collective purpose rallies the troops together for battle.

A youth ministry team that does not know why it exists is very vulnerable to in-fighting. We lay land mines for potential conflict when we fail to be focused in our purpose. We can end up at odds with one another; each member working towards his or her own understanding of success, and in the process working against other members. A team cannot win a tug-of-war when they cannot agree on which direction to pull. With members yanking in opposite directions, a team will get angry with one another, disillusioned by the amount of energy wasted, and eventually suffer attrition, or even dissolution. A shared vision ensures that individual members will multiply their impact by pulling in a common direction with their team.

2. Focus—A shared purpose provides focus and clarity. We clearly know what we are about and what we are not about. We have distinct boundaries that help us define what we can and cannot do. Every activity, event, and program is defined and measured by our mission. We are able to articulate what role each event or program plays in achieving our overriding vision. If we cannot connect it to our purpose, then we cannot program it into our calendar.

A focused mission reduces the potential for frustration.

A focused mission, therefore, reduces the potential for frustration. It keeps us from scaling foreign fences and getting lost in uncharted areas. Instead of being caught in a jungle of frenzied activity, we have a clear road map to reach our destination. We learn we don't have to do everything. We need not wear out, exhaust, and burn out our leaders with too many activities. We only need to focus our energy on the things that really matter according to our mission. Fruitful youth ministry simply focuses on doing the important things well. A clear mission helps us do that.

3. Proper Evaluation—Evaluation is an essential discipline for any successful youth ministry. Without formally assessing our efforts we can easily miss the times that we are missing our mark. On the positive side, we can be hitting bulls' eyes and not even know it. Evaluation is essential for affirmation for a job well done and for constructive change for an activity that is not fulfilling its purpose.

It is impossible, however, to evaluate a youth ministry that does not have a clear mission. If the leaders have not defined the criteria for effectiveness, there can be no true assessment. When we lack a standard for measurement, we can fall into the trap of evaluating by the default standard: the number of teens who came or the "fun" they had while there.

A friend of mine who was a pilot during the Vietnam War told me of his experience with vertigo. Vertigo is a dizziness and disorientation that can occur when one loses sight of the horizon while flying at night or in the clouds. He said you can become so disorientated that you would swear the plane is traveling upside down. Everything in you wants to grab the controls and turn that plane "right-side up." In training for the phenomenon of vertigo, he was taught to get focused on the control panel. If the control panel states you are right-side up, then you are, indeed, right-side up. It was drilled into him that the only reliable standard of measurement is your control panel, and you must go by it or otherwise jeopardize your life.

It is easy to experience "youth ministry vertigo" without the security of a clear mission. We can get dizzy and disorientated by countless events and activities and lose sight of any objective measurement of effectiveness. A clear purpose will ensure that we stay focused on what is truly important and fly right-side up.

The Mission Statement

The development of a youth ministry mission statement is essential for many reasons: it gives us a sense of meaning and purpose; it helps us clarify and concentrate our energy into the true mission of the ministry; it aids us in developing a ministry with concrete objectives; it provides programmatic and activity boundaries, and, hence, a reference point for evaluation. Finally, a mission statement becomes a rallying cry to inspire and motivate us towards completing our task.

When developing a youth ministry mission statement we must thoughtfully consider *what* we do, *where* we do it, and with *whom* we do it. The "what" is the overall mission of Christ and the church. The "where" is our local expression of this purpose. This part of the mission statement must incorporate our parish's personality and charisms. The "whom" are youth. This includes the consideration of the unique characteristics of adolescence.

In essence, the core substance of our mission never changes. Jesus has already established for us our purpose. This is a non-negotiable. The *expression* or *style* in which we carry out our mission, however, will look different depending on where and with whom it is being focused and applied.

Root the Mission Statement in Jesus and the Church

The mission of the church is always the reference point for the mission of youth ministry. We cannot be authentic in our practice of youth ministry without being true to the mission of Jesus and the church. Many parish youth ministries, however, are developed without any serious consideration of how their programs, activities and events relate to the overall mission of the church. By examining some youth ministries' offerings, one might conclude that the purpose of the church is to keep kids busy and off the streets!

The mission of the church is that of proclaiming and establishing among all peoples the kingdom of God.[7] We are mandated to make disciples of Christ (see Matthew 28:18) by being a sign to the world and an instrument of God's love and salvation to all peoples. The Second Vatican Council documents describe the church as "the universal sacrament of salvation." The sole purpose of the church was clearly defined:

> Whether it aids the world or whether it benefits from it, the Church has one sole purpose—that the kingdom of God may come and the salvation of the human race may be accomplished. Every benefit the people of God can confer on mankind during its earthly pilgrimage is rooted in the Church's being "the universal sacrament of salvation," at once manifesting and actualizing the mystery of God's love for men.[8]

The Church's Threefold Mission

The church's mission to establish God's kingdom and bring salvation to all peoples has been expressed in numerous ways. For our purposes, I have organized it into a sequential threefold mission: (1) Sowing (to proclaim the gospel through evangelization); (2) Growing (to proclaim the gospel through growth in holiness and fullness of faith); and (3) Reaping (to proclaim the gospel by loving and serving all those in need). The action of concretizing this mission in the form of a written statement is part of the preparation. What follows is more background on each step of the threefold mission.

1. *Sowing the Word*—The church was missionary from the very beginning. Jesus' final instructions to his followers included the call to proclaim the good news of God's kingdom to all nations, beginning in Jerusalem (see Acts 1:8; Mark 16:15; Matthew 28:19-20). The act and content of this initial evangelistic proclamation is known as the *kerygma*. Its message centers on God's saving activity through the life, death, and resurrection of Jesus Christ. The intended goal or response to the *kerygma* is conversion. Evangelization is an initial and ongoing activity that seeks to bring about a change of direction in one's life toward Jesus Christ. Good youth ministry, therefore, is evangelistic, calling teens to accept the person, teachings, and values of Jesus Christ.

Evangelization is an initial and ongoing activity that seeks to bring about a change of direction in one's life toward Jesus Christ.

2. *Growing a People*—A mother's responsibility does not end with the birth of her child. Birth simply begins a process of nurturing, which has as its goal the fostering of adult maturity. A farmer's role is not complete with the germination of his crop. His focus and tasks change when the fragile bud bursts forth from the soil. Likewise, the church's mission does not end with evangelization. Evangelization challenges teens to *accept* Jesus and his teachings. This second phase of the church's mission challenges believers to be *formed* in their relationship with Christ, one another, and the teaching and values of the kingdom.

Conversion to Christ creates new needs in the believer—to live the Christian life more fully by growing in the understanding and practice of the two great commandments of the kingdom: to love God and our fellow brothers and sisters. The Apostle Paul captures the essence of this phase when he says, "So, as you received Christ Jesus the Lord, walk in him, rooted in him and built upon him and established in the faith as you were taught, abounding in thanksgiving" (Colossians 2:6-7). This second aspect of the church's mission focuses on the formation of the believer. This would include spiritual, catechetical, moral, and ecclesial formation. The goal of the growth phase is Christian maturity. Paul articulates this objective when he says, "It is Christ whom we proclaim, admonishing everyone and teaching everyone with all wisdom, that we may present everyone perfect in Christ" (Colossians 1:28).

Good youth ministry, therefore, nurtures and forms teens toward spiritual, catechetical, moral, and ecclesial maturity.

3. *Serving All in Need*—The third focus of the church's mission *sends* forth teens to live the good news. A plant reaches maturity when it begins to reproduce. This aspect of the church's mission involves reproducing the good news in others by becoming an instrument of God's love to the world. Teens are called to proclaim the gospel both in word and deed. We become light and salt to the world by verbally sharing the good news, witnessing through our lifestyle and example, and serving all in need through action on behalf of justice. This dimension of the church's life, *diakonia*, or service, is aimed at those both inside and outside the church. If the first aspect of the church's mission is "come" (see John 1:38-39; Matthew 11:28) and the second phase is "form," then the third phase says, "Go" (see Matthew 28:19; Mark 16:15). Good youth ministry, therefore, equips, empowers, organizes, and mobilizes teens toward serving all in need.

The overall mission of the church could be summarized as bringing them in through evangelization, building them up through formation, and sending them out to minister.

Rooted in the Parish Mission

Parish youth ministry is not only carried out within the context of the church's overall mission, but each parish needs to consider carefully its own particular mission statement, if they have adopted one. Parish youth ministry cannot happen apart from the larger parish community. Each parish has its own personality, culture, and flavor. These characteristics should be integrated into the youth ministry mission statement. For instance, if hospitality and welcoming are of a high value and charism to the parish as a whole, this should also be reflected in the youth ministry mission statement. Also, the particular cultural context in which we are ministering should be considered.

The Uniqueness of Adolescence

After considering the broad mission of the church and its particular expression in our own local faith community, we must begin to further focus our lens upon who we are seeking to impact—namely youth. Adolescence is a unique stage in life developmentally, socially, and culturally. An effective youth ministry mission statement will reflect a good understanding of adolescence. The following is a brief overview of some of the primary developmental issues of adolescence:

1. *Identity*—The transition from childhood to adult life inevitably brings about a crisis of identity. Everything about

this process shakes one's comfortable "childhood" existence and screams, "Change is happening!" Paradoxically, the "transitioner" loves this new-found call to adulthood and investigation of his or her place in it, but hates the thought of leaving the security of childhood behind.

"Who am I?"

"What makes me unique?"

"What am I about?"

"Where am I headed?"

These are just a few of the questions that arise and demand answers during adolescence. The adolescent begins to crave, realize, and wrestle with a sense of meaningful self and uniqueness. Life itself becomes more complex, with relationships, school, employment, and entertainment taking greater precedence. In developing an identity, the adolescent must give personal meaning to the many life issues that will confront him or her.

2. *Belonging*—Foundational to our created purpose is being in relationship with God and other significant persons. We are unable and uninspired to live a vibrant life without meaningful relationships. The paradox of adolescence can be seen in the teenager's desire to stand out as an individual (not conforming to any particular societal influence or demand), but also to establish a sense of purposeful and significant connectedness to others.

The adolescent's desire to belong can be seen in his attempt to answer such questions as:

"Who are my friends?"

"How do I relate to others?"

"Where do I belong or fit in?"

Friendships and peer-relationships become more desirable than those with Mom and Dad. The adolescent who fails to connect with others and satisfy his or her natural desire and inclination to belong often sinks into a life of loneliness, isolation, and despair.

3. *Sexuality*—With greater intensity than any other personal insight, the adolescent becomes increasingly aware that he or she is a sexual person, and attempts to incorporate his or her sexuality into his or her identity. Teens strive to discover what role sexuality will play in their lives, and seek to answer questions such as:

"How do I relate to the opposite sex?"

"Will anyone love me?"

"Do others see me as an attractive person?"

"What role can/does sexual exploration and experimentation play in my life?"

Teenagers have a real need for intimacy. They need to care for others, and be cared for. This need directly relates to their desire to belong. Teens need to be affirmed in their sexuality—a gift from God—and encouraged to express it in healthy, moral, and responsible ways.

4. Values—

"What do I believe?"

"What is important?"

"What is right?"

"What is wrong?"

Adolescents seek to answer such questions in an attempt to develop personal values and convictions. At this stage in their lives, teens begin to understand that without standing for something, they will fall for anything. The adolescent on his or her way to adulthood recognizes that societal norms and standards have a functional purpose and are more than just a set of oppressive rules and regulations.

Establishing a personal set of values and convictions will give adolescents the impetus needed to respond to the world around them with great moral character and integrity. Without developing such ideals, teens will experience life as directionless and void of any significant purpose and meaning.

*5. Purpose—*Teens are hungry to make a positive contribution to society, and desire that society would validate and affirm their hope. Questions that adolescents pursue answers for with great tenacity are:

"Why am I here?"

"What is life about?"

"What will I do with my life?"

When it comes to their futures, most teens are not lethargic and apathetic, but are rather energetic, enthusiastic, and idealistic. With great passion and desire, adolescents want the world to know that they can make a positive difference.

Application

"Steps to Developing a Mission Statement" (page 84) illustrates the gradual narrowing of concepts and ideas that will be included in a mission statement for youth ministry.

Steps to Developing a Mission Statement

Developing a mission statement involves gathering the team together, preparing through study and reflection, brainstorming key concepts, categorizing broad themes, composing a statement, and testing it out. Let's look at each of these steps in greater detail.

1. Gather

Begin by gathering the existing planning team, or if there isn't one, assemble an ad hoc committee for planning purposes. Ideally, this group should be comprised of a diverse group of people, including: parish staff and volunteer leaders, male and female, adults and teens, and representation of the various ethnic cultures in the parish. The team should have between six and twelve members. The youth minister may serve as its facilitator or chair. A team approach will assure broader input in the development of a mission statement and greater ownership when implementing it. The process should be completed prayerfully. All decisions should be done by consensus or communal discernment.

2. Review

Gather together important documents and resources. These might include your parish and diocesan mission statements, chapters one and four of *Growing Teen Disciples, Ministry with Adolescents: A Vision and Strategy,*[9] and any other writings you may find useful in providing an educational foundation to what Catholic youth ministry is all about. Provide these resources in advance so members have enough time to review them carefully. Schedule a follow-up meeting to share key insights from each of the documents. This will serve as a foundational primer for the actual task of writing the mission statement.

3. Brainstorm

As a group, brainstorm various concepts that each of you feel should be considered in the statement. List all ideas on a flip chart or chalkboard so each member can see them. Do not judge the different ideas listed. This activity is like the mouth of a funnel—it is wide and broad. You will discuss far more than you will ever use, but the process will help the group sift through what is essential and what is peripheral to your purpose. Brainstorm answers to the following questions. Use the subquestions to spark additional perspectives, angles, or thought.

Who are we?

- ✔ How do we understand ourselves as church (universal and Catholic)?
- ✔ How do we understand ourselves as a parish: personality, locality, and charisms?
- ✔ What do we believe?
- ✔ How do we differ from the dominant culture? Other faiths?

Who do we wish to reach?

- ✔ Ages? (senior high/junior high/young adults, etc.?)
- ✔ Parents of adolescents?
- ✔ Family?
- ✔ Parish members?

- ✔ Larger community?
- ✔ Ethnic/racial groups?
- ✔ Specific groups of young people? (subcultures, cliques, etc.)

What is our goal?

- ✔ Why do we exist?
- ✔ What is our purpose or aim?
- ✔ What is our passion for those we wish to reach?
- ✔ What results do we hope to achieve?
- ✔ How would we know if we achieved our mission?
- ✔ Personally, what do I want to see happen for young people in our parish?
- ✔ How would I like teenagers to respond to Jesus Christ?

How will we achieve our goal?

- ✔ What do we need to be (as leadership) to achieve our mission?
- ✔ In what manner will we go about our mission?
- ✔ What words might describe our approach? (loving, accepting, etc.)
- ✔ What kinds of things will we need to do?

4. Organize

After exhausting the brainstorming process, allow the funnel to narrow into more digestible themes by organizing the contributions into several broad categories. For instance, your list might include such entries as small groups, a place where you can be you, hospitable environment, love for one another, fellowship, and communal prayer organized under many different categories. Those statements may be grouped under the broad heading of "Christian Community." After assigning broad categories, write a summary statement that captures the essence of the items under each heading.

5. Compose

Once you have narrowed all your data into broad categories or themes, you are ready to begin composing your mission statement. Use a flip chart or chalkboard so each member can work from the same draft. This is a tedious word-by-word process that should be done prayerfully. Work towards consensus on each word and phrase. Focus on the results you hope to achieve rather than the activities. Write and rewrite until the whole group feels that the statement communicates what God is calling you to do. Work together to be of one mind and unified in your purpose. Stop and pray through sticking points and snags. A good litmus test to gauge whether your team is on the right track is if they are excited about the *content* of the statement. You are in trouble if their only thrill is over the fact that they are finished with the task. There will also be a sense of God's peace when you have discovered your overriding purpose.

6. Test

Once a statement is completed, submit it to your parish leadership for comments and criticisms. This should include your pastor, staff members, and the parish council. Discuss the feedback of these people and groups and make any necessary adjustments. Additionally, consider playing the devil's advocate at this follow-up meeting (if this is difficult bring in an outsider) by challenging your team with the following questions:

- ✔ Does the statement inspire you to action? How so?
- ✔ Do you believe this statement reflects what the Holy Spirit desires for the youth of our community? Why?
- ✔ Does this statement reflect the overall mission of the church? How so?
- ✔ Does this statement reflect the mission, personality and unique charisms of the parish? How so?
- ✔ How does this statement reflect the needs of youth in our local community?
- ✔ How does the statement flow? Is the terminology meaningful?
- ✔ How does it communicate to others the direction we are heading?
- ✔ How does the statement communicate our overall purpose?
- ✔ Do you believe this statement? Why or why not?
- ✔ Is the statement balanced and comprehensive? How so?

A mission statement is complete when the above questions serve only to further galvanize the team in their convictions. Make any necessary revisions, however, if a question exposes a vulnerability in your statement.

Recall that a good youth ministry mission statement must reflect what we do, where we do it, and with whom we do it. In other words, it is rooted in the broad mission of Jesus and the church, includes the personality of the parish and community, and considers the developmental, social, and cultural characteristics of adolescence. To check the viability of your mission statement, make sure that it may be described by the following terms:

Specific—A good youth ministry statement is clear, focused and specific. The wording is precise in its meaning, and targeted on its destination. It will leave no questions in the mind of the reader as to what you do or do not do. Like radar, it verbally hones in and locks on its purpose. A mission statement should be concise (fifteen to thirty words) and memorizable. The danger of longer statements is that it is easy to get lost in all the verbiage, and, therefore, to lose the clarity of purpose. If our mission is not clearly stated, then everything that proceeds from it—our goals, objectives, programs, and activities—will also suffer a lack of focus.

Results-oriented—A good youth ministry statement will focus on the results which it hopes to attain rather than the activities in which it engages. Often, mission statements list the activities a youth ministry does (evangelization, catechesis, community-building, etc.) instead of the results that the activities hope to achieve (conversion, Christian maturity, Christian community, etc.). When we focus on results, we are better able to evaluate whether we have reached our target.

Motivating—A good mission statement not only defines a purpose, but passionately motivates its members towards its fulfillment. It should enthusiastically inspire the team, valiantly rallying them to make their vision a reality. It should bring about an excitement that helps provide the inspiration needed to press on when the going gets tough.

Beyond Paper—A good mission statement is a living, breathing, and blood-circulating document! Its words are inscribed on the hearts, and displayed through the actions of the entire team. A new youth worker should be able to pick up the mission by osmosis—by simply observing other youth workers doing their job. The way we do ministry ought to communicate what we value and what we see as important. A good mission statement is not just an activity a youth ministry team checks off their "to do list." It must move from the paper, to the heads, hearts, and hands of all the leaders.

Many youth ministries never fully benefit from the development of a mission statement. All too often, it becomes one more paper shuffled in the youth ministry file cabinet. If we think we have a mission statement, but are not sure what it is, or have to scramble through folders to find it, most likely it is not making much of an impact on the day-to-day happenings of the ministry. A mission statement must be championed by every member of the youth ministry team. It must be recited, memorized, prayed through, studied, reflected upon, and visually communicated. In short, it must be transfused into the heart and vascular system of the organization.

Developing a Strategic Plan

Our mission statement is the initial step to building a strategic plan and should vividly, yet succinctly, describe our final destination. A strategic plan is a practical and systematic process to organizing all that we do around our central purpose. The strategic planning process is key to the long-term success of a ministry. It places wings on dreams, helping transport good ideas to real-life expression. The strategic plan that follows, then, is the detailed road map that provides the directions to getting us to our mission.

Developing a strategic plan involves assessing and summarizing the needs of teens, determining focus result areas, establishing quantitative and measurable goals, and developing a detailed action plan. Let's look at each step in greater detail.

1. Assess and Summarize the Key Needs

An important step in building a teen-friendly youth ministry is coming to a good understanding of the young people we seek to serve. Before we can consider the development of any programming, we must first consider the needs of our target audience. There are two data-gathering approaches that can be used to learn more about the teens we are seeking to reach.

A *qualitative* approach helps give insight into *why* people think and act the way they do. For instance, we may know that a significant percentage of teens think liturgy is mostly boring, but a qualitative approach would help us understand *why* young people think liturgy is mostly boring. Questions are open-ended, allowing the respondent to answer in his or her own words. For example, "What characteristics of your parish's Sunday liturgies do you find boring, or hard to stay focused on?" The collective results of such a question might be summarized as: "Many teens find Mass to be boring because of 'poor musical selections.' Furthermore, the homilies are rarely directed toward issues that teens find relevant." Some common qualitative assessment methods include interviews, focus groups, observation, brainstorming, and town meetings.

A second approach—a *quantitative* approach—deals with numbers. This approach helps uncover *how many* people think and feel in certain ways. Most quantitative surveys are in a multiple choice format. For instance, a quantitative survey might have a question set up as follows:

Application

Page 85 offers an overall "Cultivation Strategic Planning Model." Pages 86-96 include several resources to assist as a "Parish Youth Ministry Strategic Planning Guide." Assembled and completed, these pages can make up an entire strategic plan.

What response would best describe your typical experience of your parish's Sunday liturgies?

A. very meaningful B. somewhat meaningful C. mostly boring

The calculated result might be summarized as: "Forty-two percent of young people think church is mostly boring." Commonly used methods under the quantitative approach include written surveys and telephone surveys.

When preparing to gather data, we should determine our critical audiences, the approaches and methods that will yield the most significant information from these audiences, and our present resources (human, financial, and timeline) to gather the information. We do not want to use approaches beyond our abilities, gather more information than we could possibly use, or spend our entire year's budget on the project. Some groups can become gluttonous with information, indulging in more surveys than they could possibly assess, then burning out while in the process, and finally, disillusioning the parish that was counting on them to build a youth ministry. On the other hand, we don't want to short-circuit the data gathering process by assuming we intuitively understand all the needs of the present-day teen. We should seek to strike a balance based on our present resources and what it is essential that we know.

Once the target audiences have been surveyed, the planning team should prayerfully summarize the key needs of these audiences.

2. Determine Focus Result Areas

The next step is to identify four to ten *focus result areas* (FRAs). These are key dimensions of ministry that must be addressed in order to reach out to our community in light of our mission. We determine focus result areas by asking, "What key areas of youth ministry must we focus on in order to attain our mission and meet the needs of our youth?" FRAs are general categories. Possible focus result areas might include: evangelization, formation, leadership, communication, or intercessory prayer. Collectively, the focus result areas state our vision. They form a visual picture of what effective youth ministry will look like as we seek to attain our mission.

For each FRA a descriptive statement is created that succinctly captures the essence of that area. For example:

> **Intercessory Prayer Base**
> To develop an organized, comprehensive, and impacting intercessory prayer base for the youth ministry of our parish.

Youth Evangelization
To establish programming, activities, events, methods, and approaches that effectively communicate the good news of Jesus Christ to all teens of our community.

3. Establish Goals

Next, establish goals under each FRA. Goals can be determined by asking, "What tangible things must we do to fulfill the focus result area?" Goals should be expressed quantitatively. They should be concrete, measurable, and time-based. They give practical expression to the ideals of the FRAs. For example:

Intercessory Prayer Base
To develop an organized, comprehensive, and impacting intercessory prayer base for the youth ministry of our parish.

Goal 1 To establish a person in the role of Intercessory Prayer Director by September.
Goal 2 To ensure that each teen in the parish is being prayed for each day by two people by August.

Youth Evangelization
To establish programming, activities, events, methods, and approaches that effectively communicate the good news of Jesus Christ to all teens of our community.

Goal 1 To establish a person in the role of Large Group Evangelization Director by September.
Goal 2 To begin a bi-monthly large group evangelization program by October.
Goal 3 To begin an annual, peer ministry-led, evangelistic retreat program by April.

4. Develop Action Plans

The next step is to create an action plan for each goal. Action plans cover the nitty-gritty details. Each goal should be broken down into small steps. Each step should include the task at hand, the date in which it is to be accomplished, and who is responsible for its completion. For example:

Goal 1 To establish a person in the role of Large Group Evangelization Director by September.

Action Plan

Completion	Task to be done	Who is responsible
Sept. 1	Write a job description	Melvin
Sept. 15	Brainstorm names of possible people	Team
Sept. 15	Prayerfully narrow down list	Team
Sept. 25	Personally contact candidates	Fazio
Oct. 15	Establish the position	Team
Oct. 30	Orientation and training for role	Gladys

Summary

There is a driving force behind every youth ministry. Whether by decision or default, it is driven by some underlying assumption as to what is important. Youth ministries can be primarily driven by numbers, fun, activities, fads, spiritual highs, or the sacrament of confirmation. A truly effective youth ministry begins by carefully and intentionally arriving at a clearly defined mission. A mission statement is the starting point for any planning process.

The benefits of developing a clear mission statement far outweigh the cost of arriving at one. A mission statement unifies a team in vision, helps them stay focused on what they are about, and provides the proper framework for effective evaluation.

When developing a youth ministry mission statement we must thoughtfully consider what we do, where we do it, and with whom we do it. Because youth ministry is a particular ministry of the church, it must reflect the mission of the church—namely to proclaim and establish the kingdom of God among all peoples by making disciples of Jesus Christ. This mission can be expressed in a threefold sequential process: bringing people in through evangelization (sowing), building them up through Christian formation (growing), and sending them out to serve all in need through ministry training (reaping).

Not only does a mission statement need to be rooted in the overall mission of the church, but it needs to reflect the particular characteristics of the parish community in which it is lived out. Finally, it needs to reflect a good understanding of the distinctive developmental, social, and cultural characteristics of adolescents.

The first step to drafting a mission statement is to gather a team together to prayerfully collaborate in discovering their overall purpose. In preparation, the team should study, review, and reflect on the overall mission of the church, the personality and vision of the parish, and useful youth ministry resources and documents. Next, the team should brainstorm important concepts they would like to see reflected in their mission. These contributions can be further categorized into broad categories or themes. These themes are then considered as the team begins to compose a fifteen- to thirty-five-word statement that reflects the youth ministry's overriding purpose. Finally, the statement should be submitted to the parish's pastoral leadership for reflection and revision.

A good mission statement is communicated concisely, targeted precisely, and stated specifically. The statement should motivate and passionately inspire the leadership towards its fulfillment. An effective purpose statement is expressed not in activities, but in results. Finally, a mission statement must go beyond paper, becoming a living, breathing document that is expressed in all that the leadership does.

A mission statement is the first step in the planning process. To go beyond simply pleasant thoughts to real teen-impacting practical expression, a team must organize all that it does around their overall purpose. This is accomplished through strategic planning. In addition to composing a mission statement, this process involves four steps. First, a planning team should determine their target audience, choose and utilize the best assessment tools, and interpret and summarize the discerned key needs. Second, a team must determine its focus result areas. This is done by asking, "What areas do we need to focus on to meet our key needs and fulfill our overriding purpose?" Next, under each focus result area, the team must develop measurable and quantitative goals that will help them meet the ideals of their FRAs. Finally, the goals must be broken down into an action plan. The action plan specifically identifies each task, when it is to be done, and who is responsible for its completion.

By following these steps, a planning team can be focused in their vision and clear in their efforts in making disciples of Jesus Christ.

Steps to Developing a Mission Statement

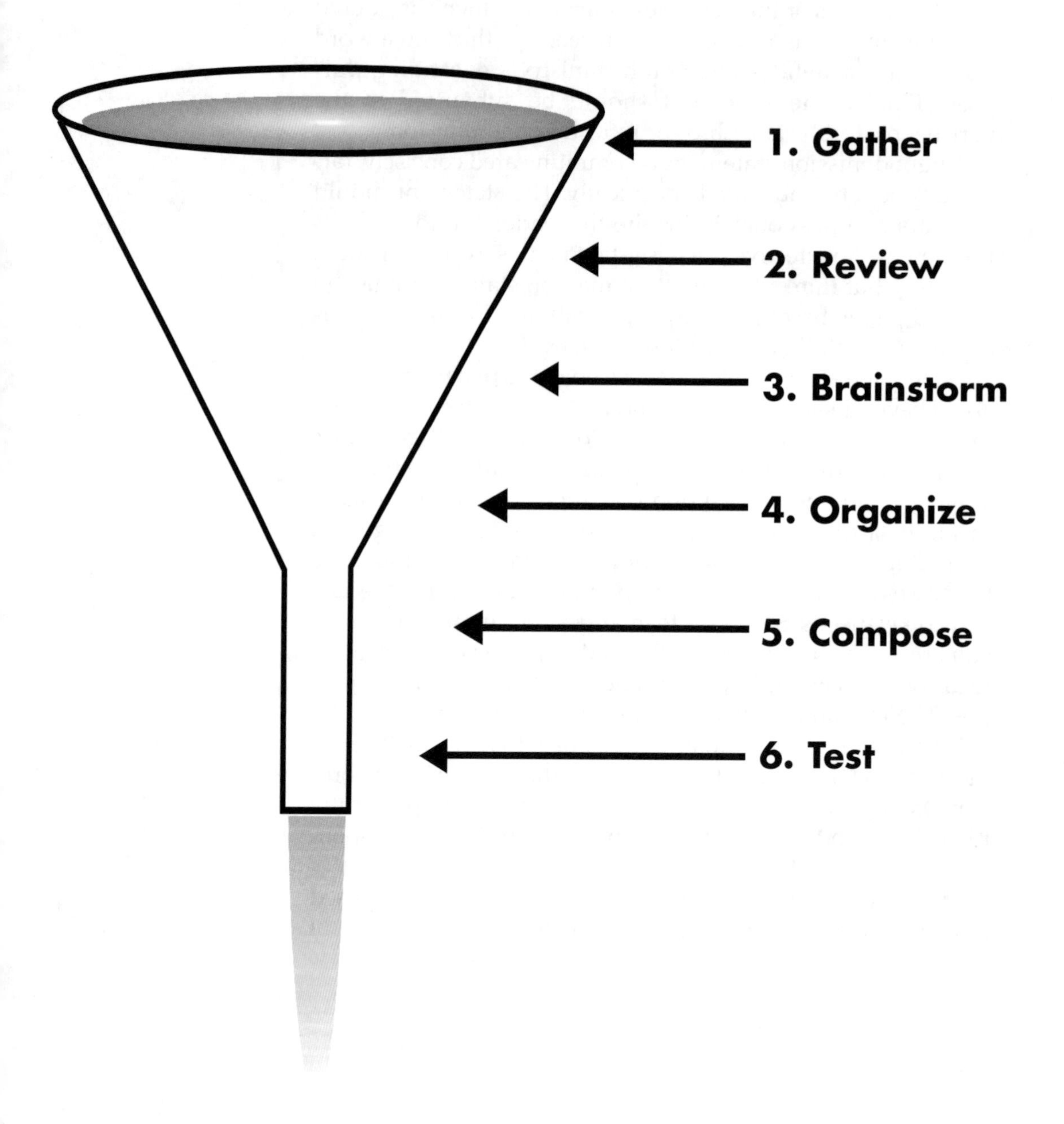

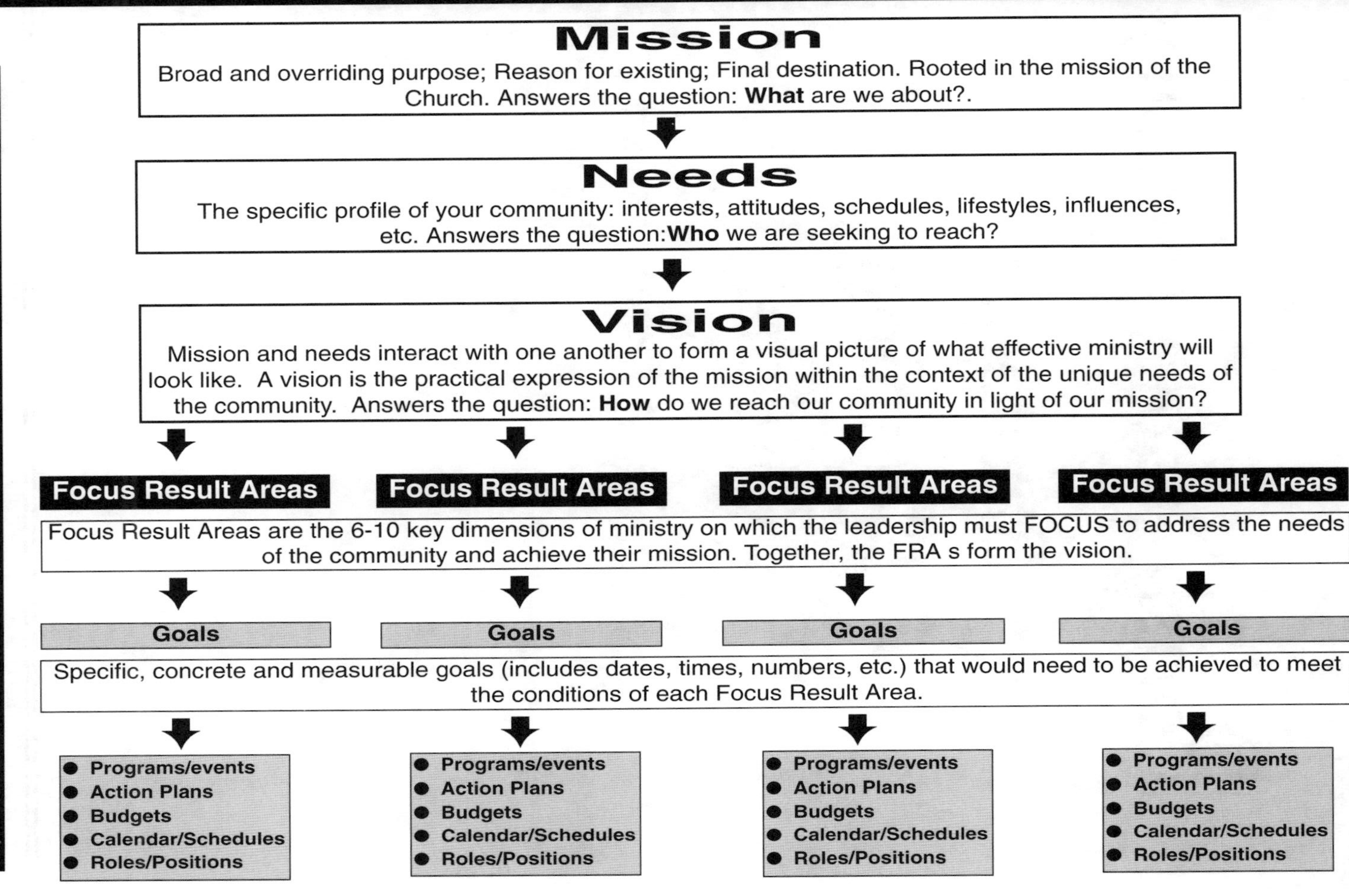
Cultivation Strategic Planning Model
Done in the context of Prayerful Intercession
Done in the context of Christian Community
Mission
Broad and overriding purpose; Reason for existing; Final destination. Rooted in the mission of the Church. Answers the question: What are we about?.
Needs
The specific profile of your community: interests, attitudes, schedules, lifestyles, influences, etc. Answers the question:Who we are seeking to reach?
Vision
Mission and needs interact with one another to form a visual picture of what effective ministry will look like. A vision is the practical expression of the mission within the context of the unique needs of the community. Answers the question: How do we reach our community in light of our mission?
Focus Result Areas
Focus Result Areas
Focus Result Areas
Focus Result Areas
Focus Result Areas are the 6-10 key dimensions of ministry on which the leadership must FOCUS to address the needs of the community and achieve their mission. Together, the FRA s form the vision.
Goals
Goals
Goals
Goals
Specific, concrete and measurable goals (includes dates, times, numbers, etc.) that would need to be achieved to meet the conditions of each Focus Result Area.
Programs/events
Action Plans
Budgets
Calendar/Schedules
Roles/Positions
Programs/events
Action Plans
Budgets
Calendar/Schedules
Roles/Positions
Programs/events
Action Plans
Budgets
Calendar/Schedules
Roles/Positions
Programs/events
Action Plans
Budgets
Calendar/Schedules
Roles/Positions

Parish Youth Ministry

Strategic Planning Guide

Our Mission

(Place Mission Statement Above)

Focus Result Area	Descriptive Statement
FRA #1 Intercessory Prayer Base	
FRA #2 Communications Director	
FRA #3 Youth Evangelization	
FRA #4 Student Leadership	
FRA #5	
FRA #6	

Focus Result Area | **Descriptive Statement**

FRA #1

Intercessory Prayer Base

Goal #1

Goal #2

Goal #3

Goal #4

Goal #5

Goal #6

Goal #7

Goal #8

Focus Result Area	Descriptive Statement
FRA #2 Communications Director	

Goal #1

Goal #2

Goal #3

Goal #4

Goal #5

Goal #6

Goal #7

Goal #8

Focus Result Area	Descriptive Statement
FRA #3 Youth Evangelization	

Goal #1

Goal #2

Goal #3

Goal #4

Goal #5

Goal #6

Goal #7

Goal #8

Focus Result Area	Descriptive Statement
FRA #4 Student Leadership	

Goal #1

Goal #2

Goal #3

Goal #4

Goal #5

Goal #6

Goal #7

Goal #8

Focus Result Area **Descriptive Statement**

Goal #1

Goal #2

Goal #3

Goal #4

Goal #5

Goal #6

Goal #7

Goal #8

Focus Result Area **Descriptive Statement**

FRA #6

Goal #1

Goal #2

Goal #3

Goal #4

Goal #5

Goal #6

Goal #7

Goal #8

Focus Result Area | Descriptive Statement

FRA #1 — Intercessory Prayer Base

Goal #___

Action Plan

#	Action Item	Person Responsible	Date

Focus Result Area

Descriptive Statement

FRA #00

Goal #___

Action Plan

#	Action Item	Person Responsible	Date

5

FERTILIZING THE HARVEST THROUGH INTERCESSION

Fresh out of college, I was hired as a full-time youth minister in a parish with little history of youth ministry and no ongoing programming for teens. My job was to build a youth ministry program from scratch.

Things were slow during my first summer. Teens were not yet hanging around the parish, nor were there any programs planned. Consequently, I found myself with a lot of time on my hands.

With the time I had, I prayed every day for each individual high school teen registered in the parish. Don't get me wrong—it wasn't simply a time-filler for a guy bored to death and desperate to justify his full-time position. I believed in prayer—at least theoretically. I had no idea, however, how practical and powerful this incredible God-given resource is. I still marvel at the power God releases through this simple investment of time and love.

The benefits were numerous. First, as a result of praying for each teen on the list, I became very familiar with their names. Consequently, it only took a quick introduction for me to remember who they were. I discovered that these teens, like most of us, appreciated the fact that I was able to call them by name so quickly.

Second, I noticed substantial numerical growth in attendance as that first year progressed. Our first evangelistic program attracted a total of twelve teens. By the end of the year we were seeing over 120 teens attending this same program. We grew over 1000 percent in numbers! That was exciting, but there was something going on that was far more significant in impact.

Amazingly, I found teen after teen attempting to articulate to me, both awkwardly and profoundly, his or her experience of a spiritual hunger. It was not uncommon for me to hear teens say things like, "I feel empty inside. I feel like that missing piece is God. How can I have a relationship with the Lord?"

It seemed so apparent to me that this spiritual hunger for a personal relationship with God was a direct answer to the hours of prayer in behalf of these teens.

I remember one young man in particular. John was a junior in high school who looked and acted well beyond his adolescent years. He was one of those teens you thought could some day be the president of the United States.

One day while talking with John, he proudly proclaimed a litany of his accomplishments—including president of teen council, grades that could land him into any college he desired, and wide popularity with his peers. What more could a young man ask for in life? Apparently, a lot.

One day, in a moment of painful honesty, John's façade cracked. He went on to tell me that he chased after these accomplishments in a futile attempt to silence a nagging chorus of doubt and insecurity that skipped endlessly through his head. "I am looking for peace and significance through accomplishments, and it feels like I am on a treadmill going nowhere. I think what I am really looking for is Christ." John's statement was reminiscent of St. Augustine's classic words, "My heart is restless until it rests in Thee, O Lord."

John has yet to be elected president, but he did become a full-time youth minister. His restless heart found in a relationship with Jesus that for which he had been searching. He chose to invest his life in sharing this same good news with other teens. John is one of over a dozen teens from my years at the parish who have followed Christ's call to full-time ministry in the church. Intercessory prayer works!

What Is Intercession?

A prayerless youth is simply a powerless youth ministry.

Intercession is a prayer of supplication, or asking. Supplication prayer has two general forms of expression: petition and intercession. Petition is asking in behalf of one's self. We transition from petition to intercession when we shift our prayer focus from our own needs to those of others. Intercession *is the act of asking in behalf of another or others.* It literally means "to go between." Any time we pray for another's need we are interceding.

Intercessory prayer is a fundamental ministry, but does not take the place of other essential elements of an effective youth ministry, such as evangelization or social justice. It simply enhances the impact of these activities. It can be likened to the fertilizer that increases the yield of a crop. A prayerless youth ministry is simply a powerless youth ministry. But it takes far more than just prayer to build a solid and impacting youth ministry. (That is what the other parts of this book are about.)

Beyond my simple definition, Walter Wink describes intercession as:

> spiritual defiance of what is in the name of what God has promised. Intercession visualizes an alternative future to the one apparently fated by the momentum of current contradictory forces. It breathes the air of a time yet to be into the suffocating atmosphere of present reality.[10]

The intercessors are, in some ways, the quality control managers for the kingdom of God. Their jobs are to measure the present situation in light of God's promises and will. That which is out of order is brought into alignment through proactive, prayerful intercession.

In other words, the teens of a parish may be turned off to God and the church. Generally, they may respond to youth ministry activities with a non-caring attitude. The intercessor is fully aware of the present situation, but refuses to passively acquiesce to this undesirable alternative to God's will. The intercessor is tenaciously motivated by God's will for his people, as clearly stated in scripture. (See 1 Timothy 2:3-4.) The intercessor may visualize a spiritual disposition radically divergent from the present indifference. He or she may envision teens spiritually open and hungering to know God deeply and personally. It is this reality that the intercessor proactively prays into existence.

Isaiah 62:1-7 describes the role of the intercessor well:

> For Zion's sake I will not be silent,
>   for Jerusalem's sake I will not be quiet,
> Until her vindication shines forth like the dawn
>   and her victory like a burning torch.
> Nations shall behold your vindication,
>   and all kings your glory;
> You shall be called by a new name
>   pronounced by the mouth of the Lord.
> You shall be a glorious crown in the hand of the Lord,
>   a royal diadem held by your God.
> No more shall men call you "Forsaken,"
>   or your land "Desolate,"
> But you shall be called "My Delight,"
>   and your land "Espoused."
> For the Lord delights in you,
>   and makes your land his spouse.

As a young man marries a virgin,
your Builder shall marry you;
And as a bridegroom rejoices in his bride
so shall your God rejoice in you.
Upon your walls, O Jerusalem,
I have stationed watchmen;
Never, by day or by night,
shall they be silent.
O you who are to remind the Lord,
take no rest
And give no rest to him,
until he re-establishes Jerusalem
And makes of it
the pride of the earth.

Intercession, as described by the prophet, is not for the passive or spiritually comfortable. It is an aggressive activity of storming heaven's gates with relentless, sacrificial, fervent prayer until the situation is in harmony with God's will.

Steps to Developing an Impacting Intercessory Prayer Base

It is not enough to believe in the power of prayer. We must make practical use of this great resource by developing an intercessory prayer base. This can be done by recognizing the importance of intercession, praying for the grace to be an intercessor, and strategizing for consistency and effectiveness. Let's take a closer look at each of these elements.

Recognize the Importance of Intercession

The first step to developing a powerful intercessory prayer base is to recognize it as an essential youth ministry activity. Most parish youth ministries have little, if any, organized intercessory prayer activity. Intercessory prayer is probably the most underutilized resource in youth ministry today. It is no wonder that few Catholic youth ministry books or approaches devote any serious consideration to the topic of intercessory prayer. Many approaches primarily focus on the "natural" side of developing a youth ministry, largely ignoring the "supernatural" element. We have been quick to implement the wisdom of the secular business world, but slower to grasp the wisdom of our faith tradition. As Catholics, we have a rich history and heritage of prayer. During this present time, however, we tend to throw money, activities, and programs toward solving all our problems. It is not that we doubt the power or even the importance of prayer. We believe in it. We just favor a pragmatic approach to things. We have adopted the Nike approach to youth ministry: "Just do it!"

Intercessory prayer is probably the most underutilized resource in youth ministry today.

At best, many of us practice what Peter Wagner calls "rhetoric prayer," but not "action prayer."[11] Rhetoric prayer involves intellectually assenting to the importance and even the power of prayer, but in reality not making much practical use of it. To progress to "action prayer" one must move beyond mental and verbal acknowledgment of the need for intercession to consistent and fervent practice of intercession.

There are several obstacles that may prevent us from moving forward in action prayer. One of these is *temporal-mindedness*. Without consistent exposure to the truth of the scriptures and church teaching, we fall prey to present-day cultural perspectives. This was also true in the early church. Note the admonition in Romans 12:2: "Do not conform yourself to this age but be transformed by the renewal of your mind, that you may discern what is the will of God, what is good and pleasing and perfect." Our mind is renewed as we allow the truth of the scriptures to become our standard for interpreting reality.

In the hustle and bustle of everyday living it is easy, if not quite natural, to forget there is more to this life than the world around us. Materialism has a stronger grip than we are willing to admit. Modern advertising masquerades consumerism as a cure to our deepest spiritual needs. Materialism and consumerism combine to blind us to the power of the gospel.

We might vigorously deny that we are controlled by the ways of the world, but the sad fact is that most of us behave like the world does. We practice youth ministry as if it only depended on us. Our tendency is to throw money, programs, and resources towards building a youth ministry that is rooted in materialism and temporal-mindedness. Our practice of intercessory prayer, or lack thereof, can be a clear give-away to our true reliance and level of dependence on God. Little prayer, little dependence. Much prayer, much dependence.

Prayer is an other-worldly, spiritual activity. It requires that we "think of what is above, not of what is on earth" (Colossians 3:2).

Another obstacle that keeps us from moving forward in prayer is *busy-ness*. I think we would all agree that as a society we are busier than in previous times. Our days are packed with activity like an over-stuffed suitcase. We can get so consumed with the trivial details of our lives that we can miss what is truly important.

This is a central message taken from Jesus' visit to the home of Martha and Mary (see Luke 10:38-42). Has Martha, the flustered host, become our patron saint for modern ministry? If your experience of the typical youth ministry is anything like mine, we must concede—yes. We, too, need to be slapped with the truth of Jesus' words to Martha. Let's stop settling for the least portion and again sit ourselves like Mary in a prayerful and attentive posture at the feet of our true Master. If those of us in ministry are too busy to pray, we are simply too busy.

Additionally, *pragmatism*—being as "American as apple pie"—heavily impacts our youth ministry. We bring a pragmatic premise to all we do, including the business of youth ministry. As a result, a significant amount of work is accomplished. The product of our efforts are clear to see: programs, activities, and events. A great sense of satisfaction accompanies a concrete accomplishment. We learned early that if you want to see something happen, you had better "take the bull by the horns."

If those of us in ministry are too busy to pray, we are simply too busy.

Prayer, on the other hand, does not seem like a very practical activity. We can spend hours praying but have little to show for it. With no concrete results to report we can't help but feel unproductive. With problems like drug and alcohol abuse, divorce, gangs, and suicide devilishly sneering in our face, how can we justify simply sitting there and praying? It feels like we are doing nothing. Everything in us screams "get up and do something about it!"

Pragmatism can certainly be a great gift. Many wonderful national accomplishments are the result of pragmatism. It fools us as Christians, however, into believing that human effort alone is our most powerful resource for change. We are like the little boy who took out his stick horse and played cowboys and Indians all day long. In the evening he slumped into his bed tired and exhausted. His father asked, "Why are you so weary?" He replied, "Real cowboys have real horses, but I have to do all the galloping myself."

Maybe we are doing too much of our own galloping. Many Catholic youth ministries, as evidenced by the mere practice of perfunctory prayer, are in reality functioning primarily through human effort. Ministry solely fueled by human strength lacks the ability to bring about a true conversion of heart, and sooner or later will result in spiritual atrophy. When this happens, we must admit that we have been better Americans than Christians.

Prayer taps into a power that far transcends the abilities of humans. As someone once said, "Prayer is the slender nerve that moves the muscle of omnipotence."

It is easy to get caught up into our own world and become indifferent to the needs of those around us. Our economic affluence makes us vulnerable to spiritual apathy. It is easy not to care enough to pray.

Basil Pennington wrote, "intercessory prayer is not a question of a lot of prayers; it is a question of a lot of love."[12] Intercessory prayer, plain and simple, is about loving others enough to embrace their needs as one's own, and on their behalf, take them to the throne of God.

Effective intercession is grounded in compassion. It was Jesus' deep compassion for the crowds, whom he described as sheep without a shepherd, that led him to teach his disciples to pray for more workers to be sent into the fields.

If we truly love others, we will want to give them more than what is naturally possible; it is this love that motivates us towards intercessory prayer. Prayer is a sacrificial act of love. We leave our own agendas, worries, and issues behind to focus our energies towards the concerns of others. What we seek for them is something we, ourselves, could never deliver: the intervention of an all-loving and all-powerful God.

As Walter Wink rightly states, "history belongs to the intercessors. . . ."[13] God has given us an incredible resource that has the potential to radically influence and change global, national, regional, and personal history.

Anthony de Mello elaborates further, "It is only at the end of this world that we shall realize how the destinies of persons and nations have been shaped, not so much by the external actions of powerful men and by events that seemed inevitable, but by the quiet, silent, irresistible prayer of persons the world will never know."[14]

God calls us to partner together and change the future through intercession. The future of our youth ministries can change as we pray a new vision into reality. Before we go on, consider the impact intercessory prayer has had in each of the following areas, large and small:

> ***World history***
>
> Many of us were raised in great fear of the Soviet Union. Through the Soviet Union's influence, many countries violently swung towards an atheistic and oppressive communism, drawing the United States into war and threatening the national security of many nations. We were nervous about this "sinister" country's potential to annihilate us through nuclear exchange. The Soviet Union was a superpower that seemed invincible.
>
> In 1991, we stood in shock and disbelief when this behemoth power disintegrated before our eyes, with hardly a shot fired. Within a few short years the Iron Curtain crumbled in domino fashion, and communism in Europe suffered extinction. We witnessed a truly miraculous event.

Since that time, many stories of fervent intercession from both within and outside of the Soviet Union have surfaced to give us a behind-the-scenes view of this historical event. Many of us remember praying for the conversion of Russia at the conclusion of Mass every Sunday. Could God have answered our prayers and changed world history? Could it be the release of God's power in response to our prayers that wrote the script that ended the tyrannical political oppression of millions? Could it not have happened through God's power?

Parish youth ministry history

One parish with which I worked had a sad history of successive youth ministry failures. Haunted by their past, they were open, even desperate for change. They decided to take the task of prayer seriously after attending our training session on intercession. Months before beginning any type of youth programming, their team prayed each day for every teen. Within two years of beginning, ninety-three percent of the teens for whom they were interceding had attended some type of youth ministry event. Beyond the numerical response, many of these same teens had life-changing encounters with Jesus Christ. Through prayer, this parish youth ministry team broke free from a legacy of failure to a future of fruitfulness.

Personal history

The future of individuals can be influenced through the power of prayer, too. Jeff was one such young man. He was entering his sophomore year of high school when I met him. I was impressed with Jeff's depth of spirituality and leadership qualities. I could envision him as a very effective peer minister in the coming years. My hope for Jeff was disrupted during his junior year as he lost interest in God and the church and discovered girls, varsity sports, and the popular crowd (a common spiritual ailment in high school).

As Jeff's heart was swept away in the swirling current of popularity, I began to regularly intercede for him in a new way. Each day I would earnestly pray, "Lord, make Jeff miserable." Before you think I am terrible, let me explain.

Those words, as harsh and cold as they may seem, were rooted in a love and compassion for Jeff. I was not all that different from him during my own high school years. I was not right with God, but I was at all the "right" parties, doing all the "right" things while with all the "right" people. Increasingly, however, I felt an emptiness and disillusionment about my life. It was on the retreat weekend I described during my senior year that I had a personal encounter with Jesus. My life took a "180." What my heart had been searching for in popularity, sports, and relationships was found in Christ. I knew firsthand the stark contrast in quality of life. I wanted Jeff, too, to experience that true peace and true joy found in a relationship with Jesus.

We were created to live life with God at our center. Jesus described this as the abundant life (John 10:10). Anything different is, at best, second-rate living. Jeff was living life second rate and my prayer was that he would have the grace to recognize it. I believed God had an exciting adventure for Jeff's life, but until Christ once again became his focus, he would miss out on the possibilities.

So, I prayed that Jeff would be "miserable" in his current lifestyle, and therefore, be able to clearly distinguish the difference between a life with Christ at the center from a life apart from him; that he would find no satisfaction until his "heart rested in Thee."

After praying this for some time, my wife De happened to run across Jeff's mother at the grocery store. After exchanging some small talk, De casually asked, "Donna, how is Jeff doing?" Donna sighed and sadly shook her head, saying, "Oh, De, he's miserable."

I was encouraged that God was answering my prayer (quite literally, no less), but misery for misery's sake was not my goal. I wanted Jeff to turn the corner. And that he did.

During much of this time of intercession, Jeff was doing things that, shall we say, were not going to land him on a list of America's Who's Who (more like America's Most Wanted). But interestingly, no matter how hard Jeff worked at having a "great time," he was closely shadowed by an internal dissatisfaction. He simply could not sin and feel good about it. After being cornered by crisis in every area of his life, Jeff turned his head back to a loving Father who was calling him home. I was right about God having a wonderful adventure planned for Jeff's life. God has used him to touch many teens and youth workers with the gospel, and today, he works with me at *Cultivation Ministries*.

In 1986, Roy Whetstine, a Texan gemstone broker, rummaged through the shoe boxes and dishes of unpolished stones among the amateurs in an Arizona mineral show. He fished out from a Tupperware dish a dusty, lavender-gray stone, about the size of a small potato. After examining it with his well-trained eye, he said to the salesman, "You want $15 for this rock?" The man replied, "Tell you what, I'll let you have it for $10. It's not as pretty as the others." Whetstine forked over $10 and brought home with him what he named the "Life and Pride of America," the largest star sapphire in the world. Its true value: 2.28 million dollars!

Whetstine had no qualms about spending only $10 for the gem. "When a man places a price on something he sells, that's what it's worth to him," he said.[15]

As youth workers, by virtue of the time we invest in intercessory prayer, what kind of worth are we attributing to it? Are we like the amateur mineral salesman who failed to recognize what he had in his possession? Imagine how different his life could have been if he only realized the value of that not-so-pretty rock. How different could our youth ministries look if we truly invested in something as simple as prayer?

Ask for the Grace to Be an Intercessor

There are many areas in my own life I recognize to be important and of high priority, but somehow I fail to give them the place they deserve. Even if we recognize the importance of intercession and are utterly convinced of its need, we may not make it a regular practice. Even if we are super-motivated, the process of building an impacting intercessory prayer base cannot be done on human tenacity alone. We need to ask God to provide us with the grace to be intercessors.

The prophet Zechariah speaks of a time when God will pour out "a spirit of grace and petition" upon the house of David and inhabitants of Jerusalem (see Zechariah 12:10). When we begin to develop an intercessory prayer base, our starting point is to simply ask God to pour upon us a "spirit of grace and supplication." In other words,

God help us pray!

Give to us the desire and ability to pray.

Provide for us the grace to earnestly pray in behalf of the youth of our community. Help motivate us to fervently pray our vision for our teens into reality.

Amen!

Develop Strategies for Consistency and Effectiveness

This third step moves us beyond simple desire to actual application. It is on this level that we leap from "rhetoric prayer" to "action prayer." Constructing an intercessory prayer base involves developing a practical strategy and organized effort towards harnessing the prayers of the community in behalf of teens. Paul was soliciting prayer support for his own missionary efforts when he wrote to the Colossians: "Persevere in prayer, being watchful in it with thanksgiving; at the same time, pray for us, too, that God may open a door to us for the word, to speak of the mystery of Christ, for which I am in prison, that I may make it clear, as I must speak" (Colossians 4:2-4).

The development of the "Intercessory Prayer Director" position and the establishment of "prayer goals" allow for the development of consistent and effective strategies.

The Intercessory Prayer Director—I believe that developing an intercessory prayer base is so essential that I recommend that each youth ministry planning team have one person serve as an Intercessory Prayer Director. Ultimately, the youth minister needs to set the tone with a leadership style that gives priority to prayer, but the role of managing the intercessory base should be led by a prayer director. This person is responsible for mobilizing the parish to pray for the youth ministry. His or her role is to ensure that the development of a consistent intercessory prayer base is built, developed, and maintained to lend sufficient prayer support for all young people, youth workers, programs, activities and efforts of the youth ministry.

In many ways, the Intercessory Prayer Director's role can be likened to that of Moses during the Israelites' battle with the Amalekites (see Exodus 17:8-13). At Rephidim the Amalekites waged war against the Israelites. Moses sent Joshua and his army to engage Amalek in battle, while he remained on top of a hill above them. As long as Moses had his hands raised, Israel had the better of the fight. When Moses' arms collapsed with fatigue, Amalek began to win. Soon, Aaron and Hur positioned themselves on each side of Moses and helped support his arms until Amalek was soundly defeated.

Military history may attribute the win to Joshua, but it was the intercessory efforts of Moses, assisted by Aaron and Hur, that won the spiritual battle. Moses may not have lifted a finger in battle, but his lifted hands in prayer supplied the needed strength for the warriors below to achieve the victory. Similarly, the Intercessory Prayer Director may not be directly involved in the day-to-day ministry with teens, but it is his or her efforts that assist the youth workers in making an impact.

What characteristics should the Intercessory Prayer Director possess? Mainly, a deep love for prayer and a consistent personal commitment to prayer. To motivate others to pray, one must be authentic in one's own practice of it. It is hard to convince others to invest in prayer if we have not yet convinced ourselves.

The Intercessory Prayer Director should also possess a mature faith. It would be essential for this person to respect and be comfortable with prayer methods, forms, and spiritualities that may differ from his or her own. As Catholics, we have a rich heritage of prayer forms and experiences. A mature prayer leader respects and appreciates this diversity. In no way does the director want to canonize his or her own prayer tradition while condemning those of others as heretical. Ideally, the prayer director is able to utilize the prayer contribution of various different groups of people, such as the rosary prayer group, the charismatic prayer group, the shut-ins, the contemplative prayer group, and so on.

Additionally, this person should have gifts in management and organization. I have worked with some prayer leaders who were exceptional in their personal practice of intercession. They were "mountain movers" in personal faith and prayer, but could not organize anything if their life depended on it. They were ineffective as directors because they lacked the essential organizational skills to get others effectively involved. Our efforts are multiplied when we are able to motivate and organize others to join with us in prayer.

Application

A resource offering a job description for an Intercessory Prayer Director[16] appears on page 111.

Prayer Goals—We are a very goal-oriented society. Establishing, working towards, and achieving goals are common experiences to most of us. We have set goals for our school and business careers and for our family life, but few among us have applied goal-setting towards prayer.

A youth ministry team's strategic planning process is in essence a discernment exercise. What results in our mission, focus result areas, and goals, are what we believe God is calling us to do to effectively reach the teens of our community. A tremendous amount of time, hard work, and energy is required to make a strategic plan a practical reality. We establish programs. We build relationships. We write job descriptions. We train leaders. However, we cannot just *work* towards achieving our mission. We must actively pray it into existence. An important role of the Intercessory Prayer Director is to establish and work towards achieving prayer goals that will unleash God's power towards the fulfillment of his will.

The goal-setting process begins by establishing targets for intercession. We must ask ourselves: If we are to achieve our mission, for whom or what should we be praying? We may begin with a group brainstorming session to surface potential targets for prayer. While brainstorming, remember it is quantity, not quality for which we are looking. Do not allow judgment or debate on any given item. Encourage the group to build off each other's answers.

Once the creativity of the group is exhausted, the next step is to narrow down our focus to a manageable number of the more significant needs. Begin this process with prayer, asking the Lord to reveal the most essential needs for prayer. As a rule, choose two to five targets. Targets may include teens, parents of adolescents, the mission statement, the strategic plan, families, schools, community problems or issues, the youth ministry leaders, or specific programs.

Next, set specific, quantitative, and measurable goals for each target. For instance, if one of our targeted needs is for the adult planning team, we might state the goal "that each planning team member has two people who are committed to pray for them each day, beginning this January." Another example might be "that each high school teen registered in the parish will be prayed for by name, each day, starting this March." Each goal should be written in sentence form. Include the target, the measurable goal, and the completion date.

When affixing measurable goals, we will want to be realistic with our present resources, yet challenged enough to stretch beyond our comfort zone. For instance, a parish with little background or experience with prayer should not suggest the ambitious goal of having a perpetual, twenty-four-hour prayer vigil on behalf of every teen in the parish. On the other hand, we do not want to excuse ourselves from any challenge by limiting ourselves to simply writing one prayer to be recited during the "prayers of the faithful" once a month.

We should begin at the place in which our parish is. An intercessory prayer base may be such a radical idea for some parishes that the best place to start might be a series of workshops or homilies that motivate and instruct parishioners on the importance of prayer.

Once our prayer goals are established, we will need to develop concrete methods, approaches, and programs that ensure we achieve our goals. One of our prayer goals may be that each high school teen registered in the parish be prayed for by name, each day, starting this March. But how will we make sure that happens? In what practical ways will this be completed?

This last step involves the formulation of a practical plan for each goal statement. The Intercessory Prayer Director should develop a team of people who work together in getting the parish praying through various kinds of programs and approaches.

Application

Several "Practical Approaches to Intercessory Prayer" are named and described on pages 112-113.

Summary

Intercession is a supplicatory prayer that involves asking in behalf of others. It is a powerful resource that God has given the church to change history. The first step to developing an intercessory prayer base is to recognize its importance. Many obstacles can stand in the way of prayer, including temporal-mindedness, pragmatism, busy-ness, and a lack of love. We must move past these barriers and beyond talking about prayer to the consistent practice of prayer. This begins with intercession itself—we start by asking for the grace to be an intercessor. Finally, we take practical steps to form a consistent intercessory prayer base by recruiting an Intercessory Prayer Director, developing quantitative prayer goals, and organizing specific prayer efforts to help achieve these goals.

Intercessory Prayer Director Job Description

PURPOSE

To ensure that a consistent intercessory prayer base is built, developed, and maintained to lend sufficient prayer support for all young people, youth workers, programs, activities, and efforts of the youth ministry.

DESIRED CHARACTERISTICS

- ✔ A personal belief in the power of prayer
- ✔ A consistent personal practice of intercessory prayer
- ✔ Organizational skills
- ✔ An ability to motivate others to prayer
- ✔ Interpersonal communication skills

GENERAL RESPONSIBILITIES

- ✔ To help build, maintain, organize, and coordinate an effective intercessory prayer support base on behalf of the youth ministry efforts, workers and teens.
- ✔ To support, encourage, and resource the leaders of the various prayer groups, projects, etc.
- ✔ To oversee all intercessory prayer ministry projects and programs.
- ✔ To help promote, educate, motivate, and mobilize youth workers and parishioners to intercessory prayer on behalf of the youth ministry.
- ✔ To gather the various prayer needs and channel those needs through the various prayer groups, programs, and projects.
- ✔ To communicate the status and progress of all intercessory prayer projects, programs, groups, and efforts to the Coordinator and youth ministry team.
- ✔ To network with existing prayer groups, projects, or programs.
- ✔ To create new avenues for prayer support for the youth ministry.

PRAYER SPONSORSHIP

One way to ensure that each teen is being prayed for every day is to establish a prayer sponsorship program. Recruit members of the parish to serve as sponsors of one or two teenagers. The names of the teens could be attached to a refrigerator magnet or business card (to be placed on a mirror) and handed out to the sponsors. The sponsors would commit to praying for their teen(s) each day. The details could be further developed to include a photo, basic biographical information, and prayer needs of the teens.

PRAYER CALENDAR

A calendar of daily prayer intentions is produced by and for the youth minister each month. A "day" might include the name or names of teens (maybe in conjunction with their birthdays), events or activities on that day, goals of the youth ministry, and youth ministry needs (such as securing commitments from additional leaders). A prayer calendar can be produced as simply as by writing requests on a blank calendar, or as elaborately as creating an illustrated, desktop publishing-designed tri-fold. Such calendars are mailed or handed out to all participants prior to the first of each month.

PARALLEL PRAYER

While a meeting, activity, or event is in progress, a parallel prayer effort is held. For instance, during the same time as a youth rally a group of parents meets to intercede for all the teens, speakers, and events of the evening. Parallel prayer can be done individually (a group of people praying at the same time, but in different locations) or in a corporate manner (a gathered group in a single location). Many retreat movements incorporate parallel prayer by establishing a chapel dedicated to intercession.

PRAYERS OF THE FAITHFUL

Not all elements of an intercessory prayer base need be newly created. Plugging into existing structures can multiply our efforts with little energy and time expended. The prayers of the faithful during a parish's liturgies can be one such opportunity. Simply include a youth ministry intention in the regular Sunday prayers of the faithful each week or month. An event, goal, person(s), or general intention can be highlighted. Parishioners will become better acquainted with what is being done and more deeply invested in the youth ministry by consistently praying for it.

PRAYER WALKS

Prayer walks are becoming a popular prayer form these days. It simply involves walking around a strategic location while praying for the needs of those associated with the site. For example, one might walk around a local high school while praying for all the teens, policies, teachers, problems, or issues of that particular school. Prayer walks can be done individually or corporately. We can incorporate many different methods of intercession from praying the rosary to spontaneous intentions. We can target troublesome areas such as a teen hangout, an area known to be a place of heavy drug traffic, and so on. Prayer walks are not public marches or protests. They should be done in a quiet manner and truly focused on prayer.

PERSONAL INTERCESSORS

A personal intercessor is an individual whose ministry involves praying for a particular person who is in leadership. A full-time youth minister, for example, might have a person or persons praying for him or her each day. The ministry of a personal intercessor goes well beyond the commitment of a prayer sponsor to include remaining in close contact with the person for which he or she is praying in order to intercede for the person concerning particular issues and challenges.

PRAYER BREAKFAST

On a regular basis a youth ministry can sponsor a corporate prayer breakfast. The purpose of the event would be to gather concerned people together to share breakfast while praying for the needs of the youth ministry. The morning meeting might include a time of worship, a simple breakfast, reports of answered prayer, current prayer needs, and a time to intercede.

PRAYER NEWSLETTER

Some parishes use a prayer newsletter to help support, inform, and encourage those participating in the efforts of intercessory prayer. The newsletter can be published monthly or quarterly and may be as short as one page or as long as four or more pages. The content can include articles on how to pray, stories of answered prayer, publicity for different prayer groups, prayer needs, and so on. The newsletter should be sent to all individuals who are in any manner supporting the youth ministry through prayer.

Section Two

SOWING THE SEED

6

WHAT IS CATHOLIC YOUTH EVANGELIZATION?

Jesus' final instruction to his followers was to proclaim the good news to all creation (see Mark 16:15 and Matthew 28:19-20). This call to *evangelize* all nations is generally known as "the great commission." The Catholic response to this call is generally known as "the great omission!" Through much of our history, we adopted the professional football approach to evangelization—where seventy thousand inactive spectators (who are in desperate need of exercise) cheer on twenty-two exhausted players (who are in desperate need of rest).

For most Catholics, the word *evangelization* is still an uncomfortable term, let alone a regular practice. We tend to associate the word with door knockers, TV preachers, or peculiar types who scream threats of hell at unsuspecting passers-by. We wonder to ourselves, "Can I be a good Catholic and evangelize? Do we even do this stuff? Are we supposed to?"

Unfortunately, these tainted images, past experiences, and negative connotations can leave us cold to what is the actual heart and lifeblood of Jesus' message. We run the risk of ignoring a central reality of our identity as church. As baptized believers, we are not invited to evangelize. *We are mandated to evangelize.* The church as a whole, and we as individuals, are called by Christ to be evangelized ourselves, to proclaim the good news to others, and to transform our society and culture. The church is missionary by nature, and, therefore, so is good youth ministry.

Before we can embrace the word and engage in the practice of evangelization, we must become comfortable with the term. Hearing the word in a Catholic context is an important beginning. With Pope John Paul II's stress on the "new evangelization," the American bishop's document "Go Make

Disciples," and the National Federation for Catholic Youth Ministry's document, "The Challenge of Catholic Youth Evangelization," *evangelization* is beginning to sound more Catholic all the time. In fact, Protestants generally use the term "evangelism" while Catholics have gravitated towards the word "evangelization."

Elements of Evangelization

In the original Greek, the word evangelization means "announcing good news." It was used to proclaim positive information such as an athletic victory or a wedding celebration. In the New Testament it was used to describe the activity of sharing the good news of God's kingdom.

Pope Paul VI essentially defined evangelization as "bringing the Good News into all strata of humanity, and through its influence, transforming humanity from within and making it new."[17] Building on this definition, *evangelization is the process of invitation for individuals, societies, and cultures, to embrace for the first time, again, or more deeply the good news of salvation through Jesus Christ.* This definition has several important elements worth looking at in greater detail.

A Process—Catholic evangelization is understood as a lifelong process as opposed to a completed event. Evangelization is not finished upon baptism, confirmation, or a significant moment of conversion. The invitations do not cease with an initial acceptance of them. During our lives we are continually invited to embrace new aspects of the gospel or revisit old elements of the good news in which we need renewal. Evangelization is a Spirit-generated dynamism that re-energizes our commitment to Jesus again and again. Each forward movement is a part of the whole evangelization process. We will always be in need of further evangelization. We cannot say, "Evangelization: been there, done that."

We cannot say, "Evangelization: been there, done that."

Even though this cultivation strategy divides the discipling process into three distinct and successive movements (sowing, growing, and reaping), one movement does not end with the beginning of another. Once established, each phase is ongoing in our lives. The only tree that can boast of being fully grown is one that is fully dead. Likewise, the only Catholic who can boast of being fully evangelized is one who is fully embalmed.

An Invitation—Evangelization is a loving invitation to accept the good news of God's reign. It is not a subpoena for inscription into God's kingdom. When we receive a wedding invitation there is always an enclosed reply card. The families request the honor of our presence, but leave the choice with us. When we are subpoenaed, we are essentially told how to respond; there is no choice without the threat of punishment.

As critical as our message is, we can never justify any form of evangelization that whittles away at the free will of others through high pressure sales, eternal threats, manipulation, or deception. Genuine evangelization respects the free will of others to decide whether or not they will accept what God is offering. Because evangelization is a message of love it must be carried out in love. Love is always respectful of others.

A Transformation—The good news of Jesus Christ has the power to transform individuals, societies, and cultures. Generally, we think of evangelization as primarily impacting individuals. The gospel certainly has the power to radically change one person's life, affecting his or her other attitudes, loyalties, values, behaviors, and lifestyle. Additionally, evangelization can bring about change to a society and culture. Gospel values often challenge the perspectives and practices of the dominant culture. When they are applied and integrated into a society's ways of thinking, its structures, and its systems, the final outcome is a transformed culture.

A Proclamation of the Good News—Evangelization is the proclamation of the good news of salvation. God calls us into joyful union with him. God invites us to be a part of his family forever. It is in Jesus and his message that the hunger of our hearts is satisfied. The goal of this message of love is conversion. We are challenged to respond wholeheartedly to God's irresistible invitation.

As evangelization is an integral part of our Catholic faith, there is also a great need for teens to be evangelized and led to conversion.

The Need for Youth Evangelization

The youth of our nation will be evangelized and converted. That is no longer a question. The more relevant questions are:

"By whom will they be evangelized?"

"To what will they be converted?"

"Will it be the church who leads the way?"

Or, will it be the contemporary American culture which packages its message with the greatest of sophistication and through the latest media? The present-day culture is an effective evangelizer which has applied excellence to its task. As each year passes, the media-promoted culture drifts further and further from Catholic values. It has progressively become more hostile to Christian beliefs. This has created a much greater need on our part to be committed to active evangelization. In many, if not most, respects the contemporary

American culture has won Catholic teens over. Its modern message can be costly and destructive in the lives of vulnerable adolescents.

Developmentally, adolescence is a pivotal season in life. Young people grapple with many important issues. Along with these issues, they are making critical choices. Many of these decisions will have lifetime consequences. Some of these decisions include or involve education, vocation, and sexuality. The church (which is the custodian of the greatest news of all) cannot stand by idly, but must instead commit its energy, creativity, and resources to becoming a significant and relevant evangelistic voice in the lives of teens. It is during this period in life that young people are asking the following significant questions:

Who am I? (the question of identity) If the church is not actively providing an answer to this question, the contemporary American culture will gladly respond. The answer teens will hear is, "You're nobody unless you have. . . ." Our consumer-based society brazenly proclaims that you need *things* to be truly satisfied and significant. An incredibly attractive man will pick up your scent and pursue you like a bloodhound if you wear this cologne. You will be transformed into a macho man with plenty of female companions if you drink this beer. The presumption is that you are a lesser person without purchasing certain products. You are what you have.

On the other hand, the gospel refreshingly states, "You are somebody because God is crazy about you. God purposed you, planned you, and he died for you. You are worth Jesus to the Father!"

When Jesus was baptized, a voice from heaven came down saying, "This is my beloved Son, in whom I am well pleased." Think about it. Before Jesus was baptized, he did nothing heroic to "earn" his Father's love. This tells us that we do not have to do anything special or possess anything of value to be loved by the Father. God loves us simply for who we are and calls us to be a part of his eternal family. God provides us with gifts to employ in the kingdom. That is good news.

What is life about? (the question of purpose) Again, the popular American culture persuasively articulates a narcissistic and hedonistic philosophy of life: "Life is about me. Look out for number one. Pursue pleasure through the accumulation of things, popularity, and good looks."

On the other hand, the scriptures teach that life is about loving, giving, and serving. True fulfillment comes not by trying to gain the whole world for ourselves, but by dying to ourselves, living for God, and loving others. When we live an other-centered lifestyle, we feel good about who we are. When we live a self-centered existence, we feel empty and hopeless.

What do I believe? (the question of values) For preadolescents and younger children, parental values are welcomed as coming from the authority and wisdom of prophets. However, once a child enters the teen years, parents somehow become cultural heretics who hold hopelessly prehistoric perspectives. As teens seek independence, they often turn to others outside the home for guidance in what to believe. Teens may seriously question what they have previously been taught. Often, their new information regarding important moral issues such as sexuality, human life, and justice comes from television, magazines, and their peers. Much of the contemporary morality from these sources is based on relativistic thinking. With the absence of moral absolutes, teens may utilize flawed moral reasoning that leaves them lonely victims of negative consequences. The present-day teenage carnage from pregnancy, abortion, drugs, violence, and suicide stands as an embarrassing societal monument to our failure to influence the youth of our nation with the values and morals of the gospel.

Like no other time in history, we need to direct and guide young people in moral choices.

Like no other time in history, we need to direct and guide young people in moral choices. There is a need for the good news of right living to be boldly proclaimed in a clear and relevant manner. Jesus' feelings for the youth are typified by the description in Matthew 9:36: "His heart was moved with pity for them because they were troubled and abandoned, like a sheep without a shepherd."

Dynamics of Youth Evangelization

We, too, feel pity when we see so many youth ravaged by the flawed moral reasoning most teens face on a daily basis. But how do we bring the good news of God's love to the youth of our day? Let's look at a helpful resource for guidance.

The Challenge of Catholic Youth Evangelization[18] identifies six elements in the evangelization process: witness, outreach, proclamation, invitation, conversion, and the call to discipleship. Theoretically, each element is sequential in order; however, in reality, a clean linear process is rare. More information on each element follows.

Witness

The first level of evangelization is the witness of our lives. We are breathing illustrations of what it means to follow Jesus. What we say and do in our homes, neighborhoods, workplaces, faith communities, and schools speaks volumes to teens regarding the validity of our lifestyles. Our witness is expressed individually as believers in Christ and corporately as a faith community.

Pope Paul VI wrote:

> Above all the gospel must be proclaimed by witness. Take a Christian or a handful of Christians who, in the midst of their own community, show their capacity for understanding and acceptance, their sharing of life and destiny with other people, their solidarity with the efforts of all for whatever is noble and good. Let us suppose that, in addition, they radiate in an altogether simple and unaffected way their faith in values that go beyond current values, and their hope in something that is not seen and that one would not dare to imagine. Through this wordless witness these Christians stir up irresistible questions in the hearts of those who see how they live: Why are they like this? Why do they live in this way? What or who is it that inspires them? Why are they in our midst? Such a witness is already a silent proclamation of the Good News and a very powerful and effective one. Here we have an initial act of evangelization. . . .
>
> All Christians are called to this witness, and in this way they can be real evangelizers.[19]

Our lives need to authentically communicate that following Jesus is most important to us. Before we can proclaim the good news, we must be good news. As the saying goes, "My life may be the only bible someone reads."

Outreach

Outreach builds upon our witness. It is the "Go" of the great commission, the building of caring relationships with teens. The teens in question include the unchurched, the inactive, and the active teen in need of conversion. We venture from the safety of our own comfort zone to the world of the adolescent. Outreach is a ministry of presence. Teens need to see us on their turf.

Often, our witness and outreach is *pre-evangelistic.* Pre-evangelization involves the process of preparing a person to consider or even reconsider the gospel message. It helps facilitate a proper disposition to accepting the seed of faith. It can be compared with the "preparing the soil" process described for preparing youth leaders in Part One. Now we are referring to preparation work with teens. The purpose of pre-evangelization is to develop a credibility that arouses an interest in faith. Before young persons will consider the Christian lifestyle, they need to be in regular contact with sincere and loving believers who demonstrate the reality and power of the Christian message.

Pre-evangelization includes modeling the Christian life, building accepting and caring relationships with youth, developing an inviting, attractive, and inclusive community, sharing common interests, attending teens' extracurricular events, and just "wasting" time together.

Theoretically, pre-evangelization precedes evangelization. In reality, it functions concurrently. Pre-evangelization can be likened to the farmer's task of plowing the soil. The winter leaves the ground hard, compacted, and unreceptive to the spring seed. To plant in these conditions would be nothing short of a waste of time and effort (unless, of course, your intention was to feed the birds). The furrowing of soil is necessary to help create the proper condition for germination.

Pre-evangelization can be likened to the farmer's task of plowing the soil.

Many teens, like the winter soil, have immediate barriers that prevent them from honestly considering Christ's message. Attempting to throw the "seeds of faith" their way is at best premature, if not foolish. To do so almost guarantees a zero yield. A smart farmer does not waste his time planting in such conditions; nor should a smart evangelist. It is erroneous to conclude that because I have seed in my hand and there is soil beneath my feet, I should start sowing. This type of practice will contribute to the already bad connotations that come with the word evangelization. Evangelization is a proclamation of love. The content of the message is love and the manner in which the message is delivered must be in love. If not for the sake of the recipient, then at least for the sake of success, we must assess the condition of the soil before we do anything. The assessment of teens and their lives and the response of the teens is pre-evangelization.

My own receptivity to Jesus and the church came only after I observed the credibility of those who took their faith seriously. I had some misconceptions about God and the church that kept me from embracing the faith of my family. These barriers had to be dealt with in my life before I could respond to the gospel.

During that time of adolescence I was beginning to ask some spiritual questions. My conversion would have stalled out if I had found myself staring down the cold iron barrel of a bible-slinging evangelist. I needed a softer approach. I needed people to demonstrate to me that you could be "cool" and follow Christ. I needed people to express care, to listen, and to accept me for who I was. Indeed, charging directly at me with the "good news" would have been very "bad news" to me.

Outreach takes the time necessary to build relationships, credibility, and the right to be heard. Our traditional approaches to catechesis have somehow presumed that our teens will ardently dash into our classrooms, each with the spiritual yearning of a thirsty man in the hot desert sun. A more realistic assumption might be that they are like reluctant children who balk at the idea of eating the mounds of gross spinach on their plates. Pre-evangelistic outreach might include accepting the child's dislike for spinach, listening to why the child hates spinach, doing some fun things together that have nothing to do with eating spinach, quietly eating the spinach on my own plate and demonstrating the "Popeye" strength that comes from such a diet. After some time, the child might reason, "This guy is pretty cool, cares about me, and eats spinach. Maybe his strength comes from that spinach. Maybe it is not all that bad after all. Maybe I'll taste it."

Proclamation

It is essential that we model the Christian life through our daily actions and lifestyle and build genuine, caring relationships with teens. However, that is not enough. Pope Paul VI made this very clear when he wrote:

> Nevertheless this always remains insufficient, because even the finest witness will prove ineffective in the long run if it is not explained, justified—what Peter called always having "your answer ready for people who ask you the reason for the hope that you have"—and made explicit by a clear and unequivocal proclamation of the Lord Jesus. The Good News proclaimed by the witness of life sooner or later has to be proclaimed by the word of life. There is no true evangelization if the name, the teaching, the life, the promises, the kingdom and the mystery of Jesus of Nazareth, the Son of God are not proclaimed.[20]

As Catholics, when attempting to express our faith to others, we have often become like "arctic rivers"—frozen at the mouth. We seem to gravitate towards being "closet Christians" or "secret agents for Christ." We like to say, "I will let my actions do the talking." With so much high profile hypocrisy around us, we feel fully justified by and even proud of this approach. It often, however, conceals our fear of verbally sharing our faith with others. In other healthy relationships, we do not make such distinctions. As a father, I verbally express my love to my children by saying, "I love you; you are a gift to me and our family; I am glad God allowed me to be your father." I also demonstrate my love through acts of kindness, provision, and protection. It would be unhealthy for me to practice one action at the exclusion of the other. I would not say to my children, "I will not speak of my love for you; I will only express it in my actions." As a father, I need to do both. As an evangelist, I need to do both.

We are called to verbally proclaim the gospel to others. This mandate is both an honor and privilege. The Apostle Paul gives us a title of esteem and prestige in this role:

> And all this is from God, who has reconciled us to himself through Christ and given us the ministry of reconciliation, namely, God was reconciling the world to himself in Christ, not counting their trespasses against them and entrusting to us the message of reconciliation. So *we are ambassadors for Christ* (italics mine), as if God were appealing through us (2 Corinthians 5:18-20).

We are ambassadors of God's kingdom—representing his reign among the teens in our communities. God honors us with the privilege of being his instruments in communicating his unfathomable love and with the gracious invitation to be a part of his eternal family.

But what is this gospel we proclaim? The good news is that God loves us (John 3:16) and wants us to experience life to the fullest (John 10:10). He has vividly and undeniably communicated this love through the life, death, and resurrection of Jesus. Jesus' life definitively reveals who God is and how God calls us to live. We are invited to be a part of God's family (see John 1:12). God has given our lives real purpose and meaning. The gospel is, indeed, good news.

Invitation

While in seventh grade, a friend of mine announced that he would be having a boy-and-girl party the following month. This was a new and exciting concept for all of us prepubescents. During the next three weeks he went on and on about this "party of the year." He openly shared with me and others who were coming what was being served, what music would be played, and a host of other exacting details. Soon, this party became the biggest single event of the whole seventh grade. Before the big night arrived, I was clear on every particular about that party except for one minute detail—a detail that was, shall we say, driving me crazy. This single decisive detail had the distinct potential to make me or break me socially. With all my friend's ramblings, he failed to articulate to me whether I was included in this mega-event. Up until the week of the party, I anxiously wondered whether or not I was invited. Somehow, he simply presumed that I knew I was invited.

We can approach evangelization in a similar manner. We may model the Christian life, build genuine relationships with teens, and even enthusiastically share the gospel. But, if we do not explicitly invite teens to share in the good news, we have neglected an essential dynamic in the evangelization process. There are, of course, times when an invitation may be inappropriate or premature, but to consistently leave it out of the evangelization process is neglectful.

If we do not explicitly invite teens to share in the good news, we have neglected an essential dynamic in the evangelization process.

Invitation includes leading teens into a new or deeper relationship with Jesus. Evangelization is Christocentric, that is, the person of Jesus is central to the process. Good proclamation leaves young people with questions of how they might personally respond to Jesus' call to them. Evangelistic invitation solicits a response from the listener. This is illustrated after Peter's evangelistic preaching at Pentecost.

> Now when they heard this, they were cut to the heart, and they asked Peter and the other apostles, "What are we to do, my brothers?" Peter said to them: "Repent and be baptized, every one of you, in the name of Jesus Christ for the forgiveness of your sins; and you will receive the gift of the Holy Spirit" (Acts 2:37-38).

Imagine if Peter finished this sermon and said, "Okay, it's lunch. I'll see ya all later." Not only would he have missed a Holy Spirit-inspired opportunity, he would also have left his listeners in a frustrated state. They were deeply touched by Peter's words and wanted to respond personally. Peter, in turn, offered his listeners some concrete steps to conversion. He explicitly provided an invitation on how to respond to the proclamation. We, too, should give clear invitations to teens on what Jesus is calling them to. After sharing our faith story, for instance, we may say to teens: "Over the years, Jesus has become my closest friend. Who is Jesus for you?" Or, "Jesus invites us to place our life in his hands. Have you ever considered what that invitation means for you?" It is at this point that we should be ready to provide concrete guidance as to how to meet Jesus or know him more deeply. When teens respond to this invitation, we might initially pray with them.

The invitation is not only to receive Jesus, but to be welcomed into our faith community. The person of Jesus and his followers come as a packaged deal. We are evangelized into a relationship with both Jesus and his church. We need to intentionally and personally invite teens to be a part of, and participate in, our faith community.

Conversion

Our efforts in youth evangelization culminate when a young person experiences a change of heart. The scriptures refer to this event as conversion. The Greek word for conversion is *metanoia*, a process of change where one breaks from the past and turns toward God as the goal and meaning of one's entire life.[21] Conversion involves two dimensions. The first is the saying of "no" to our old ways of thinking and acting. There is a death brought about through repentance. The second is our saying "yes" to God. We embrace new attitudes, behaviors, and actions that are in line with God's perspective. The evidence of interior conversion is outward change (see Luke 3:8).

Conversion is, however, an ongoing activity for a Catholic. We may have experienced an initial "Aha" moment that radically turned the compass of our lives in a new direction. But it is to be hoped that it is only the beginning of a lifelong series of successive conversions. Often, conversion is a cyclical process linked closely with issues of human development, suffering, or crisis. During the different stages of the human journey we may look at life from new perspectives. These "challenges" can rock our understanding of faith, leading us to either abandon our presently understood faith or to deepen our understanding, leading to a new experience of conversion.

At some point, teens need to experience a conversion from childhood faith to a more personalized and owned faith that reflects their adolescent developmental growth. Children tend to uncritically accept the beliefs of their parents and faith community as a given fact of life. As a child moves into adolescence, simple, ready-made answers will not satisfy the quest and need for deeper meaning. We must give adolescents the freedom to evaluate, question, and even be critical of a faith tradition that means so much to us. The journey from childhood to adult faith is one that must be made personally by teens through their own questioning, evaluating and struggling with the essential truths. Any evangelization process that fails to recognize this adolescent developmental need may actually be a cause for a teen to reject his faith. Adolescents grow out of their childhood faith. If we do not take the time to re-measure and re-fit their expanding minds, emotions, and perspectives, they will discard their childhood faith like an old, worn-out sneaker.

The Call to Discipleship

Becoming a disciple of Jesus Christ involves taking his mission to the world. It is not enough for us to personally enjoy our own salvation; we must join with Christ and the church in proclaiming the good news, living as a community of faith, hope, and love, and serving all those in need. To be authentically evangelized ourselves means to enthusiastically evangelize others.

The kingdom of God has two principle commandments: to love God and our neighbor. A disciple, therefore, focuses his life around these two central expressions of love.

When we love God the best that we can, when we make efforts to invite young people into our lives so that we can be present to them, when we tell them why we have hope and offer them a chance to respond to God, and finally, when we model and teach them how to be followers of Jesus, then we are actively involved in youth evangelization. We can make a difference, one person at a time. This personal touch is crucial to evangelization, but there are also ways to reach out to a greater number of teens.

Evangelistic Programming

Evangelization is a process. It is also an attitude, mindset, and quality that arouses faith. Its threads should weave into the entire tapestry of the youth ministry, affecting every relationship, event, activity, and program. However, in addition to a pervasive mindset, we should specifically design programs, activities, and events that are evangelistic in scope and purpose.

Evangelistic programming can be classified into two distinct categories: *gathering events* and *non-gathering activities.* Gathering events involve bringing two or more people together. Examples include retreats, rallies, small groups, one-to-one meetings, and large-group events. Non-gathering activities are not based on people physically coming together. They can include newsletters, birthday cards, videos, CD-ROMs, telephone calls, web pages, correspondence, and audio tapes.

Evangelistic programming can be classified into two distinct categories: gathering events and non-gathering activities.

A full-cycle youth ministry intent on making disciples needs to have numerous evangelistic approaches, targeting particular types of teens with different interests, schedules, and backgrounds. In past years, teens generally fell into one of three categories: "in and popular," "average but okay," or "out and excluded." Today's teens are much more diverse. There is no longer one "in group" and one definition of "cool." Friendships are formed on the basis of interests. For instance, teens belong to many social groups just on the basis of their involvement in activities like drama, music, volleyball, computer games, and youth groups. Our challenge is to think innovatively and strategically as we seek to reach out to the many diverse groups of youth in our communities.

Addressing Perceived and Unperceived Needs

Once we've targeted a particular youth audience, it is crucial to be aware that any kind of successful evangelization program needs to keep in mind both the perceived and unperceived needs of the youth. *Perceived needs* are conscious desires or needs of which young people are aware. These are desires that young people can articulate to us. They are what teens wish and want for themselves. If we do not address their perceived needs, they simply will not be interested. There are usually several things that are vying for their attention, so they typically will not attend events that are not relevant. Our drawing card is perceived needs.

An example of a perceived need is fun and good times. If there is any place that should be fun, it is the church. Unfortunately, the church is not the first place that comes to mind when young people think of fun. In most cases, it is just the opposite. Many teens think that to have fun they have to sin or do things that are wrong. We ought to reclaim what it means to have fun! God is the authentic author of joy. To attract youth to our meetings they have to be fun.

Another example of a perceived need is friendship. Young people have a strong need to interact with new people and make new friends. They want opportunities to meet and build relationships with members of the opposite sex. Before they are going to be interested and evangelized, we have to meet their perceived needs. Jesus worked in a similar manner. The perceived need of the lepers, the blind, and the lame was healing, sight, and mobility. Once Jesus met their perceived need, they were more willing to address the very real need for spiritual conversion.

Young people will attend evangelistic meetings because they meet their perceived needs. By addressing their felt needs, we communicate our love and concern. Our love goes deeper, however, as we address their very real *unperceived needs.*

Unperceived needs are unconscious desires or needs of which the young person is unaware. These needs are very real, yet not articulated or consciously understood. Many times young people cannot express everything that is going on inside them, so they may act out in certain ways due to unperceived needs.

An example of an unperceived need is personal faith. Most unevangelized teens do not recognize a deep need for a personal relationship with God. They may sense something missing in their lives, or experience a longing for more, yet few would be able to explain it as a spiritual need to be better connected to God. It is our role to help them recognize and address this essential need in their lives. This can be done at the same time we are meeting their perceived needs. For example, we might address the topic of friendship at one of our meetings. We may provide three important ingredients that make for a lasting friendship (perceived need). Building from that, we may then describe Jesus as the person who consistently exhibits these ingredients in his friendship with others (unperceived need). Jesus is a very desirable friend, the kind for whom we all long. We may end the meeting with an invitation to them to begin or deepen their friendship with Christ.

Objectives of Evangelistic Programming

Any program needs to begin with focused objectives. We need to know where we are going. Effective evangelistic programming will have the following four basic objectives. These objectives also serve well for separate meetings, events, or activities. Evaluation of all evangelistic programming is based on whether we have achieved these objectives.

Objective 1: To provide opportunities to have fun and make friends—When I ask teens whether they like school or not, I most often hear "yes." When I follow up by asking teens why they like school, I do not hear: "Because of the academic adventure, cerebral stimulation, and intellectual ecstasy I encounter within the daily rigors of the classroom milieu." Ask an average teen why they like school and they will typically reply: "Because my friends are there." In terms of adolescent development, this response is right on target, and, if we want to design evangelistic events that are attractive to teens, we had best keep it in mind. Effective evangelistic programs are fun and relational in expression.

Objective 2: To break down barriers to Christ and the church—Many young people think an exciting church event occurs as often as a solar eclipse. Or, that Christ's teachings speak to today's issues on the same level as knickers speak to today's fashions. A significant number of teens in our community will have common barriers that may prevent them from being active members of the church and having a living relationship with Christ. Effective evangelistic programming addresses these barriers both in content and practice.

For instance, a teen might think that he or she could not have fun and be a Christian at the same time. Our message

Many young people think an exciting church event occurs as often as a solar eclipse.

might address the fullness of life Christ offers, and the joy of Christian living. Beyond our words, the atmosphere and activities at our meetings should experientially demonstrate that it is a joy to follow the Lord. Whatever those barriers might be—that God is not relevant or real, the church is a boring place, or the youth group is cliquish—we need to be addressing and breaking them down by presenting and illustrating the truth of Christ.

Objective 3: To demonstrate how Christ can relate to a teenager's life—Often, young people feel Jesus and the scriptures are, at best, remote in addressing real teen issues. Effective evangelistic programming should help teens apply scriptural principles and church teaching to common teenage issues. For example, our lessons might address the following questions:

"What can Jesus do concerning peer pressure?"

"How can Christ help me with my self-image?"

"How can the scriptures address my loneliness?"

"How can my faith provide meaning and purpose in life?"

"How can Jesus help me be a better friend and choose better friends?"

Faith only becomes real when it connects to life. Our topics and themes must be rooted in matters that are important, relevant, and meaningful to teens.

Application

A worksheet for brainstorming ideas under "Four Evangelistic Objectives" is available on page 132.

Objective 4: To invite them to a closer relationship with Christ—A roomful of teens who are experiencing a good time is never enough. If we are failing to invite youth to Jesus and deepen conversion, we have fallen short of our goal. Effective evangelistic programming clearly invites teens to a closer relationship with Christ. This invitation should be integrated into the presentation's message and reinforced by the relational ministry that must take place afterwards.

Summary

Our teens have been, are, and will continue to be evangelized by our hedonistic and consumeristic culture; many stand confused, hopeless, and despairing of meaning and significance in life.

During this critical time in which they set out to develop an identity, find their purpose in life, and establish the values and morals foundational to all their present and future decisions, the church needs to rise up, become a significant and relevant voice, and fulfill the Lord's "great commission" by evangelizing its teens in a way that attracts them to Jesus.

The six elements included in the evangelization process—witnessing with our lives, reaching out, proclaiming the good news in word, inviting to a new and deeper relationship with the Lord, personal conversion, and daily discipleship—need to be accomplished in the lives of our teens with their perceived and unperceived needs in mind.

Through a variety of creative gathering and non-gathering experiences, we can provide our teens with opportunities to have fun and make friends, break down barriers to and misconceptions of Christ and the church, see how Jesus can relate to their lives, and invite them to a closer relationship with the true Lover of their soul.

Four Evangelistic Objectives

Brainstorm with an adult team some specific applications for teen programming that can help accomplish each of the following evangelistic objectives.

To provide opportunities to have fun and make friends.	**To break down barriers to Christ and the church.**	**To demonstrate how Christ can relate to a teenager's life.**	**To invite teens to a closer relationship to Christ.**

7

Caring for the Crop: A Relational Approach to Ministry

During my nocturnal young adult years, I faithfully attended midnight Mass every Christmas. Fr. John's Christmas homily was as consistent as my attendance. It did not deviate in a single detail over the years. My face grimaced as he began that oh-so-familiar bird story.

Now, years later, I appreciate his lack of fresh material. It is one of the few homilies that I remembered past communion! The tale began with a father who remained home on Christmas Eve while his wife and children attended Mass. The Christmas story did not make much sense to the father as an adult, so in his usual custom, he opted out of going to church.

While hauling in some firewood that Christmas Eve, a confused sparrow fluttered into the house through the wide open door. The bird soon became perplexed and disoriented as it flapped back and forth in the confined space. Realizing that the bird did not know how to get out, the man held open the door to give the bird a safe passageway back to the outside world, but it was afraid to fly near him. He tried to scare the sparrow out by clanging pans and yelling, but that only made matters worse. The sparrow stood frozen and terrified above the fireplace mantle. As soon as it appeared safe, the bird soared towards what it perceived to be a wide open channel to freedom—the living room picture window. The bird painfully crashed into the window several times before realizing it was not an open space. All the while the man was trying to communicate to this desperate sparrow. However, no matter what he said or did, the bird failed to trust his intention and follow his direction. In frustration, the man revealed his thoughts out loud, saying, "If I could only become a bird. I would then speak this sparrow's language and show it the way to freedom!"

No longer than the time it took for the statement to pass his lips did it take him to realize the parallel truth of the Christmas story. God took on flesh to communicate authentically his love and direction to humans. The man's life was changed. That Christmas was the last time he ever missed Mass.

Incarnational Ministry

When the Father wanted to reach us, what did he do? Did he send out a slickly produced brochure? Did he schedule a meeting? Did he create a web page? When God the Father wanted to touch our lives, he sent Jesus the Son, who became a human being like us and shared our pain. We call this the *Incarnation.*

The Incarnation stands as a foundational principle for effective evangelization of teens. As God sought to reach us by entering our world and journeying with us, so must we enter the world of young people and *journey with them.* St. Paul understood this approach well. He wrote that when he wanted to reach Jews, he became like the Jews, and when he wanted to reach Gentiles, he became like the Gentiles (see 1 Corinthians 9:19-23). He became one of them in order to "win a hearing" for the good news.

To be effective in youth discipleship, we have to "earn the right to be heard."[22] By building relationships with young people, we are seen as credible and caring people, worthy of their trust.

James was one young man with whom I had to earn the right to be heard. His mother wanted him confirmed, so to appease her, he would ride out his religious educational tour of duty; but, no bones about it, he was not going to like it. He was not buying this Jesus stuff, and made his position clearly apparent to our entire group. James's comments and actions clearly revealed his anger for having to be in the class.

Eventually, for the sake of the others, I had to ask him to leave the group as a result of his constant negativity and disruption. I gave up on him being a part of the group, but I did not give up on the relationship. He was not at all happy with me, but I continued to take an active interest in his life by attending his football games, calling him, stopping over at his house, and even having him over for dinner. As time went on,

James began to warm up to me. He began to distinguish between his negative feelings about doing something against his will and his real feelings about the person of Jesus. We finally turned the corner when I landed him the job he always wanted. James's attitude about God and church changed that year. He joined our discipleship group the following year, participated in a positive manner, and was confirmed. A decade later, I still see James, even though he lives more than a thousand miles away. When he comes back home to see his family he always stops by to say "hello."

Relational or incarnational youth ministry involves a willingness to (1) be personally present to youth, (2) enter the world of adolescents, and (3) journey with the young people. Some more detail about each aspect of incarnational youth ministry follows.

1. Be personally present to youth. We need to go where young people spend their time. Once a convicted thief was asked why he robbed banks. He matter-of-factly replied, "Because that's where the money is." As youth workers we need to ask, "Where are the teens?" Our response to this question will reveal the best locations for youth ministry. Such places might include the local high school, sporting events, plays, concerts, the mall, the park, fast-food restaurants, gyms, and arcades.

Youth need to see us on their turf. The word Jesus used for the great commission was "Go"; in other words, we must move out of our comfort zone and *initiate* outreach. All too often, we replace "Go" with "Come," and simply set up shop in the church doing our best to "save the choir." The problem with this approach is that we are only reaching a small percentage of teens, usually those who either have to or want to be there and not necessarily those teens who *need* to be there.

Incarnational or relational youth ministry is difficult for many of us to comprehend because we grew up within a different ministry paradigm. We attended CCD for religious instruction. Our classes were content-oriented and our teachers rarely got involved in our lives. The truth is that this approach was seldom effective. Content-oriented ministry rarely makes a lifelong impact. When God wanted to reach us, God initiated it. He came here to walk with us in the person of Jesus. He became present to us. Likewise, by our consistent presence in their lives, young people will recognize us as "teen-friendly adults."

2. Enter the world of the adolescent. Profoundly respecting and fully entering into the culture of the indigenous people is the trademark for successful foreign missionary work. A surefire strategy for failure is to disrespect culturally the people one seeks to reach. The "world" of a teenager is very different from the "adult world." Our aim is not to try and make young people officially authorized adults. We do not want to drag them forcibly into our world, but rather to venture forth into their domain and journey with them.

It is not only easy, but natural for an adult youth worker to forget what being an adolescent is like. A teen's world and issues can seem trivial, foolish, or incomprehensible to an adult mind. But, youth ministry is mission work. Adults are called forth from their own familiar culture and "civilized" ways of thinking into the uncharted jungles of the modern youth mindset and culture.

Respectfully entering the world of an adolescent does include seeking to transform aspects of that culture through the gospel. But to do this, we must possess a sense of credibility by first entering their "world." Youth will take us seriously only when we take them seriously. A good rule of thumb is to listen and learn first and thereby earn the right to be heard.

Youth will take us seriously only when we take them seriously.

3. Journey with young people. We must be willing to partner with teens on their journey. In order to be truly effective, we cannot simply meet with them an hour a week, attempting to catechetically saturate their minds with the glorious truths of the church. Effective youth ministry involves long-term relationships. We need to channel more of our efforts toward becoming people-centered as opposed to program-centered. In an extensive *Group/Youth for Christ* survey, teens articulated that relationships with adult Christians and parents were most influential in their initial decision to follow Christ. According to the survey:

> It's people who live out their relationship with God in a real way who make a difference in teenagers' spiritual growth. Teens grew when they were immersed in the disruptive, emotional, surprising realm of real relationships.[23]

Additionally, youth ministers commented on what led them to commit their lives to Christ when they were young, and later their decision to enter youth ministry:

> Everyone we interviewed said all the defining moments in the path toward Christian maturity were relational. For one it was a late-night talk with an adult volunteer in a tent. For another it was a youth minister who believed in him enough to give him leadership responsibilities.
>
> Here's the surprising thing: these people were impacted most by the tiny, nondescript things adult and

teenage Christians did for them. They were most powerfully influenced when other Christians revealed a kind of spontaneous Christ-likeness in the context of relationship. It wasn't the well-planned, well-presented teaching series on Colossians that changed their life. It was the tears welling up in their leader's eyes when he listened to their struggles. And twenty years later, they still remember those eyes and those tears.[24]

All too often, our relationships with the teens in our parish begin and end with the program. If we operate solely on a program-centered model, we then reach youth with only the content of the meeting. With a people-centered model, we reach them with the "content" of our love brought to life by our words, example, and actions. A people-centered model for youth ministry most certainly offers programs. The difference is that ministry goes beyond the reaches of organized church programming and into the realm of real life. This, in turn, helps teens understand that faith is not meant to be compartmentalized—that is, something one does only in church buildings—but a way of living that is integrated into all of life.

This fact is clear: a teen's involvement in church is not primarily motivated by themes or topics. Sure, we may have achieved a record attendance for that "Sex and Dating" retreat. However, long-term involvement and lasting impact comes by way of meaningful relationships. Interest in programs or topics may bring young people to a meeting one to three times. If in that period they do not develop any significant relationships with peers and/or adults, they will not continue coming back. The bottom line is: *they come and keep coming as a result of the relationships they have formed and because of an established sense of belonging.*

Characteristics of a Relational Youth Minister

Practically speaking, what does relational youth ministry look like? First and foremost, it is not what we do as much as who we are. Impacting youth ministry is not about getting the "relational techniques" down to a cause-and-effect science. We have all met the slick phone salesperson who, cued on command, has all the right words and techniques. Everything he says and does is reminiscent of a relationship with a close friend, but, he is not our friend. We feel uneasy, distrusting, and suspicious. We usually recognize insincerity behind a masquerade of concern. We sense a self-seeking, hidden agenda; and often, his hand is revealed when we express no interest in what he is peddling. CLICK!

Relational *techniques* will *not* work. Authentic relationships evolve from who we are. It is best, then, to be the kind of person who concentrates on caring rather than on simply doing all the right things. The following five personal qualities can be of help.

1. Be a Person Motivated by God's Love

We are not slick sales agents for God's kingdom. We cannot be motivated by our own emotional needs or our own eternal commission. Our inspiration comes from the One who sought nothing for himself, but gave his life in obedience to God and for the benefit of others. Like St. Paul, we must be compelled by the love of God (see 2 Corinthians 5:14). First and foremost, we are driven by the love we have personally experienced from our Lord. It is the joy of personally knowing such pure love that compels us to share it with others.

Do you remember the experience of being infatuated? Have you recently talked with a teen who is "in love?" It seems that the conversation always finds its way to that "special someone." The discourse might go like this:

> "Hi, Gladys. What's new?"
>
> "Well, Melvin called at 8:02:28 p.m. last night. I was thinking about him and anticipating his call all day—that's why I know the exact time."
>
> "Oh?"
>
> "Yes—the phone ringing jarred me out of a glorious daydream—starring Melvin, of course. As I staggered to the phone I was gripped with anxiety—what if it's Melvin? What will I say? What if it's not Melvin—how will I handle the disappointment? I picked up the phone—trembling, and squeezed out a tentative, 'hello?' My blood pressure momentarily sky-rocketed as I waited in ominous silence for what seemed like an eternity."
>
> "Well, who was it?"
>
> "The next thing I heard was, 'Hello . . . Gladys?' It was Melvin's deep, masculine voice! My throat constricted, my mouth dried, and my glands perspired! But I could not talk! My body was spazzing! Melvin, how could you do this to me?!"

Get the picture? We love to talk about the people or things we love. We want others to meet the special people in our lives. We want to share our good news with others. Our desire to share Jesus with those around us can serve as a spiritual barometer to the quality and depth of our relationship with the Lord. Experiencing afresh the reality of God's love through an active, living, and daily relationship with Christ is the best preparation for loving others.

Secondly, we are compelled by God's own love and concern for others. Jesus loves every teenager in our community. His heart is broken by Bobby's pain, Jason's struggles, and Maureen's estrangement from his love. It was his "crazy" love for them that caused him to endure the joy of the cross (see Hebrews 12:2). This terrible price Jesus paid ought to remind us of what these teens are worth to him. When we truly understand Jesus' love for his children, we are motivated to join Jesus in reaching them.

2. Be a Person Who Is Accepting

Acceptance is the admittance ramp for any relationship. When we are unaccepting and critical of teens, we pound down a sign that reads: "Do Not Enter." As with anyone, teens will not pursue relationships when they don't feel accepted.

Being accepting of others means being like our God, who "proves his love for us in that while we were still sinners Christ died for us" (Romans 5:8). Jesus does not wait until we become "acceptable" before reaching out to us. He is not put off by our idiosyncrasies, bad attitudes, long hair, multiple earrings, tattoos, or a pierced navel. Nor is he more accepting because of our dynamic personality, good looks, wealth, athleticism, or intelligence. He accepts us simply because we are children of God. We must do the same.

The scriptures clearly indicate that God looks after the poor and the oppressed. Our acceptance of others should reflect God's preferential option for the emotional, spiritual, physical, economical, or social poor. Being an accepting person means we find favor with, approve of, or freely give admittance to those the world has found unattractive and has rejected. The church ought to be a place where the "poor" find safety, refuge, and love. We must be careful not to mirror the contemporary culture by loving only the attractive. We, too, can be enchanted by what the world defines as beautiful. Without even noticing it, we can find ourselves spending most of our time with this world's "winners." Often, they will be the ones to whom we are naturally attracted. It is hard to be around those who dislike themselves, or are emotionally needy. Often, as a result of core wounds from their primary caregivers and years of rejection, needy teens have developed social mannerisms and relational patterns that only breed further pain, hurt, and rejection. Spurned by other clubs, organizations, and peer groups, these teens find themselves at the last stop—the church. Will they be greeted by accepting people?

Will they be welcomed with love? Will they be pursued with tenacity? Or, will the church be just one more negative experience in a lifelong litany of rejection?

3. Be a Person Who Listens

President Franklin D. Roosevelt got tired of smiling that big smile and saying the usual things at those White House receptions. So, one evening he decided to find out whether anybody was paying attention to what he was saying. As each person came up to him with extended hand, he flashed that big smile and said, "I murdered my grandmother this morning." People would automatically respond with comments such as "How lovely!" or "Just continue with your great work!" Nobody listened to what he was saying, except one foreign diplomat. When the president said, "I murdered my grandmother this morning," the diplomat responded softly, "I'm sure she had it coming to her."[25]

Many teens also wonder if anyone is really listening to them. No matter what age we are, we like being around people who take time to really listen to us. While in my teen years, I remember more than once my friends coming over to see me, and when they found that I was out, ending up spending hours at the kitchen table with my father. It was not that my dad was a life-of-the-party guy. He was actually very shy and quiet. But my father was a person who listened, and a number of my friends found that very attractive and inviting.

Being people who listen means putting aside our own agendas, profundities, and plans. We essentially say, "You are more important than anything else at this moment." It is amazing how much love we communicate without even opening our mouths.

4. Be a Person Who Cares

While going through a difficult time in my life, I called my pastor, Fr. Bob, to set up a time to talk with him. Fifteen minutes later, at 10:30 p.m., he was knocking on my door! On another occasion, my six-year-old daughter Deborah was crying in a very crowded parish center because one of her older siblings failed to buy her a bagel after Sunday Mass. Fr. Bob somehow noticed her among this sea of people, found out why she was so upset, and personally delivered a bagel—compliments of the pastor. My daughter Rebekah expressed interest in a motion picture Fr. Bob referred to in a homily. Two days later there was a letter delivered with two tickets for Rebekah and a friend to see the movie. Fr. Bob is a person who cares. He demonstrates this care in some very concrete ways.

Care for teens can be expressed in many ways. It might be a note of encouragement, a prayer for a teen before an important test, a phone call, a birthday card, or a ride to an event. When we take the time to do even the most nondescript things for another person, we communicate love; and in so doing we help bring praise to the God we serve (see Matthew 5:16).

5. Be a Person Who Values Others

Dr. Erikson was my professor of Greek during my undergraduate years. I admired him for his clarity of thought and intelligence. But the best gift he gave me had nothing to do with his brilliance or teaching abilities. One day after class, I was hanging in the back of the classroom pondering a few grammatical questions. Three other students were ahead of me with questions of their own. After waiting a few minutes, I thought I would head back to my room and try to figure them out myself. As I began to make my way to the door, Dr. Erikson caught my movement from the corner of his eye. He stopped his conversation with another student and yelled to me, "Frank, did you want to talk with me about something?"

I felt he was busy enough and replied, "No . . . that's okay. It's not important."

With genuine concern, he looked me right in the eyes and replied, "It may not be important, but *you* are." There was no doubt in my mind that he sincerely meant what he said. I was so personally touched by those words that they became a model for me in ministry. Whenever a teen said something to the effect of, "I'd like to get together, but I know you're so busy," I have responded with, "I will never be so busy that I would not want to spend time with you. Let's schedule a meeting."

We all want to be valued by others. We want to be with people who see past our faults and recognize and encourage us in our potential. Primary to any solid relationship is the confidence of knowing we really matter to another person. Teens especially need to be reassured that they are important to us.

Young people will also feel valued as we allow them to minister to us. Teens, too, want to experience the joy of giving in the relationship. One-sided relationships do not meet the needs of either party and eventually die. Teens should not replace our adult peers, but we should afford them opportunities to contribute to the relationship in a mutual manner. Letting down our guard in an appropriate manner and allowing young people to pray for us, encourage us, and even offer insights can go a long way in giving teens a sense of value.

Four Elements to Relational Outreach

Relational ministry is at the heart of any effective youth ministry. There is no substitute for sharing our lives and faith within the caring context of friendship. The following section identifies four sequential elements to relational outreach. Although presented here as a linear process, in reality, each step in the process is on-going.

It is also important to note that relational ministry should be generally practiced in a same sex context. If we do meet with someone of the opposite gender, it should be the exception and it should be done with others present. Youth ministers must exercise great caution and prudence in their dealings with teens of the opposite sex.

We need to work together with parents in being a support to their children.

More than ever before, parents are cautious and even suspicious of adults who take an interest in their children of either gender. Therefore, it is very critical to establish relationships with the parents of teens with whom we are meeting. When we call, we should always introduce and identify ourselves. We need to build relationships with them in order to gain their trust. We need to work together with parents in being a support to their children.

Lastly, relational outreach will not conform itself easily to a "neat and tidy" plan. Getting involved in other people's lives and letting others get involved in our lives involves risk and vulnerability. When we truly love, we chance rejection; but by establishing relationships with young people and truly caring for them, we bring the reality of the gospel out of the sterility of the church classroom and into the live action stage of real life. Four elements of relational outreach follow:

1. Make Contact

What do football, wrestling, and rugby have in common? They are all contact sports. Contact lenses are named similarly because they touch you, make contact with you. In an analogous way, we need to interact and touch the lives of young people. This step involves being present to teens and initiating and establishing relationships with them.

Contacting teens begins with going where they can be found. As we attend events and go places where teens are present, our face becomes more familiar to them. We lose the "stranger" status and become a "friendly face." We further broaden our base of relationships as teens we know introduce us to their friends.

Some practical ways in which to make contact with teens might include:

- ✔ Attend (or possibly assist in coaching) varsity and lower level athletic events and practices. Don't neglect the lower levels.
- ✔ "Hang out" in the school cafeteria (bring snacks).
- ✔ Attend band and choir concerts and recitals.
- ✔ Participate in school pep rallies. (If you really want to be noticed, paint your face in the school colors. Or at least dress in school colors.)
- ✔ Watch dramatic practices and presentations.
- ✔ Chaperone school events such as homecoming, field trips, mixers, and prom.
- ✔ Become the advisor for school clubs like Key Club, Natural Helpers, Cheerleading (okay, this one is a sport), Peer Mediation, Fellowship of Christian Athletes, Chess Club, Ski Club, Computer Club.
- ✔ Visit teens at their places of employment (be a paying customer).
- ✔ Work out with them at the local gym, spa, or YMCA.
- ✔ Volunteer to tutor local teens who struggle academically.
- ✔ Attend high school art exhibits and shows.
- ✔ Observe school debates.
- ✔ Sit in on teen council meetings.
- ✔ If possible, spend time at the nearest juvenile detention center.
- ✔ Occasionally be present at the local malls and arcades (as well as other various hangouts).
- ✔ Send birthday cards, holiday greetings, and notes of encouragement (call too!) when the occasion arises.
- ✔ Make "pump you up" calls on the eve of big events.
- ✔ Shoot hoops at popular outdoor/indoor courts.
- ✔ Volunteer time with some aspect of the local park district program in the summer.

Some of these ideas require the establishment of relationships with parents, teachers, principals, and/or other authority figures in the lives of our teens. This is essential and opens the door for other opportunities to minister as well.

When you are first making contact, the most awkward moments occur during your initial time together. Questions like "How do I start? What if I go blank? What if the conversation dies?" cross our minds. The acronym I.N.V.I.T.E. can be a helpful tool in initiating a conversation and talking to a teen for the first time.

"I" stands for *introduction*. Enthusiastically introduce yourself. We might extend our hand saying, "Hi, my name is Dorcas. I am a youth minister at Our Lady of Perpetual Penance. What's your name?"

"Uh . . . my name is Elmo."

"Well, Elmo, it's a real pleasure to meet you."

"N" stands for *name*. Remember their name! When someone calls us by name or remembers our name the next time they see us, we feel important and valued. When others seem continually to forget who we are, we feel insignificant, devalued, and unimportant. We think, "Gosh, what kind of insignificant loser am I that he still can't figure out who I am!" Make a point of remembering names. It will go a long way in initiating and establishing relationships with teens.

This little gesture makes twice the impact of the effort invested. We can further our ability to recall names with some simple practices. The first is association. For instance, we may associate Elmo with the *Sesame Street* character of the same name. Or, we can make an association by attaching an adjective that describes some aspect of the person's personality and begins with the first letter of his or her name. Maybe Elmo twitches a bit as if he had too much sugar. You might then think of him as "Energetic Elmo." When you see him the next time, and he is again hyper—click—"Energetic Elmo!"

Secondly, use the person's name in conversation both to personalize the exchange and memorize their name: "What are some of your interests, Elmo?" After using their name several times we are better able to recall it later. Beware. Too much of a good thing can turn it sour. We do not want to overuse a name during our conversation. That can get obnoxious and artificial and will actually secure the opposite effect we desire!

"V" represents *value*. We want to communicate to young people in the course of our conversation that we value them. One simple way to do this is by making good eye contact. Giving a young person our exclusive attention goes a long way in saying, "You are important." Remember, only a small percentage of our communication is verbal. It is essential that our tone, gestures, and body language agree with our words and also say, "I value you." Be careful not to deny what you are trying to say verbally by sending a contradictory message nonverbally.

Additionally, when we hear something interesting or fascinating, we should sincerely affirm, encourage, express more interest, or compliment that person. For instance, Elmo might state, "I broke the gender barrier by becoming the only male on my school's synchronized swimming team." We might respond with, "Wow, I can't imagine being able to hold my breath as long as you have to in that sport. How do you do it?"

"I" stands for *interests*. Ask teens questions about what they are interested in. For example, we might say, "Besides synchronized swimming, Elmo, what do you like to do?" Other questions might include:

"What kind of sports do you like to play?"

"What kind of sports do you like to watch?"

"What school do you attend?"

"What are your hobbies?"

"What do you like to do with your spare time?"

"What kind of books do you like to read?"

"What was a movie that you really enjoyed?"

We can talk about all kinds of things—extra-curricular activities, favorite subjects, or future ambitions. Remember: Teens usually won't volunteer information, so we will have to work at getting it through asking questions.

"T" is for *tribe.* Find out about the teen's family. Inquire about his or her ethnic and cultural background. Again, we may ask questions like:

"How many kids are in your family?"

"What are your mom and dad like?"

"Where do you live?"

"What are your brothers and sisters like?"

"Where do you stand in the birth order?"

"How do you like being the oldest?"

"Do you like being the youngest?"

"How do you get along with your brother?"

"Has your family always lived in the area?"

"E" of course designates the *end*. Eventually all good things must come to an end (some sooner than others). We should be sensitive to the comfort level of the teens with whom we are conversing. If we can see that they are very uncomfortable, we should not prolong their misery by ignoring their nonverbal signs. They will dart in the opposite direction the next time they pick up our scent. Bring the conversation to a gracious ending. It may take several encounters over a period of time before they feel comfortable around us. End the conversation in a manner that communicates that we enjoyed talking with them and hope to see them again. We should close in a manner that expresses our desire to talk again in the near future or get together and pursue a common interest. For instance, as we end our conversation with our friend Elmo, we might conclude with, "It was a real joy meeting you, Elmo. Maybe sometime we can get together and you can show me those breathing techniques you use for synchronized swimming." Also, we should not be afraid to end a positive conversation with an invitation to a youth group event that would be appropriate.

Remember:

I ntroduction
N ame
V alue
I nterests
T ribe
E nd

2. Develop the Relationship

Being present and initiating contact with teens is an important beginning. Once we have done that, however, we will want to consider ways to further develop the relationship. Prayer is an important beginning. We need to pray that God will lead us to pursue and deepen the relationships into which he is calling us. Our time is limited and, therefore, we need to invest it in a manner that is according to God's leading. Second, when we pray for people, we grow to love them more because we invest in their lives.

Application

A sample of a "Teen Profile" is on page 153.

A helpful tool in remembering what to pray for and what we learned about a new teen is a "Teen Profile." After meeting a new teen we can record the information we discovered on a Teen Profile. Not only does this help us recall the details of our conversation, it can also assist in building a deeper relationship in the future. For example, we might call Elmo the next week and say, "I was just watching television and saw—you won't believe this—a synchronized swimming event! It reminded me of you. How are things going on the team?" Elmo sadly responds, "I just found out I was cut from the team." At this point we have an opportunity to deepen our friendship and move it beyond an informational level. We might say, "Oh, Elmo, I am so sorry to hear that. How do you feel about being cut from the team?" Sensing that we really care about him, Elmo may open up in a manner that ushers the relationship to a deeper realm. We might let him know we care by listening and encouraging him. We could redirect our prayers, and even let him know we will be praying for him. Later we can follow up the conversation with a note of encouragement or an appointment to get a soda together.

Other actions that deepen relationships with teens include:

- ✔ Greet teens by name and refer back to our last conversations with them. When we remember important details of someone's life it demonstrates our interest and care. We might say, "Last time I saw you, Baxter, you were worried about your algebra test. I prayed for you that day. How did you end up doing?"
- ✔ Read the local papers with a watchful eye for any articles that highlight the athletic, academic, artistic, or activity achievements of familiar teens. Write a note or make a call to congratulate those teens.
- ✔ Invite a teen over for a meal or dessert. This will give them an opportunity to meet our families and get to know us in our familiar surroundings. It helps take the stiffness and formality out of new relationships.
- ✔ Make a practice of recording the birthdays of teens and sending them cards on their day. We tend to appreciate cards from people we don't normally expect to remember us. Be sure to write a short personal note as opposed to simply signing a name.
- ✔ Make a phone call in the middle of the week to check on a teen who seemed down the last time we were together.
- ✔ Treat a teen who just made it through finals, SATs, or a particularly stressful time to a soda or ice cream.

To make an impact in a teen's life we have to move the relationship beyond simple information swapping to a deeper level of sharing and trust. This is a natural process that cannot be forced or done insincerely. It will look different with each teen. Some teens almost begin there, while others may never arrive there. No matter how long it takes, we cannot lose our focus of genuine love for a young person. I have met individuals who have esteemed "evangelization" more than the teens with whom they were seeking to share the good news. The results are often less-than-desired. The "evangelized" teen feels used, like an impersonal statistic within a sales quota. We should evangelize teens out of a love for people, not out of a love for evangelization.

No matter how long it takes, we cannot lose our focus of genuine love for a young person.

3. Share Our Faith

Once we make contact and develop a relationship with a young person, we then have a very natural context in which to share our faith. If being a disciple is central to our identity, and if Jesus is part of our everyday life, then we will have much to share. God's action in our lives, answered prayer, and instances of his providence will simply be part of our normal conversation. Some rules for faith-sharing follow:

Always be ready to share—Some of the best evangelistic moments in my life were not planned. The Holy Spirit definitely has a schedule of his own! Our role is to discern what the Spirit is doing and to follow that guidance. We must, as St. Paul writes, "always be ready to give an explanation to anyone who asks you for a reason for your hope, but do it with gentleness and reverence . . ." (1 Peter 3:15-16). To be effective in youth evangelization we must possess an openness to the movement of the Holy Spirit. We must be willing to put aside our own agendas and cooperate with whatever the Spirit is doing.

It is rare when I am unable to identify which one of my children is about to enter my room. I cannot see them coming down the hall, but I have learned to recognize the distinguishing characteristics of their approach. I can tell by the manner in which they breathe, the length and speed of their stride, and the weight of their step. Over time I have come to know my children's movement. We, too, must learn to recognize the Spirit's movement and direction in our life. When we walk with the Lord throughout the day, prayerfully interacting, our chances are much greater that we will see, hear, and understand what our Lord expects of us.

In addition to being open to the Holy Spirit and recognizing his movement, we must also be prepared to share our faith. Ideally, this is a natural process that flows from our daily lived experience. For most of us, however, we must prepare and work at communicating the good news. One of the most useful and effective tools in sharing our faith with teens is our own faith journey. Each of us has a story of how God has touched our lives. A faith journey, or story, communicates God's ongoing interaction with us. Mary, the mother of Jesus, communicated the purpose of a faith journey when she said to Elizabeth, "My soul proclaims the greatness of the Lord . . . the Mighty One has done *great things for me*" (Luke 1:46, 49). The main objective in sharing our faith story is to proclaim to others the greatness of our God as illustrated through the great things he has done for us. Being prepared to share the hope that is within us includes an ability to present succinctly our faith journey to others.

For some of us, our faith journey resembles the Apostle Paul's: a dramatic, 180-degree conversion (see Acts 26:9-23). Paul always had an excitement for Jesus Christ. His initial excitement was enthusiastically expressed by arresting and approving the death of those who followed Jesus. After a personal encounter with Jesus on the road to Damascus, Paul articulated his zeal for Jesus in a new way: the bold proclamation of the gospel to the Gentiles. Paul's conversion was sudden, dramatic, and life-changing. If our own story is similar to Paul's, we might express our faith journey in the following three-part movement:

1. Describe what my life was like before the "aha" moment.
2. Describe my experience of meeting Christ and the "aha" moment.
3. Describe how my life has been transformed and changed by Christ.

Others are more like Timothy. That is, we experience a gradual growth in faith throughout our lives (2 Timothy 1:4, 5; 2:15). Timothy was described by Paul as one might describe "a good Catholic boy." Timothy knew the scriptures from his infancy. His faith was passed down from a faith-filled mother and grandmother. He was an apple that did not fall too far from the tree. He steadily progressed in his faith as he grew from a child to an adult. If our own story is similar to Timothy's, we might express our faith journey in the following three-part movement:

1. Describe my faith environment, family values, and Christian experience.
2. Describe how my faith grew to become my own.
3. Describe the differences Christ is making in my life and my experience of following him.

Whether we are a Paul, a Timothy, or a combination of the two, we should be able to articulate confidently and concretely the story of God's personal interaction in the way we live. The story of God's movement in our lives can take the abstract truth of the gospel and enflesh it with a concrete illustration of how it positively works for someone. This ability will prove to be one of our most helpful tools in sharing the good news with teens.

Application

For concrete examples of the "Timothy" and "Paul" profiles that can be shared with adults or teens, see "Examples of a Faith Journey" (pages 154-157).

Share the good news in light of a teen's need—Jesus chose the particular strand of good news based on the audience or individual he encountered. He tailored his message to the need of the moment. Given our particular situation, personality, or circumstances, some aspects of the good news will be more meaningful or pertinent than others. The "one-size-fits-all" approach to youth evangelization simply does not work.

As we build relationships with teens, the Holy Spirit will help us understand the nature of a teen's spiritual need. Jesus demonstrated this in his own interpersonal evangelistic encounters with the different people he encountered—for example, Zacchaeus, Nicodemus, and the Samaritan woman.

Jesus told Zacchaeus (see Luke 19:1-10), the unpopular tax collector, who was short in stature as well, to come down from his tree. Jesus went to Zacchaeus's home and shared a meal with him. Zacchaeus's greatest longing was for acceptance, dignity and love. Jesus sensed this need and delivered a message that addressed the cravings of Zacchaeus's heart. The result was conversion.

Nicodemus (see John 3:1-21) was a Pharisee and a member of the Jewish Sanhedrin. In other words, he was a "somebody" of Jewish Palestine. Jesus told Nicodemus that even though he was a son of Abraham, something was missing from his life. A change of heart and a new birth was what Jesus prescribed for Nicodemus. A change was needed on the interior, not simply in external practices. This was an approach tailored to Nicodemus' needs, and it brought about conversion. After Jesus died, it was Nicodemus who went with Joseph of Arimathea to bury Jesus.

The Samaritan woman (see John 4:4-26) had passed through a series of broken marriages and was presently in an illicit affair. Her heart hungered to be cherished, loved, and cared for. She had a nagging spiritual thirst, but was futilely seeking to quench it through the right man. She was thirsting but never satisfied.

Jesus uses the well as a powerful image to illustrate her condition. He offers her living water—a water that would satisfy her restless heart. She was trying to fill a God-shaped hole with temporal relationships and Jesus offers her the truth that would fulfill her longing.

Jesus related to the Samaritan woman in a very different manner than he did with Zacchaeus, or Nicodemus. In each case Jesus diagnosed their particular needs and brought forth the strand of good news that best addressed their real hunger.

Jesus' style of interpersonal evangelization illustrates an essential evangelistic principle. Instead of using a standard or "canned" approach, we need to identify a person's need and tailor the message to address it. For someone who is lonely, we may present the gospel as a relationship with a Good Shepherd who cares for each one in his flock. To another who feels inferior, we may present the Jesus who validates human existence by his death on the cross. Another teen may always be anxious and worried about life. We may share how our Lord cares so much about us that he has the hairs on our head numbered to show us how he cares for us to the most minute detail.

The good news we share must be based on the scriptures and church teaching. We do not have the liberty to make up what *we* think is good news. If our message is contrary to the scriptures and church teaching we are in error. Our own human compassion can sometimes be an enemy to the good news. It is important, therefore, to know the scriptures and church teaching well. The Holy Spirit will then be able to draw from our previous deposits during the present time of need (Mark 13:11).

Also, it is not enough to present the good news. We need to invite young people to a response. Like Peter, our teens need to personally respond to Jesus' question, "But who do you say that I am?" (Mark 8:29). We need not be afraid to ask a teen:

"Who is Jesus in your life?"

"How would you describe your relationship with Christ?"

"Have you ever committed yourself to serving the Lord?"

We should also be open to pray sensitively with teens and lead them into a closer or new relationship with Christ.

4. Follow Through

Whether a teen responds to our invitations to God's kingdom or not, we should follow up on the relationship. If a teen responds negatively, or is not ready to open her or his life up to Christ, we should continue to love and pray for that teen—even if he or she never responds. We should not attach a condition to the relationship.

If a teen does respond to the invitation to give her or his life more fully to Christ, we should help support and nurture the person's growth. Appropriate follow-up includes directing a spiritually hungry teen to the appropriate parish programming, resources, and events that could help foster spiritual and faith growth. Our own role may change from evangelizer to spiritual mentor.

Summary

When God the Father decided that something had to be done to bring us back into relationship with him, he did not send a program into the world to do so, but rather he sent the person of his only Son, Jesus Christ. If we are going to "earn the right to be heard," we must do so through relational ministry, as opposed to a model that is primarily programmatic in nature.

As beacons of the good news, we must be willing to learn how to be present to our teens in the grease, grime, and grit of their lives, as well as the glorious moments. We need to break into their fast-paced world, not superficially as "pseudo-adolescents," but as willing learners and participants. Just as Jesus journeyed with his apostles through their discipling, so must we with our teens.

True relational ministry, put in context, naturally flows out of our personal lives and experiences. We may not be experts in evangelization, but we are worthy to do ministry nonetheless because we, too, are in the process of becoming Jesus' disciples. The most effective ministers to teens are motivated not by selfish ambition, but by the Lord's love for them. The viewing lenses of our ministry glasses must be bifocal in nature: we see and accept teens for who they are as well as for who they could become. Teens need to be genuinely listened to, cared for, and valued.

The four elements of relational outreach testify to the fact that true ministry is a process that takes great time and concentrated effort and attention. After making initial contact with our teens, we begin to develop a relationship with them, share our life and faith with them, and follow up in whatever way necessary. This entire process does not begin and end at an evening youth ministry program; it develops over time.

We must always keep in mind that our personal lives may be the only "gospel" our teens see. If they choose to accept the good news, it won't be because they were "turned on" to an awesome program, but rather because a real person shared in a real way the real message.

Teen Profile

The following worksheet can be an effective tool for developing relationships with young people in your community. It can serve as your personal database for each student under your care. Compile, refer to, and revise your information through phone conversation, personal meetings, etc.

Name:	Phone Number:
Address:	City:
Birthday:	Parish:
School:	Grad. Year:
Parent's Names:	
Brothers & Sisters (Ages):	
Favorite Sports:	
Interests:	
Hobbies:	
Favorite Classes/Subjects:	
Least Favorite Classes:	
Future Ambitions:	
Major Issues:	
Miscellaneous:	

EXAMPLES OF A FAITH JOURNEY

The Timothy Faith Journey

Like many children in this melting pot called "America," I grew up in a culturally-mixed family. From my mother, I received a Jewish heritage, although this was more of a cultural connection than it was one of religious practice. Her side of the family did not faithfully adhere to the majority of the Jewish rites and rituals. As a matter of fact, the kosher laws were about all they observed regarding the faith. In addition, my mom grew up with a mother who taught her to believe that Jesus was the Messiah. So, in a sense, Mom was a Messianic Jew.

My father grew up in a very orthodox, pre-Vatican II Catholic family who faithfully adhered to the teachings, doctrines, practices, and obligations of the Church. Because my mother believed in Jesus, she and Dad had no qualms about having me baptized into the Catholic faith and training me up in it.

As a young child, several experiences impressed the reality of God on my fresh mind and heart, although it obviously takes hindsight to see God's movement in my toddler and early childhood years. I remember being given the opportunity as a family to bring the gifts to the altar during the offertory at Mass one Sunday. The usher placed in my hands what would become the Body of Christ and told me to "take good care of it." I remember feeling a sense of awe, although I really did not understand why at the time. I remember to this day (word for word) the bedtime prayers my mom and dad would say with me every night which included a spoken blessing on every one of my immediate and extended family members, including the pets! Family prayer was also an upheld tradition before dinner and during special seasons such as Lent and Advent. Together we would say the Rosary, and Dad would let me look at the paintings that corresponded with the mysteries in our family bible. I can remember being very intrigued by Jesus' life, although the Rosary was sort of a bore.

As a child I even contemplated (as do most boys) becoming a priest and would go so far as to play "Mass" with my sisters. I would be the priest, they would be my congregation, and Wonder Bread would be our nourishment.

When I hit my junior high and early high school years and began to think more critically, there was a brief interlude where the call to Christianity became somewhat tainted and misconceived by natural developmental issues as well as my observation of "Church" around me.

The Church did not seem all that exciting or relevant to me. I briefly questioned the legitimacy of the Christian life. I did not necessarily pursue rebelling against the Church or the faith foundation my parents helped to establish in my life, I just wanted something real.

As a part of my confirmation preparation, I was required to attend an overnight retreat. On this retreat, young adults shared with me through skits, talks, and other activities what Jesus Christ meant to them. They gave me an impression of Jesus unlike any that I ever had before. They spoke as if they knew him personally (they showed me something real), and for the first time in my life, I began to understand that Jesus wanted to be a part of my life twenty-four hours a day, seven days a week, 365 days a year. He did not simply want to be put into a compartment called "Sunday Mass" or "Youth Group."

I also had a youth minister who took time to spend with me in my areas of interest. He would take me down to the local ballpark where we would play home-run derby, discuss life-issues, and talk about Jesus Christ. He showed me through his example that Jesus desired to be in a regular, consistent relationship with me, and I gradually became "sold out."

My final two years in high school, I served as a peer minister at my parish and discerned God's call for me to take Jesus' message to teens through youth ministry as my life's vocation.

I love Jesus Christ. As I look back on my life, I can see his protective, firm, loving, and providential hand guiding me into a relationship with him through the influence of countless people, experiences, and events. My walk with Jesus did not begin as did the apostle Paul's, with a radical 180 degree about-face, but rather like the disciple Timothy's, through a gradual process of growing and learning—a process that will span my entire life!

EXAMPLES OF A FAITH JOURNEY

The Paul Faith Journey

Although I grew up in a Catholic home with wonderful parents and a good support system, my commitment to my faith came through a "Paul" type of experience. During my college years at a Jesuit University, I all but left the Catholic church. It was during this time that I began to participate in many deviant behaviors that lead to much pain and disillusionment. I transferred to the school halfway through a semester; everyone seemed to already be in their own groups, and I desperately wanted to fit in. A few guys invited me to go "out for a beer" and I slowly began to drink regularly. The following school year, I whole-heartedly began a lifestyle of loose living and partying. I began participating in activities that only a few years earlier, I despised.

Toward the end of my junior year, with poor grades, poor dating relationships, and not a very good relationship with my parents, I decided it was time to straighten up. Instead of living with five other guys, it was time to move in with someone that was more focused on graduating. I found an engineering student to room with for my senior year, the only guy from my dorm floor that didn't drink.

I returned from summer break with a resolve to stay away from the bar scene and study daily. I even worked on a few "I will . . ." statements such as: "I will study every evening for at least two hours," and "I will consume only what is good for my body." It seemed to be working . . . for about the first week, anyway. I stopped by my buddies' place, and they were all sitting around getting high . . . and I joined in. For the next month, I lived with wanting to follow through with my commitments, but not having the willpower. Around mid-term when grades came out, I was at my lowest point ever—angry and frustrated with myself, not to mention pulling a couple of D's.

I remember calling home and talking with my mom about this time. I expressed that she just would not believe the things I had gotten into during college and I was having a very difficult time. Then she said, "Ever since you've been going to school up there, you have turned away from God and become a different person." I knew she was right, but I really did not think God could help me.

A week or so later, I went with seven friends to a Van Halen concert. As we arrived, I mentioned to a friend that I was bummed we were so far back and that I had forgotten my glasses. Nevertheless, we were having a great time jamming along on our air guitars. About halfway through the concert I started thinking to myself, "I have so much... a good education, a good family, lots of friends, a cool VW bus, and lots of other things. If I have so much then why do I feel so empty inside?" Then Van Halen began to play a song called "Best of Both Worlds."

The song begins, "I don't know what I'm living on, but it's not enough to fill me up." I could not believe my ears—they felt the same way I did! The song goes on to say, "We want the best of both worlds." I thought to myself, that's like me. I want to party and do whatever I want and in the end I hope to go to heaven. The song continues—"You don't have to die and go to heaven or hang around to be born again, just tune into what this world has to offer because we'll never be here again." At that moment it hit me: is it possible we are both missing the same thing... God? Then I immediately felt a voice in my head say, "Do you see how clearly you see the truth?" At that moment for about ten seconds, I could see the sweat on Sammy Hagar's face and read their t-shirts and banners. I started to tear up and Chris said, "What's going on with you?" I responded, "I'm OK, this is a great concert."

That evening I dropped my friends off at the bar and went home. I took a few jeers for it. When I got back to my apartment, I dusted off my bible and got down on my knees. "God," I prayed, "if you are real and what happened tonight was real, I want to know it." I spent the next few hours, until early in the morning, crying and repenting for all I had done, reading scripture through the eyes of faith, and asking God into my life. The Lord revealed Himself to me in wonderful ways. My life changed drastically! What I could not accomplish with "I will" statements, God accomplished in me through His power! My addictions were gone immediately. I stopped going to the bars. I started going back to Mass and spent time daily with the Lord. I got involved in a senior retreat and bible study. I individually shared what God had done in my life with many of my partying friends. One commented that he thought I was maybe a prophet sent from God, to which I responded, "We go to a Catholic school, and I am simply living out our faith!" The last semester of my undergrad experience, I received my best grades ever, including high school.

Since that time the Lord has called me to full-time youth ministry to share the love that He has shared with me. I have been blessed with a beautiful Christian wife and two wonderful daughters. The Lord has taken care of my every need and I truly want for nothing. The meaning, purpose, and belonging I hungered for I found in Christ and His church.

8

Acres at a Time: Large Group Evangelization

I can still remember boarding the bus to go to CCD (which was affectionately understood to stand for "Central City Dump"). None of us were thrilled. As a matter of fact, we all looked miserable—as if our mothers had died earlier that day. Upon arriving we were "warmly" greeted by our teacher with furrowed brow and ruler in hand. We knew there was only one escape route—and it was called "confirmation." Once confirmed in fifth grade, I tenaciously resisted any invitation to church events. I had nothing against God—it was church programming that I disdained.

When it comes to youth ministry programming, we are often like the dog food company president who gathered all his employees for a big corporate rally. As he stepped to the podium he was greeted with spirited applause. He began his speech by asking his employees, "What dog food company has the best marketing program in the entire nation?"

His workers shot back the name of their company with the kind of enthusiasm, excitement, and morale that would turn even an Amway convention green with envy.

On a roll, the president inquired, "Who, of all the dog food companies in the world, has the best employee incentive package?" One could physically feel the energy level rising in the room, as the entire throng exploded forth with the name of their organization.

Again, the president threw out another question to his faithful employees, "Who manufactures the most nutritious dog chow in this entire world?"

At a near frenzy, his audience screamed out with great pride the name of their beloved company.

The president paused for a moment as his employees leaned toward the edge of their seats. Surrounded with great anticipation, he lowered his voice and tempo, and quietly asked, "Why, then, are we not selling the *most* dog food in the world?"

Silence.

A stunned work force slumped back into their chairs.

Finally, a man in the back of the room slowly stood to his feet and shouted in response, "Because dogs don't like it!"[26]

Often, our youth programming is similar to that dog food. We have the greatest news in the world, financial support, ministry resources, and even dedicated youth workers, but kids taste what we offer, don't like it, and fail to return.

As a result of my own experience, I heartily agree with Jim Rayburn, the founder of *Young Life,* when he said, "It's a sin to bore a kid with the gospel." When I first started in youth ministry, I wanted to construct a program that addressed the perceived needs of unevangelized teens. I wanted it to be a place where teens could have fun, develop friendships, hear the good news in light of their issues, and experience the love of Jesus Christ. I also wanted it to be a place where teens *wanted* to come and even a place where they would be proud to invite their friends. Over the years we watched our large group evangelization program grow from about twelve teens to over 300. But more importantly, it became a vehicle that the Spirit used to touch many teens with the good news of Jesus Christ.

"It's a sin to bore a kid with the gospel."
—Jim Rayburn
Young Life

Defining Large Group Evangelization

One of the most effective ways to reach a significant number of young people from a good cross-section of social groups is through *large group evangelization.* Large group evangelization can be defined as *a regular large group gathering that addresses perceived and unperceived needs of youth for the purpose of evangelizing as many teens as possible.*

"Regular" is a key part of the definition. Irregularity is not only a disturbing experience for the human digestive system, it also constipates the momentum of large group evangelization! A large group evangelization program needs to be consistently planned on the same *day,* during the same *time,* at the same *location,* and with the same *quality* to make maximum impact on teens' lives.

We are creatures of habit. Most days I have little recall of how I arrived at work. I know, of course, that I drove my car, but I remember little about making turns, stopping at lights, or going down streets. As a result of consistent repetition, I put very little thought into getting to work. (Some might say that's true about me in a lot of things!) Likewise, consistency in programming builds routine in young people's lives. Teens are very busy. Working at remembering something lessens the chance of attending. If we have to look at a calendar, find a schedule, or call a friend to find out where and when a meeting is, chances are greater that our attendance will slip. Establishing the same day, time, and location reduces the amount of effort it takes to get to an event. Meetings that are every Sunday at 7:00 p.m. in the church gym have less of a chance of falling through the cracks of daily living than sporadic programs. Additionally, when we switch days, times, or locations, we have to publicize the event all over again.

A helpful trick is to name the program after the night it is held. For instance, we might call a program held on every second Sunday of the month, "Second Sunday." If it sounds too generic, what about combining the program name with its meeting day, like "Second Sunday Jam." Names like this will publicize our meetings for us in themselves.

We are more apt to attend a meeting that is held in a location in which we are familiar and comfortable. Teens who are not members of our parish might be hesitant to come to a place in which they feel they do not belong. This may not be a significant factor if most of our visitors are accompanied by teen members, but if our parish is in a remote area, or nonmembers are uncomfortable, we may consider a more centralized, neutral, or well-known location.

Momentum, carried forth from one meeting to another, is an important dynamic of large group evangelization. Large group evangelization works optimally on a weekly or bimonthly pattern. Monthly meetings, though possibly effective in themselves, usually risk stopping any momentum gained from a previous meeting. After a month layover, it is easy to lose any trajectory effect through the friction of daily life. We forget the fun, the relationships, and the impact.

Besides consistency in time and place, we need consistently to deliver meetings that are of the highest quality. Unfortunately, many young people presume a church-sponsored event will be boring. These impressions are not the result of innate natural instincts. We must concede that over the years we have inadvertently formed teens in these negative perspectives. We haven't been known for our programmatic adventurousness, sense of innovation, or exciting meetings. Instead we have served a steady diet of lifeless liturgies, meaningless meetings, and smelly small groups! In many ways we have earned our reputation.

It should not be that way! Excellence should be our standard for programming. Young people are surrounded by quality today. We live in a fiercely competitive environment and most institutions know that if they are to survive, they must provide a high quality service or product. Furthermore, young people today have a wide array of dazzling opportunities from which to choose. There are many different movies, channels on television, sporting events, and social activities at their disposal. There is a very real competition taking place for their time. If we are going to hold large group evangelistic events, then we need to do them with "typical excellence." If there is any message that deserves to be presented with the highest standard of quality, it is the good news of Jesus Christ. Teens expect us to apply ourselves and make the things we plan for them worthwhile. We must put time into praying, planning, and preparing for our meetings in order to make them creative and impacting.

Teens live in a fairly closed environment. Word travels fast through their schools. Creating a positive and attractive image and reputation in the minds of young people is critical to the survival and growth of our large group gatherings. If our youth ministry has a reputation for being boring, disorganized, and lifeless, we will sooner or later suffer extinction. We can produce a positive image by doing things with "typical excellence." This not only includes programming content and process, but even more importantly, an inviting and hospitable atmosphere.

Large Group Dynamics

A large group evangelistic gathering characteristically involves twenty to several hundred teens. Because of the potential for participation by large numbers of teens, the dynamic of large group evangelization differs from what takes place with other smaller groups. For instance, the "wave," a common event at large stadium gatherings, might look rather pathetic when performed by eight teens in Mrs. Flemdrop's living room! Large group evangelization has its own activities, personality, and dynamics that make it a unique form of programming.

Before we look at the specifics of this dynamic, a word of caution. Because we plan a program for large numbers does not mean that hundreds of teens will necessarily attend. The program is not magical. Its growth will be proportionate to our practice of relational youth ministry. A large group evangelization program becomes a gathering place for teens with whom we are building friendships. If both adult and teen leaders are invested in the program, actively inviting newcomers, and building relationships with those teens who attend, we will reap a great harvest. *Remember:* The foundation to successful large group evangelization is the development of one-to-one relationships.

The large group dynamic includes the following qualities: (1) opportunities to meet new people; (2) fast-paced and action-filled programming; (3) an enthusiastic tone; and (4) the message expressed through a variety of mediums. Let's look at each quality in greater detail:

1. Opportunities to meet new people—For the majority of teens, it's fun to go places where a lot of other youth are present. Large group evangelization capitalizes on this dynamic. It becomes part of the drawing card for teens who may not necessarily be thinking about their relationship with God as much as with regular attendee Drop Dead Darla. Getting to know Darla is a perceived need; getting to know Jesus is a very real, but unperceived need. Most unevangelized young people will attend events because of who will be there—not because of what will be presented.

Teens will keep coming back to a program because they have made friends with other committed teens or met some adult leaders who care for them.

Large group events should be designed to help young people build friendships with each other. Teens will keep coming back to a program because they have made friends with other committed teens or met some adult leaders who care for them. We want to create a good and positive sense of interaction.

2. Fast-paced and full of action—Today's youth have cut their teeth on television. They have been reared on *Sesame Street* as children and MTV as adolescents. Scenes, camera angles, and perspectives change every few seconds. Consequently, today's adolescent has the attention span of a mosquito. Therefore, a large group of teens will get bored and lose interest quickly if our programming fails to keep moving. Large group programming should be fast-paced and full of action. It is essential to move from one event or activity to another at a relatively quick pace. Most activities should not last more than five to fifteen minutes. Any lull between events can prove to be deadly. Quick transitions are critical for success in the large group setting. If we fail immediately to direct teens from one activity to the next, we will lose the group to side conversations. A night of wrestling their attention back after each activity can be exhausting to the leadership and give the appearance of chaos to the participants.

3. Enthusiastic tone—Typically, young people have a lot of energy to burn. Most youth are not willing to sit for two hours on a hard floor listening to Dr. Sedation prove that even the most advanced insomniac is no match for his speaking skills. Something is wrong if teens are responding to our meetings with the same energy level of one suffering from carbon monoxide poisoning. Often, we, the leaders, are our own worst enemies when it comes to breeding a glacial climate. If we project reluctance and a lack of confidence in our program, and explain activities with the enthusiasm of the back room library clerk, we will surely suffer from low morale and attrition.

Attitudes are contagious. When I wake up in a negative mood I often spread my poison to other family members. Next thing I know, we are all in a bad mood. Likewise, a positive attitude is contagious. Large group evangelistic meetings, therefore, must be carried out in an enthusiastic tone. As leaders, we must set a standard. Activities should be introduced and led with high energy and excitement. Our attitude must emphatically proclaim: "It's great to be here!" Sooner or later, those attending will also feel positive and energized by the meetings.

4. *Variety of activities, media and events*—The large group dynamic capitalizes on variety. Before a teen has a chance to be bored with one activity, we should move on to another. Each teen has a different learning style. If we use a variety of approaches, our chances increase in touching the lives of a greater number of teens. When our meetings become as predictable as a Chicago Cubs season, we know that we are in trouble.

A variety of activities and media to convey our message should be employed: skits, dramas, mimes, interactive activities, talks, witnesses, music, games, video, slide shows, multimedia, and so on. Variety for its own sake is not helpful. But, when we use a number of diverse media to shed light from a different angle on a common topic, we have a greater chance of holding the attention of the average teen. Activities should be carefully chosen to achieve the content objectives for that meeting and should be sequenced in a purposeful and meaningful manner.

More About Perceived and Unperceived Needs

We cannot hold to the "take your medicine" philosophy of youth ministry. (You know, "It tastes bad, but it's good for you.") On the other hand, we should not sugarcoat or water down the gospel message in any way. Paul clearly cautions us against appealing to "tickling ears" (see 2 Timothy 4:2-4). Youth ministries that solely entertain are not worth existing.

Effective large group evangelization addresses both the *perceived* and *unperceived* needs of young people. Many of those who came to Jesus did not arrive with spiritual conversion in the forefront of their minds. They were seeking a more apparent need. They wanted to see because they were blind; to walk because they were lame; relief because they were hemorrhaging; a miracle because a loved one was dying. Perceived needs fully absorbed their attention and moved them towards Jesus. Once he met their perceived needs, they became open to addressing their also very real, but unperceived need for conversion.

I have found that many teens operate in a similar manner. They are primarily motivated by a conscious need for fun, action, friendship, and interaction with members of the opposite sex. Ignoring these developmentally appropriate needs and leapfrogging to their spiritual needs is like preaching to a man who is dying of thirst. Gripped by the need for water, he is deaf to our "life-giving" message. In reality, he may get further turned off to us because we callously ignored his very obvious need for water. By addressing his need we demonstrate that we truly care about him. Our message, in turn, becomes credible. With our credibility comes a greater probability that he will return again and address his spiritual needs.

Fruitful large group evangelization enables teens to spend time with existing friends and make new friends. In a culturally relevant manner, large group evangelistic programming addresses common teenage issues such as loneliness, self-worth, peer pressure, stress, the future, friendship, family life, and dating (perceived needs) in light of scripture and church teaching, and draws teens into a meaningful encounter with the person of Jesus Christ (mostly an unperceived need of the unevangelized teen).

We must resist the temptation to do too much in any one program.

A common mistake made while developing a youth ministry is trying to meet the needs of every level of spiritual maturity in a single, all-purpose large group program. We must resist the temptation to try to do too much in any one program. It is impossible to design a program that evangelizes new teens, fosters faith maturity in older teens, and equips teen leaders to minister to their peers. The "one-size-fits-all" program usually falls short in meeting any one need. Students lose interest and the program often defaults into a youth group that solely exists to meet its own needs.

The primary focus of large group evangelistic programming is, as its title states, *evangelization.* The principal audience is the active unconverted, inactive unevangelized, and the unchurched teen. The program content is aimed at breaking down barriers that teens might have toward Jesus and the church, presenting the gospel relevantly and in light of contemporary teen issues, and inviting teens to a deeper relationship with the person of Jesus Christ.

Though large group evangelistic programming content is designed for the unevangelized teen, this does not mean, however, that an already evangelized teen should opt out of attending. On the contrary, these meetings play an important and meaningful role for an already evangelized teen. Once a young person's faith becomes personal and committed, it is essential that we, as leaders, pass on to them the importance of sharing their faith with others. An evangelized teen does not attend large group meetings to address his or her own spiritual needs (there are other programs for that), but uses the meetings as an organized means of sharing his or her faith with the peers in attendance. If large group evangelization is to be fruitful, teens with a growing faith must be committed to supporting the program by inviting their friends to be a part of their faith community and sharing their faith both interpersonally and programmatically. Large group evangelistic meetings multiply in attendance and spiritual impact when evangelized teens enthusiastically support their vision and purpose.

Reaching Out to Many Teens

Reaching as many teens as possible with the gospel of Jesus Christ is an important element of large group evangelization. Large group evangelization is designed for numerical growth—but not simply for the sake of numbers. (Remember, success in God's kingdom is not measured by numbers in attendance, but by the quality and quantity of spiritual fruit.)

Large group evangelization is designed for numerical growth—but not simply for the sake of numbers.

While keeping our focus on fruitfulness, we still have the responsibility to reach as many young people as possible. The following questions can serve as evaluative tools for our outreach efforts.

Are new people coming? A sign of life is that new people are regularly coming. If we are not attracting any new teens, then we should ask, "Why?" Are we providing an inviting and inclusive climate? Are we publicizing? Are the peer ministers inviting their friends? Do those attending know they can invite their friends? Would they even want to invite their friends? Are we dealing with relevant issues in teens' lives? Are we holding meetings on a night that is convenient? Are we praying? If new teens are coming, what is it that is attracting them?

Are new people returning? Do teens come once and never return? Do new teens feel welcome? Are they being incorporated into the community? Do they feel like they are part of things? Are we following up on new teens in an organized manner? Or, are they falling through administrative cracks? Are teens so unimpressed that they have no desire to return?

Do regular attendees invite their friends? Are regulars proud and enthusiastic about including their friends? Is it so enjoyable and fun that they want others to take part in it? Or, are they reluctant? Do they perceive their friends are welcome? Do they think their friends will benefit from the meeting? Does the evangelized teen see the meetings as an event to which he or she can bring friends to hear the gospel message and experience a sense of belonging?

Are regulars returning? Did we lose the regulars along the way? Are we still meeting their spiritual needs, or have the regulars lost interest? Have we incorporated evangelized teens into growth-oriented programming to meet their spiritual needs, and encouraged them to use large group evangelization as an avenue for sharing their faith?

Meeting Format for Large Group Evangelization

A large group evangelistic meeting lasts from an hour and a half to two hours. It is planned and carried out in partnership with both teen and adult leaders and is divided into six movements that operate as if preparing a meal for consumption. As the food must be defrosted, preheated, marinated, cooked, and sliced before it can be digested, so, too, may the process of taking teens through a meeting from beginning to end be described. The six movements and their purposes are listed in the chart and explained in more detail in the text that follows:

Movement	**Purpose**
Pre-Meeting Hospitality	To create a warm and friendly environment.
Welcome	To help participants feel welcome.
Warm-Up	To reduce discomfort and create an openness.
Message	To communicate the gospel message.
Closure	To wrap up the evening.
Post-Meeting Follow-Up	To relationally follow up.

Pre-Meeting Hospitality (Defrost)

One afternoon a mother called my office. Her son attended our large group evangelistic meetings. She began the conversation by telling me of her son's unusual request. He asked her to be dropped off at least five minutes after the start of our large group meeting.

"Why is that?" I asked.

"He says that it's too painful to stand by himself before the meetings begin. No one talks with him or even acknowledges his presence. He could only look busy for so long by hanging out in the bathroom and by the drinking fountain. If he has to go, it would be easier for him to arrive late," she painfully disclosed to me.

My heart sank. I wondered how many other teens had the same experience as her son. It was at that moment that I made some very intentional efforts to change the atmosphere at our meetings. There was no excuse for a teen to feel unwelcome, uncomfortable, or alone among a group of people who were supposed to be known for their love for one another (see John 13:35).

Providing an hospitable climate is absolutely essential to being effective in reaching out to teens. As the saying goes, "You don't get a second chance to make a first impression." If a young person feels insignificant, unwelcome, or unnoticed, there is little chance that he or she will return. Who wants to go where they feel unwanted?

On the other hand, who does not want to go where they feel welcomed, wanted, and important? The impact of a warm, accepting, and hospitable atmosphere cannot be underestimated in its power to attract and hold the participation of teens.

An hospitable climate does not come naturally. As a matter of fact, hospitality is quite unnatural. What is customary are cliques and exclusive groups. We are naturally attracted to the people whom we know and with whom we are acquainted. To be a welcoming group requires constant attentive effort on the part of the leaders. We must consistently sacrifice our own comfort for the well-being of our participants. Leaders huddling contentedly together at the start of a meeting is a large group evangelization cultural taboo.

Stationing leaders at the entrance to greet teens enthusiastically as they arrive will help to ensure that young people feel welcome as soon as they walk in the door. We should make contact with each young person before the meeting ever begins. We can create a positive and warm atmosphere by playing some upbeat contemporary Christian music in the background. Additionally, several leaders should be "hospitable roamers," that is, on the lookout for teens who are standing alone or looking out of place. This is a great time to use the "INVITE" method for initiating relationships (see chapter seven). Leaders can later record details about any new people met on their teen profiles (see page 153).

Pre-meeting hospitality usually begins about fifteen minutes prior to the starting time of a meeting. If a meeting begins at 7:00 p.m., pre-meeting hospitality would start at 6:45. We should complete all preparations and set up at least twenty minutes prior to the start of the meeting. This ensures that we give full attention to those teens arriving at our gathering.

Welcome (Preheat)

Most people walk in the door of a meeting room stiff and uncomfortable—like a cold lawnmower. A grass cutter's engine won't roar unless the carburetor is properly primed. Likewise, the welcome phase primes the atmosphere of a meeting by helping the participants feel comfortable and welcome in their surroundings. Pre-meeting hospitality sets the climate; however, the meeting officially begins during the "welcome" phase. The purpose of this movement is to foster a sense of familiarity and ease in those present. It gives participants an opportunity to meet and interact with other people in the room, and therefore reduces the tension associated with unfamiliarity. Activities in this phase might include:

- ✔ an enthusiastic welcome and opening comments
- ✔ an opening prayer
- ✔ identifying newcomers and officially welcoming them
- ✔ videos or slide shows of participants from past meetings
- ✔ mixers that get teens interacting with one another
- ✔ fun music or songs with actions that get people moving around
- ✔ introductory skits or drama that are fun and make people laugh
- ✔ activities that help young people feel welcome and a part of the group.

The welcoming phase usually lasts anywhere from ten to twenty minutes. It builds off the informal warmth of the pre-meeting hospitality phase and leads to the warm-up phase.

Warm-Up (Marinate)

The purpose of the warm-up phase is to continue fostering a sense of familiarity, to have some fun, burn off energy, and to prepare teens for the message. Warm-up can last anywhere from fifteen minutes to a half an hour. It often consists of games, crowdbreakers, funny skits, relays, or fun songs—all the better if these activities can somehow relate to the topic of the evening.

We should choose games and activities that fit the personality of the teens in our community. Some groups are wild and crazy and enjoy games accordingly. Other groups are sophisticated and stick their nose in the air to "silly, childish" games.

A good game is both fun to play and enjoyable to watch. Games should be carefully planned and tried out beforehand. We should articulate the directions clearly, provide concrete examples, and possibly play a practice round so our audience is not left confused. In today's day and age, it is essential to consider safety issues. Do not play games that put teens in risk of serious injury, or potential embarrassment. The warm-up phase should be fun for everyone and successfully lead the group to a greater receptivity of the following message phase.

Message (Cooking the Main Entrée)

It is during the message phase that we creatively communicate the good news of God's kingdom. It is not our message that we are proclaiming. Our presentation must reflect God's transforming word as revealed through the scriptures and church teaching. Our message should be prayerfully planned (a great focus for our intercessory prayer team), designed in a developmentally appropriate manner, creatively and relevantly expressed, and situated within the common experiences and issues teens face.

The message phase should be a good mix of presentation, reflection, and small group interaction.

The message can be communicated through many different mediums and activities that are sequenced in an order that build upon one another. Media and activities include:

Skits	Mimes	Shadow mimes	Multimedia
Video	Role plays	Case studies	Simulations
Music	Witnesses	Talks	Discussions
Activities	Reflection	Scripture reading	Storytelling

The message phase should be a good mix of presentation, reflection, and small group interaction. The larger group can be divided into smaller discussion teams led by adult and/or teen leaders. Even though the tempo of the meeting slows down during the message phase, avoid activities that keep teens sitting for long periods of time. Our minds can only absorb what our bodies can endure. The message should be presented in an experiential manner and include an opportunity for teens to respond.

Closure (Slice)

The last movement in the organized program is closure. It is a basic summary of the main points of the message. It can be stated as a simple verbal wrap-up of the evening, or can be expressed in an emotionally impacting manner through a skit, song, or slide show. It can even be done through a closing prayer.

Post-Meeting Follow-Up (Digest)

After the meeting, we do not want teens stampeding toward the door in a wild frenzy to escape. It is to be hoped that our atmosphere, message, and community life will influence teens to stick around a few minutes after the planned programming ends. We should leave the last ten to fifteen minutes of our scheduled time for the purpose of follow-up interaction. The best stuff usually happens after the meeting. We do not want to give teens the impression that the meeting is over and they should go home so we can get home. Instead, provide some simple and inexpensive refreshments after the meeting to motivate the teens to stick around. (It's a well-known scientific fact that teens are always hungry.) It is during this time that we can continue to develop relationships with teens. We can also get more personally involved in their lives with questions such as, "What did you think about the message this evening?" We should be open to any interpersonal evangelization opportunities that present themselves after the meeting.

Smaller Groups in the Large Group Setting

It is easy to get lost in a crowd. In a sea of teens it is easy to get overwhelmed by numbers and lose teens through the cracks. Experiencing a sense of belonging is a very important need of any adolescent. One way to impart a sense of belonging to participants is to use team competition in the large group setting. Establishing various smaller groups or teams within the large group structure can help young people feel better connected and a part of the community. Being a member of a team is a built-in way of developing community, friendship, and ownership. These three elements are essential to holding the interest and participation of the teens in outreach programming. Competition among teams helps to motivate teens to come back. In addition, it promotes outreach to their friends. Team competition can be incorporated into the welcome and warm-up phases of the large group evangelistic format.

How to Use Team Competition

It is important to strike a balance when using team competition. We do not want an atmosphere of cutthroat, win-at-all-costs competitiveness. On the other hand, we do not want teens to be apathetic and bored with every competitive incentive. Competition should be fun, good-natured, and motivating. It should help draw people together, not tear them apart. Competition can be used in the following ways:

Attendance—Teams should be awarded points for participation of their members. Teens will be motivated to attend meetings because it will directly help their teams. Members will also encourage fellow members to come because the whole team will benefit. Adult and teen leaders will spearhead this effort initially, but as times goes on we will want to get the entire team invested and committed.

In addition, points should be rewarded to those teams whose members bring visitors. These visitors are given an opportunity to become members of the team. The opportunity to invite friends can help members take part in the outreach process and even strengthen their own attendance as the result of having a good friend being part of their team. It is critical that the leaders of the team emphasize people-centeredness as opposed to point-centeredness. We sincerely invite teens to our meetings because we want them to be an active part of our team—not because they are points to be had so we might win a competition. There is nothing more demeaning then feeling used in the name of "Christian love." Our plea is: "We have a great team, but it could only get better if you join us."

The point structure is as follows:

First-time Visitor	1000
Second-time Visitor	2000
Third-time Visitor	3000
Team Members	5000 (become team members at fourth meeting)

Games—Choose a mix of games that use intellectual skills, athletic skills, other unknown skills, and complete luck. Do not overuse games that favor any particular skills. Make the games fun to participate in and fun to watch. Some games might involve the entire team, others might call forth representatives of a certain class, gender, and so on. Encourage teams to cheer on their members to boost morale and investment. Award points for the top three places. Enthusiastically announce the score standings at the beginning of each meeting. Have a first-place trophy that is given to the team who occupies that position. Other incentives could include: a pizza party for the team who accumulates the most points during the month; first in line for refreshments after the meeting; an ice cream party; or, if your budget is like most parishes, an all-expenses-paid trip to Disney World (okay, I'm joking).

Special Events—Special events or activities for team points can be used to motivate teens to apply the content of a meeting. For example, you may give a team 250 points for each teen who memorizes a scriptural passage that pertains to last week's message. Other points might be awarded for service involvement and attendance of other events.

When team competition is done well, it motivates personal involvement, increases attendance and outreach, builds a sense of ownership and community, helps leaders focus their ministry upon a particular group of teens, and provides fun in an electrically-charged atmosphere.

Subjects should be based on real teen issues.

Steps to Planning and Evaluating a Meeting

The planning process for a large group meeting should be done in a spirit of prayer. We should always seek the Holy Spirit's particular guidance on behalf of the teens we are seeking to reach. In that spirit, the following steps apply:

1. Determine the Topic—Our topic or theme for a meeting should be prayerfully discerned. Subjects should be based on real teen issues. We might surface ideas through needs assessments, program evaluations, or brainstorming sessions with teens. It is helpful to choose topics for an entire year of scheduling to have time to gather ideas and resources well in advance. Topics should be publicized using creative titles, as opposed to generic names. For instance, a meeting that addresses our common misconceptions of God might be entitled, "God: Mirage or Real Deal."

2. Formulate Objectives—Our next step is to state specifically what we hope to achieve through our content. To hit our mark, we must take aim. Again, our objectives should be prayerfully discerned and rooted in scripture and church teaching. Our objectives should be evangelistic in scope, and stated in terms of what we hope our participants will come to value (affective), know (cognitive), or do (behavioral). Be cautious not to cover too much in one sitting. It is best to keep it simple. One to three content objectives is realistic.

3. Pool Resources—Once we know our destination, we can consider the paths to arriving there. Pooling our resources involves brainstorming for new ideas, examining books, programs, and catalogs for appropriate materials, and networking with other youth workers to borrow from their creativity and experience. Based on our situation, we may create new material from scratch or pull out scripts, learning activities, or videos from published sources. Even the most creative groups experience blocks or time crunches. Therefore, it is important to develop a library of youth ministry resource materials to support our efforts.

4. Choose Activities—While pooling our resources we may have identified two outside speakers, a video presentation, three topical discussion sheets, a teen willing to give a witness talk, a couple of good songs that cover the topic, three skits, and a learning activity. Our next step is to narrow down our options to those that best help us achieve our objectives in light of our resources. We may discard some ideas because they do not fit our objectives, they are not financially feasible, we are short on time, we do not have the expertise, or they duplicate an earlier activity. Pick those activities that are best suited for the objectives and circumstances.

5. Sequence Events—The effectiveness of what we do is dependent on the order in which we do it. Activities must be placed into proper sequence within the program if it is to move in an intelligent and meaningful progression. For example, beginning a session with a powerfully emotional skit might put teens into a mood that prohibits any further discussion or movement. Or, they might not have been prepared for this powerful skit, so it makes little impact and is mistaken as funny because the previous activity was light-hearted.

Good sequencing generally begins by introducing the topic in a non-threatening manner. Any of the following can provide a light-hearted introduction to the topic: an introductory skit, a story that illustrates the theme, or a video that records teens' comments concerning the topic at hand. This type of introduction might be followed up with a small-group discussion that allows teens to share their experience with the topic. Next, something a little more content-driven might take place, like a witness talk by a peer minister, and then a powerful slide show, and finally a closing prayer service. Proper sequencing usually begins light-hearted and general in focus and progressively moves to greater depth, a more detailed focus, and deeper personal application.

6. Assign Responsibilities—Once the activities are chosen and sequenced, it is time to assign responsibilities. Break down your meeting into smaller action steps and detail who will do what by when. Follow up with each other to ensure that everything is completed on time.

7. Implement Plans—This step moves the meeting from paper to reality. Begin the evening praying for each person involved and activity scheduled. Follow the plan for the evening, yet do not be afraid to adapt things according to changing circumstances or the promptings of the Holy Spirit.

8. Evaluate—At the end of the evening or at the next leadership meeting, take a few minutes to evaluate the program. Evaluation makes us vulnerable and at times can be painful. However, the long-term result is progressive growth and further excellence in programming.

Application

The are four resources included after this chapter that provide aids to planning and conducting a large group evangelization event. Each may be reproduced and distributed to team members involved in the preparation and leadership of these events.

Always keep an ear to what teens think about the meetings. Talk to them after meetings, and periodically do formal, written evaluations.

Summary

If we desire to move forward acres at a time in our efforts to evangelize teenagers, we need to present them "food" that is digestible. We will lose them indefinitely and do the cause of Christianity a major injustice by boring them with what is meant to be understood as the greatest message humanity has ever received and known.

Large group evangelization will have optimum results if it becomes an established regular weekly or bimonthly event, occurring at the same time and location with consistent quality. It is important to build momentum in ministry and help teens form attendance habits. The program should have a catchy and easy-to-remember name, and excellence in programming ought to be the norm. A variety of innovative and creative tools and media should be utilized to share the good news. Such a large-group approach has a dynamic that allows teens to meet new people, experience a fast-paced program, and tap into a contagious enthusiasm.

As ministers, and in the footsteps of our Lord, we must strategically meet the perceived and unperceived needs of our teens. Large group programs must have an evangelistic purpose, and leaders should use such gatherings as stepping stones to doing relational ministry with the teens who attend. Large group events serve a functional purpose of reaching out to as many teenagers as possible. However, numerical growth should not be sought simply for the sake of numbers, but rather, to bring as many into Christ's fold as possible. Are new people coming? Are new people returning? Do regulars invite their friends? Are regulars returning? These questions can help in evaluating the desirability of a large group gathering.

Effective meeting formats typically include pre-meeting hospitality, a welcome, a warm-up, a message, closure, and post-meeting follow-up. Attendance, games, and special events can be used competitively as a means of attracting teens to large group programs. Finally, determining the topic, formulating objectives, pooling resources, choosing activities, sequencing events, assigning responsibilities, implementing plans, and evaluating outcomes are all necessary steps to planning a meeting.

Planning Steps

PLANNING STEPS

1. Determine Topic
2. Formulate Objectives
3. Pool Resources
4. Choose Activities
5. Sequence Events
6. Assign Responsibilities
7. Implement Plans
8. Evaluate

OBJECTIVE TYPES

1. Affective
2. Cognitive
3. Behavioral

OUTREACH FORMAT

1. Pre-Meeting Hopitality
2. Welcome
3. Warm Up
4. Message
5. Closure
6. Post-Meeting Follow-Up

ACTIVITIES/COMPONENT

Introduction	Slide show
Crowdbreaker	Skit
Lg. Gg. Game	Mime
Lg. Gg. Mixer	Shadow Mime
Compet. Game	Live Music
Sm. Gr. Game	Rec Music
Sm. Gr. Mixer	Lg. Gr. Discuss.
Witness Talk	Sm. Gr. Discuss.
Keynote Talk	Role Plays
Film/Video	Theme Activity

OBJECTIVES

TO DO LIST

MATERIALS NEEDED

Large Group Evangelization Planner

Program____________________ Date________________ Theme_______________

Time	Activity / Component	Purpose	Format / Element	Person Respon.
6:45				
6:50				
6:55				
7:00				
7:05				
7:10				
7:15				
7:20				
7:25				
7:30				
7:35				
7:40				
7:45				
7:50				
7:55				
8:00				
8:05				
8:10				
8:15				
8:20				
8:25				
8:30				
8:35				
8:40				
8:45				
8:50				
8:55				
9:00				
9:05				
9:15				

Good News Guaranteed

The following statements are guarantees that we, as a team, are pledging to any student who may come to one of our large group meetings. These guarantees will help us lovingly demonstrate the good news to any student who frequents our gatherings.

GUARANTEE
#___

Strategy

#	Strategy Step

GUARANTEE
#___

Strategy

#	Strategy Step

Relational Ministry Organizer

	Name		First Timer Follow-Up	Birthday Card	Miss You Card / Note	Student Profile	Prayer Needs	Reminder Calls	Card / Note / Letter	Activities / Contacts
1.										
2.										
3.										
4.										
5.										
6.										
7.										
8.										
9.										
10.										
11.										
12.										
13.										
14.										
15.										

9

Expanding Our Harvests

Jesse had a widespread reputation throughout our city as a young man extraordinarily skilled in the fine art of trouble-making. He was well known for his frequent fighting feats. He was a martial artist who liked to practice his craft on any victim with whom he could pick a fight. Jesse was not interested in attending any church events. Being seen in places like the church could cause irreparable damage to his macho image. Besides, he was not a Catholic nor was he friends with any churchgoers who might invite him to a meeting.

He was, however, in great need of the Lord.

There are Jesses in every community. Surrounding our parishes are vast numbers of teens who do not see church involvement as an attractive option. How do we reach the Jesses of our community? What strategies can we employ to touch the lives of these teens?

More often than not, our energies are consumed by our ready-made audience. However, we need to go beyond attracting those who are already interested or parentally coerced. We need to expand our vision by focusing on unreached adolescents in our community. These may be jocks, troubled teens, unchurched kids, skaters, and even juvenile criminals. As church, our responsibility far exceeds the teens who want to or have to come to our events. To reach beyond this group, we must begin to think innovatively and strategically.

Five Steps to Reaching Uninvolved Teens

Expanding our harvests beyond the borders of our present crops requires some thoughtfulness and planning. A five-step process is explained below.

1. Target unreached teens—First, we must identify those teens who are not being touched by our present outreach efforts. Adolescents travel in groups that are usually assembled by common interests. Wrestlers are likely to hang around other wrestlers, drill team members with other drill teamers, burn-outs with burn-outs, gang-bangers with gang-bangers. There may be entire groups of teens who have not been affected by our efforts. Some of these teens may be uninvolved but registered members of our parishes. Others may be totally unchurched. Our first question to reflect on is, "Who are we not reaching?"

Our first question to reflect on is, "Who are we not reaching?"

A few of years ago I asked myself this question and found that I was not making much impact on juvenile offenders. There were a significant number of young people in our community who were in trouble with the law. They represented to me the lost and wandering sheep that Jesus pursued, leaving the other ninety-nine behind (see Matthew 18:10-14). They were playing on lethal ledges and grazing on dangerous grasses. Most of these teens had little, if any, church affiliation. Many came from either single-parent families or homes with little supervision. Others came from good homes but acted irresponsibly. They were not necessarily hard-core criminals, at least not yet. It was the "yet" that was my primary motivator. They were on a crossroads. Many were flirting with a lifestyle that could lead them down a path of destruction. If there was a critical time in their lives for intervention it was certainly now.

2. *Create a common turf*—To encounter the "unreached teens," we need to think creatively and find a turf, or common ground, on which to meet. It is important to ask ourselves what would particularly interest this group. How can we gain access to their world? In what ways can our paths meaningfully cross? What can we do that would specifically appeal to them?

I learned that many teens convicted of juvenile crimes were sentenced to do community service hours. The county provided the teens with some options in which to work these hours. I had found a turf. I offered the parish as a place where juvenile offenders could work their community service hours.

3. *Plan the program, activity, or event*—Once we have found the turf, or contact point, we need to develop the program, event, activity, or relationship. We need to think carefully and consider all the practical details. We should consider the following questions:

- ✔ Where and when will the event be held? Is it ongoing? One time? Annual?
- ✔ Do we need any special equipment, supplies, or purchases?
- ✔ What will it cost? Do we need to prepare a budget? How will we raise any needed funds?

- ✔ What are our personnel needs? What positions or roles need to be filled? How and who will we recruit?
- ✔ How will we publicize the event, activity, or program? How will our target group know what we are doing?
- ✔ What will the program look like? What activities will comprise the event? What is the agenda? How will the activities be sequenced?

While developing an outreach to juvenile offenders, I had to answer many of the above questions adequately to plan the project. My first step was to call the county office and inquire if we could be approved as a site for community service. Next, I had to look at who would supervise these teens. What would the teens do? How would I keep them busy? I made myself the supervisor and collaborated with the entire church staff to assemble a workload for each teen. I scheduled their hours in conjunction with the tasks to be accomplished. Teens would do things like mailings, janitorial services, filing, and organizing. I kept track of their hours and reported back to the county when they were completed.

4. *Integrate an evangelistic impact*—Program planning is not complete until we consider its evangelistic implications. We need to ask ourselves, "How will this program evangelize our target teens?" We must determine whether we will simply prepare the soil by providing a positive church experience and initiating new relationships, or clearly proclaim the gospel message during the event.

Sometimes building and creating a positive awareness and new openness is sufficient in itself. One good experience can lead to others. However, we should have a plan in place to build on that foundation. Other times we may program for more direct evangelization.

The first hour of community service was simply an orientation. Basically, we would get to know each other. I almost always found the opportunity to share my own faith story. We also took care of some of the organizational issues. Throughout their service, I continued to build on the relationship. While preparing mailings or other mindless activities, I invited them to view any of our youth ministry videos. Most of the teens were more than eager to watch anything. I purchased some videos solely for this purpose. My favorite was a *Power Team* video. It featured a team of muscle heads who would wow audiences with incredible feats of strength and athleticism. The tape concluded with these guys sharing their own faith journeys. It was very impressive to the macho types. Afterwards, we would discuss the message. The conversation often led to deeper exchanges regarding their life and faith.

Furthermore, I was able to introduce them to teen leaders with whom I thought they might relate, or programs in which they might be interested. A number of these teens moved to greater involvement and commitment beyond their service hours.

5. *Follow-up*—Whether an event's purpose is direct evangelization, relational door-opening, or positive awareness, we should have ready some type of follow-up plan. Our goal should not end with the event. Rarely does an activity, in and of itself, make a lasting impact in a person's life. Ultimately, the best evangelization occurs within the context of an ongoing relationship. Our plan should include the details on how to transport the relationship from a mere one-time appearance to active involvement. For instance, if we sponsor a one-time event, we might follow up with an immediate thank-you card to those who attended for the first time. We may then call with an invitation to another upcoming activity, or schedule a one-to-one meeting at a fast-food restaurant. We may send a youth ministry calendar and flyers for upcoming programs. Depending on the nature of the group targeted, we may or may not want immediately to integrate a teen into the mainstream youth ministry program. Nevertheless, we should have a follow-up plan of some kind.

Some Examples of Innovative Outreach

The following section includes some practical examples of targeting a specific group of unreached teens and developing an outreach event or program to impact them.

Slam-Dunk and/or Three-Point Shoot-Out

Let's say we want to reach a group of jocks. Why not sponsor a city-wide slam-dunk and/or three-point shoot-out contest? Specifically, invite varsity basketball players on both the boys' and girls' teams from the regional high schools to compete. Adjust the hoop size by height, age, or level of experience for the slam-dunk contest. Pick judges from the community and include prizes for the winners in each category. Publicize it throughout the city, inviting everyone to come as spectators. This is a big event that not only attracts the targeted group, but, if done well, the entire city!

The evening can be used as an opportunity to create a turf onto which previously unreached teens might venture. Participants have a fun evening, some new relationships with the targeted audience are built, and a positive awareness of the parish's youth ministry is established. We can integrate a more direct evangelistic approach by including a guest appearance of a college or professional basketball player who shares his or her faith story with the crowd. In either case, follow-up with relational ministry and invitations to upcoming events is essential.

Youth Gym/Center

An ongoing program that could potentially attract a wide range of teens is a youth center. Teens are often looking for a place to go or hang out. A center could be located on the church grounds or on a conveniently-situated neutral site. A store-front or municipal building might draw a more diverse crowd of teens as opposed to a church-based outreach. Often, city officials or even private entrepreneurs will consider donating space for a needed cause, even if it is sponsored by a religious institution. In our case, our city gave us the basement of the Municipal Center smack in the middle of the downtown district!

Our center appealed to a diverse crowd of teens. We offered weightlifting, boxing, and exercise equipment, a gaming area with a pool, ping pong, air hockey, and a bumper pool table. Other possibilities include foose ball, pinball, video games, a large-screen television, a VCR, computers, and a stereo. Some centers include a quiet study area for teens who want to work on school projects together. A youth center's equipment can be acquired through item donation and fundraising. Most of our gaming equipment was donated by parishioners.

A center's offerings and open hours should be based on the particular needs of the community. If the community does not have any work-out gyms, or those available are too expensive for the average teen, we might consider developing a teen center around weightlifting and exercise equipment. Each community has its own particular "itch niche." Our teen center should be scratching an itch—not simply doing what we think would be good. For example, if a school district announces it will be discontinuing its intramural athletics due to cost cuts, we might consider offering them at the church the following year. We would have a ready-made audience. We need to discern prayerfully our community's needs and build a center around them.

In our youth center, we had trained adult supervisors. Their role not only included a knowledge of weightlifting and exercise equipment, but involved building relationships with teens and sharing their own faith stories. Many of our regulars were unchurched teens who wanted a place to work out and hang out. It was not unusual for a supervisor to share his or her faith story between sets of a workout. Sometimes we planted seeds, other times we saw a harvest. Some of these teens became integrated into our mainstream youth programs because of the invitation of our supervisors and peer ministers.

Summer Camps

Many teens in our communities are involved in school sports. Some look for opportunities to further develop their athletic skills through summer camp opportunities. We can sponsor a camp for soccer, football, basketball, wrestling, or any other sport that might draw the interest of teens. The camp should be staffed by experienced athletes and coaches who are faith-filled and have the abilities to address both the athletic skills and spiritual hungers of teen participants. Working with a well-known Christian coach or athlete could help in filling the camp with participants.

It should be clear in our promotional literature that the camp has a spiritual component. We do not want to surprise unsuspecting athletes with evangelistic meetings. Our camp should integrate an evangelistic component into the week's offerings through athletes' testimonies, presentations, services, and discussions. Camp experiences do not have to be confined to athletics. Similar offerings might include drama, writing, or computers.

Other ways of reaching the target audiences include tutoring programs, computer or Internet training, biking trips, aerobic classes, drama workshops or presentations, coffeehouses, career fairs, art classes or tournaments. The key to successful innovative evangelistic programming is having a clearly articulated evangelistic dimension that is understood and practiced by the leaders involved.

Application

The "Innovative Evangelistic Events Planner" on page 186 is an aid to identifying teens in your community and parish who need special attention, as well as offering ways to minister to them.

Summary

When Jesus commanded his followers to "go and make disciples of all nations" (Matthew 28:19), he was calling them to expand the harvest to every corner of the earth. This would ultimately include people from every walk of life. As can be gleaned from Jesus' example, no one is to be deprived of hearing and receiving the good news.

In youth ministry, it is very easy for leaders to gravitate toward teens who are attractive in personality, appearance, and various competencies. Oftentimes, the "fringe" kids get left out of the equation of the "great commission." If we are to be truly comprehensive in our ministry, we must think of innovative and strategic ways of reaching every teen on our church roster (if not the city!) with Jesus' transforming message.

When attempting to expand the harvest, we must deliberately target unreached teens, discover a common meeting ground, plan enticing and effective programs, activities, and/or events, integrate the gospel message within such events, and follow up with relational ministry.

Perhaps this can be accomplished through such opportunities as a city-wide slam-dunk and/or three-point shoot-out contest, or participation in a youth gym/center or a summer sports camp. The sky is the limit when it comes to creating innovative and strategic ways of reaching out to our teens; and underneath that sky are millions of teens of every race, culture, and economic condition, family situation, and personality who long for the meaning and significance that only Jesus can give.

Innovative Evangelistic Event Planner

1. Identify teens (groups, cliques, etc.) from your parish and/or community that have yet to be reached by your present evangelistic efforts.

2. Prayerfully choose one group whom you feel God is leading you to reach.

3. Brainstorm common turfs, interests, or meeting grounds in which you can effectively connect with this group. Choose the approach(es) that would be most effective.

4. Based on these approach(es), develop a program, activity, or event that will attract these teens. Work out the details of planning, including publicity, program development, resources, dates, etc.

5. Integrate an evangelistic dimension. Will there be a direct evangelistic message? Will it be pre-evangelistic in scope? Will the evangelistic impact grow over time? If so, how? State your evangelistic objectives.

Section Three

Growing Mature Disciples

10

Plotting for Growth: Fostering Adolescent Faith Maturity

It was the most anticipated day in our two-and-a-half-year marriage. We were about to embark on a trip that would forever change our lives. My wife, De, and I were driving to Chicago to take home our tiny twins. Their previous car ride (and first, for that matter), was aboard an emergency vehicle that safely transported them to a hospital equipped for their medical conditions. The road that took us to this day was not an easy one. Michael and Sarah were supposed to be our *first* child. Instead, we were caught off guard with a two-month-premature delivery of undetected twins!

For five-and-a-half weeks we had made a daily 110 mile round trip to visit our sickly little newborns in a neo-natal intensive care nursery. After much prayer, many scares, and more roller coaster emotions than we thought possible, our twins were now finally coming home.

We were thoroughly prepared for our precious little cargo's big trip home. The diaper bag was weighted with enough nursery supplies to give Arnold Schwarzenegger a hernia. Two infant seats, receiving blankets, and brand new outfits sat neatly arranged in our car. We signed the release papers, took some pictures, buckled them into their car seats, and carefully drove home. Now, they were really ours!

When we arrived home we placed the car-seated twins on the kitchen table, looked at them, looked at each other, and then De nervously asked, "Now, what do we do?"

I was at a complete loss and brilliantly replied, "I don't know—you'd better call your mother!"

Michael and Sarah recently started high school. Over the years, De and I have learned that there is a lot more to raising children than simply giving them life (and driving them home). Responsible and loving parents do all that is necessary carefully to nurture their children toward maturity.

Fruitful youth ministries are similar. Our work goes beyond evangelization. As a matter of fact, it is spiritually irresponsible to ignite the spark of faith in teens through evangelization without the intention, plan, and leadership to kindle that spark towards Christian maturity.

Evangelization is devoted to creating the right conditions to facilitate the germination of faith in one's heart. The goal of evangelization is *conversion*, and this second phase of the discipling process picks up where evangelization leaves off. The conversion experience presupposes an initial personalized adherence to the gospel message. This phase helps foster a deeper understanding and experience of an already "awakened faith." Paul speaks of this growth when he addresses the Colossians: "So, as you received Christ Jesus the Lord, walk in him, rooted in him and built upon him and established in the faith as you were taught, abounding in thanksgiving" (Colossians 2:6-7).

This does not, however, preclude the presence of an evangelistic element. Igniting and reigniting the flames of faith is an ongoing need throughout every disciple's formation. Good catechesis has an evangelizing dimension that re-energizes and renews our first love (see Revelation 2:4).

The religious formation I am proposing primarily seeks to sponsor an adolescent towards deeper faith maturity. So what is faith maturity? What does it look like within the developmental framework of adolescence? I believe maturity has two primary aspects. First, it is characterized by the ability to reproduce, or bear fruit for God's kingdom. This occurs through self-sacrifice. When we speak of mature individuals in the natural realm, we are not simply referring to those who have the ability physically to reproduce or conceive. We are referring to those who have the kind of character qualities that lovingly nurture the new life they bring into the world. Therefore one aspect of spiritual maturity is the ability lovingly to sacrifice on behalf of others for God's kingdom.

The second aspect of faith maturity involves imitating Christ. Jesus is the standard for measuring the fullness of spiritual maturity. Jesus is the ultimate model of self-sacrificing love. St. Paul states that full maturity for a member of the body of Christ is to be like Jesus the head (see Ephesians 4:15). Jesus fully poured out his life for the benefit of others. Simply stated, the goal of Christian life is to imitate our Lord (see 1 Thessalonians 1:6; 1 Corinthians 11:1; Ephesians 5:1-2).

The "growing mature" phase is the ongoing process that transforms one from a *spiritual consumer* ("What can you do for me, Jesus?") to a *life changer* ("What can you do through me, Jesus?").

Characteristics of a Maturing Faith

Becoming like Jesus is also part of a lifelong process. When I was in my teens and twenties I liked myself a lot. I thought I had the time, enthusiasm, energy, and idealism to someday have it "all together." If I worked hard enough at it, I would someday achieve perfection. Now, in my thirties, I do not like myself as much. My six beloved children effortlessly mirror to me my self-centeredness, impatience, and lack of sacrificial love. As I grow in love and knowledge of my Lord, the gulf between his character and mine only seems to widen. It's not that I am retreating in the opposite direction. It is just that the tea was already in the bag, and it only took some hot water to extract its contents (children can do that).

The longer we walk with the Lord, the less we trust in ourselves and the more we rely on God's grace. This appears to be the experience of St. Paul as he initially described himself as "in no way inferior to the super apostles" (see 2 Corinthians 12:11), only to later refer to himself as the "worst of sinners" (see 1 Timothy 1:15). However, it often takes years of striving to begin to realize that we do nothing by our own power. Spiritual maturity spans all of human development. Spiritual maturity looks different in each stage of growth, including the stage of adolescence. We must be careful not to expect from teens what has taken us twenty additional years to learn.

Adolescence is a time of energy, enthusiasm, and idealism. These qualities are a teenager's gifts to the church. Their spiritual growth and maturity will be expressed through these developmentally appropriate characteristics. But what does the spiritually-maturing adolescent look like? What are some practical qualities of the adolescent who is growing in faith and spiritual maturity? This chapter identifies five characteristics we can use as a guide.

1. Growing Relationship with God

Adolescence is a time when interpersonal relationships take on a new significance. Friendships become all-important and central to a teenager's life. Relationships begin to move beyond the superficiality of childhood (doing things together) and into the deeper realms of intimacy (sharing feelings and issues). This movement should also impact a teen's spirituality, that is, his or her relationship with God.

Spiritual maturity is incompatible with what modern culture identifies as the "balanced life."

The road to adolescent spiritual maturity is marked by a growing depth in a teen's relationship with God until Jesus becomes the hub of life, not just one of many spokes. Spiritual maturity is incompatible with what modern culture identifies as the "balanced life." The balanced life assigns a piece of the pie for all worthy endeavors. Jesus stands in the same line for his ration of time and attention as do a teen's soccer coach (physical), math teacher (intellectual), and friends (social). However, Jesus never afforded the first disciples this liberty. Instead, he said:

> If anyone comes to me without hating his father and mother, wife and children, brothers and sisters, and even his own life, he cannot be my disciple. Whoever does not carry his own cross and come after me cannot be my disciple. In the same way, everyone of you who does not renounce all his possessions cannot be my disciple" (Luke 14:26-27, 33).

To be a disciple means making Jesus life's number one priority. Jesus does not demand of his followers what he, himself, has not modeled in his own relationship with the Father. Jesus placed the Father's will above everything else. Jesus always made time to be in communion with the Father (see Mark 1:35-39).

Any healthy and intimate relationships are achieved through *intentional* efforts. For example, a married couple who exert little energy into their relationship with one another soon become divorced singles. On the other hand, successful marriages are fostered by couples spending time communicating, sharing, and enjoying one another. Making the relationship work is a top priority. A committed relationship with Jesus also involves our putting our love for Jesus above every other pursuit. Transforming our relationship with Jesus into our highest priority is a lifelong task that is lived out through daily habits or disciplines. We need to help teens understand the commitment and effort it takes to make any relationship work.

To take this analogy further, evangelization can be compared to infatuation between a man and a woman. Just as this phase helps them to notice one another and attracts them to one another, evangelization helps initiate or awaken a teen to God's loving friendship, often through evangelistic meetings, camps, or retreats. However, as a couple's relationship moves from infatuation to more committed love, a teen's faith must rise beyond an emotional or communal level. To assist this process, we must provide teens with both spiritual tools and the knowledge to use them skillfully.

Tony Campolo tells a story of a young man who was a member of a Pentecostal church.[27] Each week the pastor would finish his sermon and invite anyone who so wished to come forward to commit or recommit his or her life to Christ and be prayed for. Week after week, this young man would unabashedly rush his way to the front, repeating in a loud voice, "Fill me, Jesus! Fill me, Jesus!"

One Sunday, the pastor finished his message and gave his typical altar call. And, as always, this young man began to make his way to the front of the church, loudly chanting, "Fill me, Jesus! Fill me, Jesus!"

An older woman in the back stood up and disgustedly shouted, "Don't fill him, Lord—he leaks!"

Like that young man, we leak. We are like uninsulated homes; our interior warmth escapes through the cracks of daily living. If we do not have any regular way to replenish the fire in our hearts, we soon grow spiritually cold. The practice of spiritual discipline is like a thermostat that kicks out heat when our spiritual temperature dips below an appropriate level.

A good indication of that growing spirituality in teens is the knowledge and ability to feed themselves spiritually. What would a dinner guest think if he sat and watched my wife and I scurrying around the kitchen table painstakingly feeding, spoonful by spoonful, each of our six, able-bodied children? Kind of a weird family, huh? This is certainly normal and acceptable for infants, but for high schoolers? Unfortunately, many senior high teens have neither the understanding nor the spiritual skills necessary to grow their own relationship with Christ. Many live from retreat to youth group meeting to youth liturgy. Don't get me wrong, these activities are good, and we absolutely need to be rooted in community. Sadly, though, they have never been taught to feed themselves. Most teens are spiritually malnourished and consequently linger in spiritual immaturity. The author of Hebrews spoke of a similar condition when he said: "Everyone who lives on milk lacks experience of the word of righteousness, for he is a child. But solid food is for the mature, for those whose faculties are trained by practice to discern good and evil" (Hebrews 5:13-14)

We accept the fact that to excel in any sport one must devote a significant amount of time and effort to conditioning, practicing the basics, and developing advanced skills. We rarely, however, ask our young disciples to put forth much effort in their own spiritual training. By our own lack of challenge, especially in light of what today's athletic coaches are demanding, we concede to our teens that their religious training is secondary in importance. The scriptures, however, teach the opposite:

> I continue my pursuit toward the goal, the prize of God's upward calling, in Christ Jesus. Let us, then, who are "perfectly mature" adopt this attitude. (Philippians 3:14, 15)

> Do you not know that the runners in the stadium all run in the race, but only one wins the prize? Run so as to win. Every athlete exercises discipline in every way. They do it to win a perishable crown, but we an imperishable one. Thus I do not run aimlessly; I do not fight as if I were shadowboxing. No, I drive my body and train it, for fear that, after having preached to others, I myself should be disqualified. (1 Corinthians 9:24-27)

If the old adage "nothing good comes easy" is true, then we could logically deduce from the "light and easy" practices of many youth ministries that spirituality is not all that "good" or worthwhile. Many youth ministry programs could honestly be entitled: "Jesus Lite: Faith That Tastes Good but Is Less Filling."

To spur a young person's relationship with God to maturity, we must train teens in specific spiritual disciplines or habits. Spiritual disciplines are consistent activities or practices that lead us to inner transformation and spiritual growth. Just like adults, teens need to develop a practical competence in the disciplines of *solitude, silence, prayer, study,* and *reconciliation.* Without a consistent practice of these spiritual disciplines, a teen's relationship with God is at serious risk of drying up, or remaining at a superficial level. It is important to note, however, that the practice of the disciplines in and of themselves are of no spiritual value. We do not want to produce young Pharisees who are filled with religious pride based on external practices. The purpose of the disciplines is to place a young person in a position to hear and obey God.

Solitude, silence, prayer, study, and reconciliation need to be taught, practiced, reflected on, and integrated into the daily life of the growing disciple. This needs to be done with the guidance of a mentor who has a great depth of spiritual maturity, and in the company of other teens who are on the same journey. Consistent involvement in a faith community can aid teens in the practice of these disciplines. Through the assistance

Application

More information on the disciplines of solitude, silence, prayer, study, and reconciliation is presented in the resource "Five Spiritual Disciplines for Teens" on page 204.

of group discussion, mutual support, prayer, and holding one another accountable, teens can grow and mature in their relationship with God.

2. Growing Knowledge and Understanding of Their Faith

The USCC document *Renewing the Vision: A Framework for Catholic Youth Ministry* identifies numerous assets that serve as a foundation for healthy faith development and growth in adolescents. Among these are to:

- ✔ Develop young people's critical thinking skills that empower them to analyze contemporary life and culture in light of the good news of Jesus Christ and the teachings of the church.
- ✔ Develop the biblical and doctrinal literacy of young people and a deeper appreciation of the importance of the Scriptures and the teachings of the church in the Christian life.[28]

The ad hoc committee to oversee the use of the *Catechism of the Catholic Church* recently pointed out that there is a crisis of catechetical literacy among children and teens. In the area of teens this is not surprising; most youth ministry efforts are being invested on immediate needs. We are either putting out the wildfires of personal teen crises, or forever trying to ignite a spark of life through our evangelistic efforts. This leaves little time to stoke and feed an existing flicker of faith. Consequently, many of our youth are ignorant of some of the most basic doctrines and beliefs of the church. Most Catholic teens lack a scriptural and church teaching foundation in which to root their lives. To grow towards faith maturity, an adolescent disciple needs a steady diet of faith content. Teenagers need to know what they believe and why they believe it. Without a reasonable understanding of the scriptures and church teaching, teens cannot achieve any real depth of commitment. A faith knowledge that rests solely on the authority of the faith community, or worse, the authority of the contemporary culture, is still immature.

Adolescence is a time when teens seek to make sense of the mess of the world surrounding them. It is a time of questioning and testing, as they seek to liberate themselves from their parent's identity and arrive at their own sense of self. Finding meaning, purpose, and consistency to view, understand, and interact with the world is an important developmental task. Eventually teens *will* arrive at a world view—a set of assumptions and philosophical underpinnings that serve as a base to understand, interpret, and act upon the world around them. But, how will they arrive at it? Who or what will be the primary formers of this view?

For many teens, a world view comes by default as they acquiesce to the most resounding voice in their lives—the contemporary media. Most teens have consumed a steady, gluttonous diet of television, motion pictures, advertisements, and music. Although a mixture of both good and bad, the dominant philosophies of life inherent to much of popular programming are consumerism, narcissism, and hedonism. Few teens would recognize these terms or possess the ability to articulate their meaning, yet many are interpreting life through this lens.

On the other hand, the teen who is growing towards faith maturity is developing a Catholic Christian mindset from which to interpret reality. Instead of blindly accepting contemporary secular understandings of truth, the spiritually maturing teen is being challenged to shape his or her attitudes, assumptions, and values by the truth of the scriptures, tradition, and the teachings of the magisterium. St. Paul wrote: "Do not conform yourself to this age but be transformed by the renewal of your mind, that you may discern what is the will of God, what is good and pleasing and perfect" (Romans 12:2).

Moving teens to a biblical and doctrinal literacy is an overwhelming challenge in light of our present cultural landscape. Many teens, even evangelized teens, may express little interest in our catechetical offerings. Like the old saying goes, "You can lead a horse to water, but you can't make him drink." So what does the wise cowboy do? He salts the oats and makes him thirsty!

My daughter Sarah was comfortably plodding along in her Catholic faith until she was challenged by a zealous evangelical Protestant camp counselor regarding the beliefs and doctrines of the Catholic church. Her first defense was, "My parents are intelligent people and they wouldn't steer me wrong." Not impressed by her response, the counselor persisted by presenting some common misrepresentations of Catholic teaching.

Not knowing how to answer these "heretical" charges, Sarah again fell back on the authority of her parents. "My dad speaks all over the country about youth ministry—why, he is even writing a book. *He* knows what he's talking about."

Her second defense did little to intimidate her challenger. Sarah's dad knew why he was Catholic, but Sarah could not articulate to this young woman why she was. This crisis caused her to take a step beyond her parent's faith (affiliative faith), ask some tough questions, and arrive at a deeper, more personally owned faith. Prior to this experience, Sarah did not feel the need to explore why she believed what she believed.

The water was there for the drinking, but she wasn't very thirsty. Our evangelical Protestant sister salted her oats!

We, too, can salt the oats by creating crises that challenge teens in their beliefs. By playing the role of devil's advocate and reversing sides, I have found that I can (in a safe environment) challenge the belief systems of teens, and therefore create an interest and desire to learn. I have played a formidable apologist for atheism, abortion, anti-Catholicism, agnosticism, pre-marital sex, and may other hot button topics. It may be done in an artificial manner, but the exercises serve a purpose in making young people think about what they believe and why they believe it. Often, teens realize they have yet to establish consistent principles on which to base their understanding of life, moral issues, values, and beliefs.

Teens need to learn about what they believe. Issues that should be addressed include the creed, the sacraments, the liturgy, scripture, social justice, Christian lifestyle, ecclesiology, and moral teaching. An excellent resource in this area is *The Challenge of Adolescent Catechesis: Maturing in Faith.*[29] Content needs to be made practical and connected to the everyday life of the teens.

On our way to a personalized and owned faith, we must go through a period of searching. To ignore or not address this stage of faith can be disastrous. If we do not provide a positive forum that reasonably articulates the views of the church, in an environment of open discussion, we risk two equally negative effects. First, a questioning teen who feels he or she does not have the freedom to raise issues, or does not receive reasonable responses when he or she does, can reject the faith on the basis that it is irrelevant or is deficient in substance. The second risk could affect teens who are generally more accepting of the faith. Without an opportunity to explore their Catholic faith, this type of teen can settle into thoughtless acquiescence to a superficial faith.

Young people need the freedom to question, raise objections to, and wrestle with the doctrine and teachings of the church. We need to teach them critical reflection skills. Blind acceptance will only lead to shallow comprehension and commitment. One cannot be an effective Christian witness to the world, providing adequate Catholic Christian apologetics, without a depth of understanding and personalized conviction about what he or she believes.

Young people need the freedom to question, raise objections to, and wrestle with the doctrine and teachings of the church.

3. Committed to Christian Community

As mentioned earlier, discipleship is experienced in the context of community. We were never meant to live the Christian life alone. When we became a child of God at baptism, we were born into a family of faith. Teens who are advancing toward faith maturity are growing in their commitment to Christian community.

First, the growing disciples value Christian community. They recognize that even though they know how to feed themselves spiritually, they will always need the support of other believers to grow, and the other believers will need their support, too. As alluded to in Galatians 6:2, the maturing disciple has grown past dependency (you take care of me), beyond the illusion of independence (I can take care of myself) to the truth of interdependence (we take care of each other).

Second, the disciples who are maturing as members of a Christian community have come to know, appreciate, and utilize their own gifts for the benefits of others. On the flip side, they have come to affirm, to identify with, and to benefit by the gifts of others (see 1 Corinthians 12).

Maturing disciples are discovering and appreciating their own gifts. We leaders need to facilitate this process. Teens need to see themselves as useful to God's kingdom. They need to realize that Jesus has given them purpose in his body and gifted them to express this purpose practically. No one is more valuable to God than another because of his or her giftedness. We each play an important role in God's overall plan (see 1 Corinthians 12:7). The key is to be faithful and obedient to what God calls us to do and to affirm, without jealousy, the gifting of others in the community.

Spiritual maturity is dependent on an understanding that our gifts were given to us by God and given for the benefit of others. Immaturity is characterized by an infatuation with our own gifts and ascertaining them as proof of our own self-importance. If our gifts are to be gifts, their focus is always aimed at the benefit of others.

The gifts of teens obviously should be utilized in youth programming. But, beyond this, their gifts should be used in the larger parish community. Adults should identify, employ, appreciate, and benefit by the gifting of our teen members. This will help them feel connected to the larger parish family, and will also help to develop within them a deeper sense of ownership.

A third characteristic for a teen growing in commitment to community is accountability. When we become accountable, we voluntarily open up our lives to one another. We share our victories and failures within a safe and caring environment that serves as a greenhouse for growth. Secrecy, on the other hand, is the soil of deception. If we can keep others out of our lives, we do not have to be honest about who we are.

Ever since I almost crushed myself while weightlifting alone, I have had a work-out partner. I know myself well enough to know that if it is up to me, I will ignore the alarm clock when it jars me in the morning to get up early and work out. I do much better when a partner is waiting for me. Because I do not want to disappoint my friend, I get up even when I do not feel like it (which is almost every morning). Additionally, I work much harder when someone is challenging me and pushing me to greater heights. If I work out alone, I find it very easy to skip repetitions and sets, lighten my intensity, and go home early. This point is driven home well in the letter to the Hebrews:

> We must consider how to rouse one another to love and good works. We should not stay away from our assembly, as is the custom of some, but encourage one another, and this all the more as you see the day drawing near. (Hebrews 10:24, 25)

We need to guide teens in encouraging, inspiring, challenging, and even admonishing one another. Accountability helps egg us on and takes us to heights we would never consider on our own.

Finally, growing in our commitment to Christian community means growing in our love for one another. Our love for God can be measured by our love for others. The first letter of John makes this clear:

> Beloved, let us love one another, because love is of God; everyone who loves is begotten by God and knows God. Whoever is without love does not know God, for God is love. (1 John 4:7, 8)

Christian community teaches teens how to relate to and love each other. It is a training school on how to encourage, confront, exhort, serve, build up, admonish, and challenge one another—all in the name of love.

4. Depth of Commitment

> This is what is needed: a church for young people which will know how to speak to their heart and enkindle, comfort and inspire enthusiasm in it with the joy of the Gospel and the strength of the eucharist; a church which will know how to invite and to welcome the person who seeks a purpose for which to commit his whole existence; a church which is not afraid to require much, after having given much; which does not fear asking from young people the effort of a noble and authentic adventure such as that of following the Gospel.
>
> (Pope John Paul II, 1995 World Day of Prayer for Vocations)

The Holy Father provided a recipe for world-changing impact. However, at present, very few teens are leaving the church because they feel over-challenged by its demands. I have yet to hear a teen storm out of a church complaining, "You want too much from me! What you ask is too demanding. I am leaving!" (see John 6:60-66; Matthew 19:21-22). In most cases, teens' athletic coaches are asking far more, and getting it without question! If anything, like a lifeless movie, we are boring young people right out of the pews. We fail to challenge their natural enthusiasm, energy, and idealism with opportunities to change the world through the transforming power of the gospel. We need to offer teens a worthy adventure in which they can fully invest their lives. We need to issue a call that captures their imagination.

The radical Christianity Jesus expressed is simply normal discipleship.

Jesus did just that. He called his disciples to an extraordinary commitment and challenge. He called them to put the gospel before everything, so they might be in a place to impact the world. The radical Christianity Jesus expressed is simply normal discipleship. The teen who is growing in spiritual maturity is growing in his or her commitment to live as a dedicated disciple of Jesus Christ.

The disciple maker must offer young people a "zesty" Christianity. If Jesus had come to Mexico instead of Palestine, he would have used different images to get his point across. "Jalapeño of the earth" may have replaced "salt of the earth!" His native listeners would have oohed and ahed with knowing smiles, realizing, "He wants us to spice up this earth!"

Too often, however, we are in the business of making "cottage cheese Christians." Cottage cheese is not known for its zesty, memorable, and spicy flavor. Actually, it is quite bland, uninteresting, and tasteless (at least that's what I think). On the other hand, when you bite into a jalapeño pepper, you will remember your encounter! A jalapeño makes an impact on your taste buds. Adult leaders need to call, and to provide the opportunities, for teens to be "jalapeño pepper Christians" to their community.

Young people are not lazy. They are full of energy and up for an exciting challenge. Growing teens are looking for opportunities to apply their idealism to the cause of God's kingdom. I remember first-hand. After my own adolescent conversion, I had a great desire to share the good news that transformed my own life with anyone who might listen. Prior to my conversion, I spent Friday nights going to all the best parties for all the wrong purposes. After my conversion, I spent Friday nights randomly evangelizing anyone the Lord placed in my path. My friend Paul and I began our night in prayer. We specifically asked the Holy Spirit for guidance. We surrendered our evening for God's purposes and prayed that he would lead us and guide us to anyone he wished for us to serve. Every Friday, without exception, was an absolute adventure! The fun began as we put the car into drive and trusted in the Holy Spirit's ability to navigate our way. We would always find ourselves in a divinely appointed encounter either to serve or share our faith. We learned how to discern and trust the Lord's voice in our life and share our faith through these events. Besides, it was just plain fun!

I remember one particular evening when I questioned the Lord's choice of assignment. We hooked up with a guy, Ted, whom I had worked with in the past. In a few short days he would be leaving for Marine boot camp. During the course of the night I shared with Ted my faith journey. I described in great detail the difference Jesus made in my life, and how he could do the same for Ted. As I shared, cobwebs formed on Ted's face. His most enthusiastic response to my good news was long drawn-out yawns. He appeared utterly bored with my heartfelt presentation, and eventually he changed the subject to avoid slipping into a coma.

On the way home that night, I remember asking God why he wasted our night on such an uninterested soul. I thought maybe I did not discern God's direction clearly. Ted went to boot camp and Paul and I were on to new adventures the next Friday.

Months passed, and I saw Ted walking through a shopping center sporting a fresh crew cut. His face lit up when he saw me. I never knew him to be so excited. He grabbed my arm and said, "Remember that night we went out before I left for boot camp?"

"Yeah, I remember, Ted."

"Do you remember those things you told me about God?"

"Yes, Ted, what about it?"

"It was God who got me through boot camp!" he enthusiastically disclosed. "There was a time when I didn't think I would make it. It was then that I appealed and clung to the Jesus you spoke of. Thanks so much for telling me!"

Over the years, I have been amazed at the energy and idealism teens have applied to living out their faith. There was Tim, who was so excited about his faith that he contacted over four hundred peers in one month to invite them to an evangelistic gathering at his parish. Or Steve, who was the teen council president and who had more than enough credits to graduate by the time he was a senior. Nevertheless, he took a class out of the college-prep track in order to share his faith with a group of teens he had yet to meet during his high school years.

We get what we ask for. Ask little, get little. Ask much, get much. Commitment grows by challenge. The spiritually maturing adolescent is growing in his or her commitment to Christ. The leaders who are fostering this growth are those who are asking teens to commit themselves to grow. Teens *will* commit themselves. The question is: to whom or what will they commit? Their lack of spiritual growth is usually not a matter of a lack of commitment, but of misplaced commitment or over-commitment. If we fail to ask anything great from them, they will conclude that there is nothing great about who we are and what we do.

Some motivational speakers in the business world jack up their prices because it actually increases the volume of their engagements. Their reasoning? People want the best. If it costs little, it must be worth little. We look at our commitments in a similar manner. Something that asks little must be of little importance. And that is exactly what we communicate when we cower to every other commitment asked of a teen. Sometimes we think we are doing them a favor by not asking much of them. "Why add to their stress?" we reason. The gospel does not enslave; it liberates! Jesus said:

> Come to me, all you who labor and are burdened, and I will give you rest. Take my yoke upon you and learn from me, for I am meek and humble of heart; and you will find rest for yourselves. For my yoke is easy, and my burden light. (Matthew 11:28-30)

> But seek first the kingdom of God and his righteousness, and all these things will be given you besides. (Matthew 6:33)

We need to guide teens toward responsible commitments to the things that really matter in life. The best way to capture the passion and commitment of the present generation is to offer them a vision of living that harnesses their idealism, gives expression to their enthusiasm, and navigates their need for meaningful purpose.

A growing commitment to Christ's kingdom does not mean a teen has to quit every other involvement. That would be a serious mistake. What it means, however, is that a teen places Jesus as rightful Lord over all that he or she does, and every other commitment is discerned through prayerful guidance.

5. Application of Faith in Daily Life

In our tendency to compartmentalize life, religious faith can be reduced to just another aspect of our existence. For the adolescent disciple, however, maturing faith must grow to penetrate into every aspect of life, and then transform life. Jesus called us to be a salt and light to the earth (see Matthew 5:13-14). We must challenge teens to live the gospel in their homes, schools, neighborhoods, work places, and social lives. The gospel message must be integrated into all of life.

However, teens tend to practice hypocrisy with the same intensity they judge it in others. For example, two teens might complain to one another for hours about a peer whom they describe as "such a gossip."

Often, because teens believe in something, they tend to think that it is also true in their lives. David Elkind calls this "apparent hypocrisy." He attributes their hypocrisy more to intellectual immaturity than moral shortcomings. As teens begin to enter into formal operational thought, they grapple with abstract principles and ideals and have a difficult time connecting theory with practical expression. It is an intellectual awkwardness similar to the physical uncoordination of a fast-growing preadolescent. As it takes time for this person to grow into his or her bigger body, so will it take time for an adolescent to grow into his or her new mental abilities.

This does not excuse us from making the connection between moral principles and moral behavior. Teens need to be challenged to see and understand the importance of coupling their faith's ideals to its practical expression through the actions of daily living. We need, however, to realize that their hypocrisy may only be an expression of intellectual uncoordination rather than of moral weakness.

To help foster a connection between our faith and daily living we need to assist teens in making practical application of what the scriptures and tradition teach. The content of our meetings should never result in head knowledge alone. Head knowledge becomes "dead knowledge" when it is all we possess. The knowledge of our faith must be acted upon, applied, and lived in order to result in a changed life. As we disciple young people, we need to challenge teens creatively and concretely to integrate what they are learning into their lives. The disciple maker must illustrate, enflesh, and bring to life the gospel through his or her own life application.

Summary

As critical as evangelization is, it primarily serves the functional purpose of spurring on the "evangelized" to lifelong conversion to the way, truth, and life of Jesus Christ (see John 14:6). Evangelization is not the final destination. In fact, evangelizing for evangelizing's sake alone can be equated to giving someone a million-dollar jet and encouraging him to enjoy it, when there are no plans whatsoever for teaching him actually how to use it. The gift at best will go unused as intended, and at worst could kill him! Seed planting void of strategic plotting for growth has sent countless directionless people back into their "pre-evangelized," despairing existences, with greater disappointment and disillusionment about Christianity than they ever had before.

Following conversion, and through constant, daily faith formation (discipleship), the destination is faith maturity. Faith maturity is the lifelong task of becoming like Jesus. The goal is being able to live in a manner that says, "Yes, I love the Lord my God with all my heart and all my soul and all my mind; and I love my neighbor as myself!" (See Matthew 22:37-39.)

Viewed through the contextual lens of adolescent development, the maturing adolescent disciple also is developing a relationship with God. His or her relationship with the Lord is becoming a top priority. He or she is learning how to intentionally utilize spiritual disciplines such as solitude, silence, prayer, study, and reconciliation.

The maturing adolescent disciple has a growing understanding and knowledge of faith that enables him or her to apply scripture and church teaching to practical living. The maturing teen disciple values and is committed to a Christian community which can be seen through the desire to use his or her personal gifts for the good of the "body," his or her understanding and practical application of accountability, and his or her growing love for others.

Evidence that a teen is maturing in faith can also be seen in the depth of commitment. The person's life shows spice that can only come from someone who wants to be the flavor of a "jalapeño" to a spiritually bland world. Jesus does not simply fit into a compartment labeled "Sunday Mass" or "Youth Group," but, rather, infiltrates every aspect of the disciple's daily life.

Teens will commit their lives to a meaningful cause. They want to be challenged and not lulled into a coma. They have what it takes to become mature disciples. If we ask much of them, they will give much; if we request little . . . we will reap what we sow.

Five Spiritual Disciplines for Teens

The discipline of **solitude** is the practice of being alone, in order that we can listen and create a space in our hearts where God can reach us (see Psalm 130:6). Solitude provides the means to distance ourselves from the ways, priorities, and the interactions of the world in order to gain a kingdom perspective.[30] To create in young people a spiritual maturity and depth that enables them to deal with the complexity of problems in today's culture, we need to train our youth in the practice of taking time and finding space away from other people, possessions, and concerns to be alone with the Lord.

The discipline of **silence** is often practiced together with solitude. Silence seeks to remove us from words, noise, and music, so we might better distinguish the voice of God. Jesus said that his sheep would follow him because they recognize his voice (see John 10:4). Silence helps us differentiate between the voice of a "stranger" and the true word of the Good Shepherd (see John 10:5).

Both solitude and silence may represent a particular challenge to teens. Our culture is fast, noisy, and busy. The experience of solitude and silence can be like entering an alien country with both a foreign culture and language. In addition, especially for the younger adolescent, it can open the door to the anxiety of loneliness. Our challenge is to introduce the disciplines of solitude and silence where teens can experience their benefits, yet minimize their risks. Healthy solitude is always practiced in the context of a caring community. Additionally, especially for the younger adolescent, solitude can be experimented with within group settings, with teens separating from one another into "alone areas," but able to return to the large group for communal support.

The discipline of **prayer** is fundamental to the life of the disciple. Prayer is communicating with God. There are many forms, methods, and stages of prayer, but what is critical for the growing teen is to begin the practice of prayer. Young people need to be introduced to different methods and styles to find what works best for them.

Study is the application of one's mind upon verbal and nonverbal realities. Specifically, we need to provide young people with the tools to study the scriptures and church teaching. If teens are to *think* Christian, and therefore, critically reflect on the culture around them, they must have a good understanding of God's revealed word.

The sacrament of **reconciliation** is a great gift to our church. The book of James, known for its straightforward and practical wisdom, says: "Therefore, confess your sins to one another and pray for one another, that you may be healed" (James 5:16). Providing teens with opportunities to receive the sacrament and integrate it into their daily lives will help them positively deal with the sin in their lives by leading them to discern their choices, experience forgiveness, and move forward with accompanying works of penance.

11

Growing Small-Group Communities

A few years ago, I gave a retreat for the senior class of a Catholic high school. One young man, Peter, stood above the crowd. He was handsome, athletic, and very charming. He carried himself with a self-assured confidence. When Peter said something, everyone listened. When Peter walked out of the room, there were a trail of other students behind him. It did not take me long to realize that he was the leader of his class. Here was a kid who seemed to have life by the tail.

During the evening of our first night, we had an opportunity to break down into smaller, more intimate groups. Peter was in my group. I found out that he was the school's star fullback and dated the most popular girl in his class. I also watched a fog of façades melt around us as our atmosphere warmed and members began to open up. The safety of the environment gave Peter permission to reveal his heart—maybe for the first time. We sat dumbfounded as he tearfully painted a surprising portrait of the real Peter. He revealed his constant struggle with loneliness, and his feelings of abandonment by God through the death of his father. I could see a visible sense of relief and even healing in Peter as he disclosed to those around him how he really felt. We were on holy ground. The presence of our Lord was evident in the breaking open of our lives. In this small-group setting, Peter finally found a safe place to talk about what was *really* going on in his life.

The Significance of Small Faith Communities for Teenagers

Over the years, I have met many "Peters"—teens, who, like swollen dams, ache to release their pent-up feelings to friends who truly care. Finding a safe place where a teen can truly reveal his or her fears, struggles, and feelings is a rare luxury. Even surrounded by "friends," teens often feel lonely. (Our research has indicated that twenty-five percent of senior high teens report that they experience loneliness *very often or every day*.[31]) Masks that guard a teen's true identity have become essential protective gear for the teen environment. Without the defense they provide, a teen might suffer wounds that leave painful, even lifelong scars.

Spurred by a real need for belonging, many youth settle for superficial relationships. They may be counted as a part of a group, but they exchange their true identity for group identification so as to be acceptable to the group's norms. Many teens find themselves surrounded by friends on the outside, but lonely and isolated on the inside.

Unfortunately, family life is not the refuge it used to be. As a result of the busyness of our culture (for example, two-career households and single-parent homes), children are not spending as much meaningful time with their parents. Author H. Steven Glenn compares the typical interaction between parents and children in the 1930s with today:

> Older readers will recall that in 1930 children spent three to four hours a day personally involved with various members of their extended families—parents, grandparents, aunts, uncles, and others who lived close by. Today's typical youngsters have a very different home experience. The extended family has been reduced to what we call the nuclear family—one or two parents plus the children. Relatives live typically far away.
>
> And interaction within nuclear families today amounts to only a few minutes a day. Of these few minutes, more than half are not true interaction. Rather they are one-way communications delivered in a negative tone: parents' warnings or reproaches to children for misbehavior.[32]

Major Transitions in Lifestyles[33]

The following table is a summary of the drastic reduction of dialogue, collaboration, and bonds of closeness and trust among family members.

Characteristic	Norm 1930	Norm 1980
Family interaction	high	low
Value system	homogeneous	heterogeneous
Role models	consonant	dissonant
Logical consequences	experienced	avoided
Inter-generational associations	many	few
Education	less	more
Level of information	low	high
Technology	low	high
Non-negotiable tasks	many	few
Family work	much	little
Family size	large	small
Family dominant	extended	nuclear
Step/Blended/Single parent families	few (10-15%)	many (35-42%)
Class size (K-12)	18-22	28-35
Neighborhood schools	dominant	rare

In the midst of this culture of isolation, the church needs to offer an attractive alternative. We need to provide a place where a teen can take off her or his mask at the door and truly be herself or himself. A small faith community is an important and appealing niche that youth ministry programs can offer to teens. A small faith community not only helps meet a need for human intimacy and belonging, it also is an effective environment for spiritual growth and Christian action. If young people's spiritual needs are met in an environment of Christian love and acceptance, teens will clamor at our doors to gain access.

The growing stage of the discipling process can effectively be facilitated in a number of different formats, such as mentoring, small groups, large groups, and retreats. Ideally, a combination of all the formats is optimal. Each has a specific purpose and strength, and when used in combination, can provide a holistic formational experience. Most parishes, however, lack the needed resources to do this. In such a case,

I would recommend small Christian communities as the best single choice for effectively establishing a young person in his or her faith and providing a positive experience of the church. There are many different models for small-group ministry, including support/healing, growth, fellowship, catechetical, evangelistic, and sharing groups. The model that I will emphasize in this chapter is a *small faith community*. This model is simply a smaller expression of the larger church community. It contains all the elements or dimensions of the larger church within its smaller cell.

Defining Small Faith Community

A small faith community is "a group of five to ten youth who meet intentionally and regularly, together with adult mentors, to share life, deepen their faith, and actively live out the mission of the church." Let's break down this definition further.

A small faith community is generally comprised of five to ten teens. Theoretically, we can go as low as three teens and as high as twelve. But practically speaking, going below five members places difficult demands on each member to carry the group. Additionally, if one or two teens are absent, this wipes out both the dynamic and the morale of the group. When the numbers go beyond ten, it becomes more difficult to maintain interpersonal relationships, stay on task, and accomplish goals. Groups can be larger than ten, but the probability of success is decreased in proportion to the expanded size.

The small faith community meets intentionally. It is a planned activity designed with a specific purpose in mind. It is essential that the group has a clear purpose, that objectives are developed, and that the curriculum and format flow out of the intention and design for the group. With the recent popularity of small groups, many will rush forward to join the fad without careful thought or consideration. Small groups are not magic. There will be no fruit without clear and deliberate roots.

Some groups may emphasize a specific aspect of a small faith community. For one, the primary purpose may be spiritually to deepen the faith of the group. Another group may be more geared toward sharing life issues together. A healthy, whole group, however, will resemble a microcosm of the church herself, exhibiting all five of her dimensions (see pages 210-213).

A small faith community should meet in a consistent manner, with regular frequency and at a uniform time and place. There has to be enough regularity and momentum to develop intimacy or community. Optimally, groups should gather once a week for a duration of one and a half to two hours, in the comfort of a member's home. At minimum, groups should meet twice a month. The likelihood of success is reduced in proportion to the increased length of time between meetings. If gatherings are so spread out and inconsistent that members can hardly remember each other's names from one meeting to the next, chances are that meaningful sharing will not take place. If a small group meets only once a month, it is difficult for members to maintain any type of connection. The only way that a monthly meeting can work is if the group has a significant common experience to draw upon (like a retreat) and then meets weekly for a period of time following the bonding event (six months or so). During this time, they may be able to develop rapport and a sense of community that can be maintained by the monthly meeting.

A small faith community is facilitated by adult leaders who are appropriately trained, spiritually mature, and emotionally healthy. Teens not only need positive peer relationships, but also greatly benefit by the support, experience, and leadership of mature adults. The role of the adult leader is to keep the group on task, facilitate interaction, present the content, and help guide the group toward achieving its purpose. We will discuss these skills in a more detailed manner in Chapter 12. If a parish has a strong peer ministry program, teen leaders can partner with adults to work together as co-facilitators.

The small Christian community shares life together. One reason for the collapse of many catechetically-based programs is that they fail to recognize the need of teens to experience significant and meaningful contact with one another. Young people need, want, and greatly benefit from meaningful interaction with each other. Sharing life means to "Rejoice with those who rejoice, weep with those who weep" (Romans 12:15). The concern of one member becomes the concern of all. Members share the good and the bad of their lives and know that others will pray and care for them.

A group does not instantly share life with one another. The trust needed to break open one's life with fellow group members takes time and effort. Often groups begin by getting to know one another through games, mixers, and low-risk activities. As the comfort level grows, so does the depth of sharing. Over time, teens will share their struggles, victories, faith, and even their lack of faith.

The small faith community is a place where faith is deepened and young people learn what it means to be Catholic Christians. Teens learn to know, follow, and serve Jesus, and to love, support, and minister to one another. These things happen through systematic and planned catechesis, but also through

The small faith community is a place where faith is deepened and young people learn what it means to be Catholic Christians.

modeling, example, and interaction with faith-filled community members. An important purpose of a small faith community is to sponsor teens towards greater spiritual maturity.

Finally, *the small faith community sends people out to live the mission of the church.* Members are challenged to change the world as a result of being together. The mission of proclaiming the word, living as a faith community, and serving all in need is both internally focused among the members as a community and externally applied toward the world outside the community.

Integrating the Dimensions of the Church in the Small Faith Community

The small faith community functions as a cell of the universal church. A small faith community's members live out the overall mission of the church by integrating all five dimensions of the life of the church into their regular gatherings. The five dimensions of the church are known by their Greek designations: *kerygma* (proclamation); *koinonia* (fellowship); *didache* (teaching); *lietourgia* (liturgy); and *diakonia* (service). These dimensions may not be equally balanced in emphasis during any one meeting, but over the life of the group each element must be appropriately integrated. The following sections examine how each of these dimensions are experienced within the framework of a small faith community of youth.

Kerygma

The *kerygma* is the initial evangelistic proclamation of the gospel. It represents both the act (communicating the good news) and the content (the message of God's saving activity through the life, death, and resurrection of Jesus Christ). The intended goal or response to the *kerygma* is conversion—a change of heart, mind, and action more closely conformed to the teachings, values, and lifestyle of Jesus Christ.

The *kerygmatic* dimension of the small faith community represents its evangelizing power. The *kerygma* has both an internal and external expression. First, we, the members of the small faith community, are renewed from within. We will always need to be re-evangelized. We never grow beyond the basic message of the gospel. The flames of our heart are in constant danger of being extinguished by the storms of life. The spark of the *kerygma* reignites our hearts in renewed love for the Lord.

Second, the spiritual strength that comes from being in a small faith community sends us forth in proclaiming the good news to those outside our community. As we grow more deeply in our love for Jesus and one another through our experience of community, we are compelled to share this joy with those who have yet to experience it.

Good small faith communities have the energy of the *kerygma* interwoven into the tapestry of their gatherings. As members share their faith with one another, care for one another, pray, and open the scriptures, the *kerygma* is proclaimed within and is the energy that motivates members to share the good news outside of the group.

For example, when I was in my late teens, I belonged to a small group of peers who gathered weekly to study the scriptures, pray, worship, and share life. After discussing a passage during one meeting, we were energized and renewed in our own faith. After praying together, we felt compelled to go out and share the joy of our faith. Most of us left the meeting to share the gospel with peers at a local hangout, while a few stayed back to pray for our efforts.

Koinonia

The inner life of the church is meant to be a sign to the world, illustrating in vibrant, living color the full life of which Christ spoke (see John 10:10). The two greatest commandments, to love the Lord with all our heart, soul, and mind, and to love our neighbor as ourselves (Matthew 22:37-40), are first expressed within the interior life of the church. Fruitful outreach begins with effective inreach.

Before we can call others to embrace the good news of God's kingdom, our communities themselves must be good news. The church proclaims a horizontal dimension of the good news to the world through *koinonia*, or "the fellowship we share together." Jesus said that the world would know we were his disciples by our love for one another (see John 13:35). How we live in relationship to one another as brothers and sisters in Christ is an important expression of the power of the gospel. Our unity, acceptance, and care for one another, expression of gifts to build up one another, and communal life not only benefit the members of the small Christian communities, but also serve as an evangelistic message to a world that craves real love, intimacy, and community.

Central to the meaning of *koinonia* is the practice of sharing.

Small communities of faith celebrate *koinonia*. Central to the meaning of *koinonia* is the practice of sharing. In essence, we share life together by caring and ministering to one another. *Koinonia* goes beyond the formality of the "gathering" to the informalities of daily living. It begins by establishing a safe environment and a commitment to confidentiality. Within this refuge, we bear one another's burdens (see Galatians 6:2). Teens will come to meetings with deep pains, hurts, problems, and struggles. Our community is a place where teens can unload these burdens in a nonjudgmental and caring environment. Members support, encourage, and build up one another. In addition, we pray for one another (see James 5:16), lifting each member's concerns to God as if they were our own. One of the greatest expressions of love and care for another is to pray with deep compassion for them. The shared life also includes admonishing one another (see Colossians 3:16). There are times when we need in gentleness and humility to confront one another (see Galatians 6:1). The book of Proverbs says it well: "Better is open rebuke than hidden love. Wounds from a friend can be trusted, but an enemy multiplies kisses" (Proverbs 27:5-6, NIV).

Each of the above elements of *koinonia* (sharing burdens, prayer, encouragement, and admonition) are integrated into the life of the small faith community. Teens do not arrive on the scene with innately born expertise in these practices. Leaders model *koinonia*, teach teens how to share, and provide opportunities to practice what they have learned within the safety of the group.

Didache

Members of the small Christian community are further formed and grow through the *didache*, or teaching. The *didache* builds off the *kerygma*, or initial understanding of the faith. The *didache* includes instruction on the basics of the faith, the values of the kingdom, ecclesial life, and the beliefs and practices of the church. The goal of *didache* is to bring teens to catechetical literacy, solid moral decision-making, a deeper spiritual life, and growing faith maturity. This is best achieved through focused, intentional efforts expressed through a systematic approach to themes and topics. These topics must be addressed with the felt needs of teens in mind and expressed in a developmentally appropriate manner.

In other words, the focus of the teaching should be presented in a highly relational manner. Members of the group should have an opportunity to interact with the topic and one another. Discussion, sharing, and a variety of creative learning activities should be utilized during the meetings. Meetings should be less concerned with informing and more concerned with forming. The learning environment must reflect an awareness of the freedom and dignity of each member of the group. The road to personal and owned faith is often paved with searching and questioning. To place a "detour" or "road closed" sign on this vital stretch of the adolescent faith journey would be disastrous. Over the years there have been many teens who rejected the faith because they felt rejected by church leaders when they had some serious questions. Good teaching allows for good questioning.

The adult leaders of small faith communities certainly have the responsibility to communicate the teachings of scripture and the church. But more importantly, they must witness to these teachings with the example of their lives, strength of their convictions, and depth of their love for Christ.

Lietourgia

As a community, the church comes together for worship, or *lietourgia*. Worship involves celebrating God's presence in our lives by engaging our minds, hearts, memory, and imagination. It is through worship, especially in the communal celebration of the eucharist, where the larger community comes together and expresses love, praise, and thankfulness to God. Likewise, worship is integrated into the life of the small faith community through shared prayer, songs, scripture reading, meditation, and reflection.

Small faith communities can help teens expand their vocabulary for prayer and worship by introducing different forms, styles, and expressions of prayer and worship. Our Catholic tradition has many treasures to offer and we do our teens a disservice by not allowing them to experiment with different methods, both introverted and extroverted, of prayer and worship. By offering various expressions and experiences of prayer and worship, we can help teens find a spirituality that is best suited to their personality.

Diakonia

An essential element of the church's mission is to be like Jesus and serve all those in need. Small faith communities "consider how to rouse one another to love and good works" (Hebrews 10:24). *Diakonia* is rendered from the Greek word for "service." The spiritual calories taken in through the gatherings should be expended through Christian action outside the group. Small faith communities should both inspire and equip teens to go forth and serve others and should hold their members accountable for their service. The true maturity of the group is measured by its ability to integrate its faith into daily acts of love and service. These acts can be accomplished through many individual and communal projects in service of the larger community.

Small Faith Community Meeting Format

A small faith community meeting generally includes the following sequential elements:

Element	Purpose	Dimension
Opening Prayer	To place Christ at the center of the gathering through communal prayer and worship.	*Lietourgia*
Life/Faith Sharing	To open our lives and minister to one another by sharing our struggles, victories, and faith.	*Koinonia*
Message	To learn what it means to follow Jesus as a Christian within the Catholic tradition.	*Didache* *Kerygma*
Application	To implement the good news in our lives by living it out in a practical manner.	*Diakonia*
Closing Prayer	To pray for the needs and concerns of one another.	*Lietourgia* *Koinonia*
Fellowship	To informally interact with one another while sharing refreshments.	*Koinonia*

More information on each of the elements follows.

Opening Prayer (5-15 minutes)—Most teens will arrive at the meeting after a very busy day with a lot on their minds. Opening prayer helps transition members from the hustle-bustle of the daily grind into the calming presence of the Holy Spirit. This can be achieved through a number of different avenues based on the spirituality and personality of the group. An opening prayer might be a scripture reading, a spontaneous opening prayer lead by one person or shared among members, a guided meditation, a song, quiet journaling, or any combination of these types.

Life/Faith Sharing (10-20 minutes)—The second movement encourages members to share their lives with one another. This can be done in dyads, triads, with the entire group, or in any combination. An important distinction of faith sharing from other forms of dialoguing is that it is done through the eyes of faith. Instead of asking, "What is going on in your life?" we ask, "What is God doing in your life?" Small faith community members might tell about a recent prayer that was answered, an experience of sharing the gospel with a friend, a scripture passage they found meaningful, an inspired thought or insight, or a personal struggle or victory that has occurred in their lives since the last meeting.

The purpose of faith sharing is five-fold: (1) to grow closer as a community by sharing God's activity in our lives; (2) to inspire and challenge one another with stories of God's movement in our lives; (3) to minister to one another by way of support, encouragement, and prayer; (4) to recognize God's daily presence in our lives; and (5) to become accustomed to sharing a daily living faith with others.

It is unrealistic to expect groups to be able to share openly until a level of trust is developed among the members. Initially, small faith communities should plan for less threatening mixers and exercises in order to help members feel comfortable with one another. Once this comfort level is achieved, leaders can begin to introduce faith sharing. Additionally, the adult and/or peer leaders of the group have to model faith sharing. For some teens, looking at life through the eyes of faith may be something very foreign to their experience. Like radio signals, God is always present, but teens may need some assistance in learning how spiritually to tune in. Leaders need to demonstrate and witness to God's everyday presence in their lives, using current as opposed to outdated examples.

It is also important during faith sharing that the leader facilitates ministry among the members. For instance, if a prayer need is revealed by a member, the leader should not hesitate to pause and lead the group in prayer for that individual.

Finally, faith sharing can be used to discover how each member fared in his or her attempt to apply the message of the last meeting. It is important to have some type of continuity from meeting to meeting, in addition to exercising some type of healthy accountability.

Message (40-60 minutes)—The message of the meeting should address adolescent interests, needs, and concerns, in light of the core Catholic teachings expressed through the scriptures and church tradition. The *Catechism of the Catholic Church* provides a thorough synthesis of themes. The message is best communicated informally with interaction among all members. The small-group environment does not lend itself to formal lectures or preaching.

The following five-movement learning process—adapted from the "Shared Praxis Model of religious educator Thomas Groome"[34]—can be utilized as an effective tool to promote growth and learning among teens. Four of the movements fit under the message phase. Here is a brief summary:

First, hook the teens by *grabbing* their attention. Effective communicators are well aware that the first few moments of a presentation are critical. It is during this time that an audience decides to listen attentively or daydream. Set the stage for the topic by focusing on it in a way that will be impossible to ignore.

For example, during a meeting on Christian love, I began by bragging to the group on how God has used me in the past. I followed the argument that St. Paul gave in 1 Corinthians 13:1-3 ("If I speak in human and angelic tongues but do not have love, I am a resounding gong or a clashing cymbal . . . "). While I cited my accomplishments, a teen sat next to me blowing a party horn in my face (arranged before the meeting). Eventually I was drowned out by the noise and had to stop. After the teen stopped blowing the horn, I then asked the group, "So, what do you think of my spiritual accomplishments?"

Most teens' comments reflected their inability to hear what I was saying because of the distracting party horn, or the conceited tone in which I shared my accomplishments. I transitioned to the next movement by referring to Paul's words in 1 Corinthians 13:1-3, and said, "We may do some very heroic things in life, yet if they are not done in love they can be a turn-off."

Second, allow the teens to *dabble* with the topic by sharing their own lived experiences. What is their understanding of the theme? How have they experienced the topic? How do they feel about it? Do not only invite teens to name their experiences, beliefs, feelings, and understanding of a given topic, but facilitate reflection by asking teens to reflect critically on their meaning.

For instance, in the small faith community meeting based on "love" and 1 Corinthians 13:1-3, any of the following questions may be used as a follow-up:

- ✔ When was an occasion when you felt you were loved by someone or when you felt you loved another?
- ✔ How do you define "love"? How does your definition of love compare to your expression of love? What would the world be like if everyone practiced your definition of love? What would the world be like if everyone practiced your model of love?

The third movement of the message portion of the meeting expresses the wisdom of the church regarding the topic at hand. It is described as the *gab* movement, as it is done using a significant amount of interaction among teens and leaders.

It is critical that leaders understand and clearly express the teachings of the church. Leaders, however, need not be advanced degree theologians, but should have appropriate training and resources for their roles. The tone of the leader should not be authoritative or dogmatic. We need not "assist" the credibility of church teaching by presenting it in a manner that communicates, "This is the way it is—now shut up and adjust!" This kind of "assistance" is a recipe for resistance. Scripture and church teaching are innately compelling.

For example, we might read 1 Corinthians 13:1-3 verse by verse. With each verse we might ask the teens to reflect on its meaning. The leader might intersperse some insights from a reliable biblical commentary as the group proceeds through the passage.

The fourth movement is known as *jab* because it represents an impact point between the wisdom of the church and a teen's present life experience. It helps facilitate a dialogue between a teen's understandings, beliefs, values, and actions with the truth of the scriptures and church teaching. Teens are led to apply the message to their own situations, circumstances, and world. This is done on all three dimensions of faith—trusting, believing, and doing.

While considering the topic of love, we might do a quiet self-evaluation of our lives based on the definition of love in 1 Corinthians. We may consider a particular relationship and ask, "What in the scriptures affirms my manner of loving? What challenges it?" We may seek to go beyond personal implications and consider communal, political, or economic ramifications to the topic.

Application (10-15 minutes)—The application phase of a small faith community meeting seeks to challenge members to make a connection between the message and their personal lives. (This is similar to the fifth movement—*lab*—in Groome's schema.) In other words, how can we live the message in a meaningful and practical manner? How can we integrate the truth of the scriptures and church teaching into our daily existence? The application phase can take several forms, including the following:

- ✔ Allow the group to reflect quietly and prayerfully on the message and then individually share ways they can apply the message in their particular circumstances. A variation might include meeting in dyads to discuss one another's plan of action, checking in with one another midweek, and holding each other accountable during the next meeting.
- ✔ Organize a group project that gives practical expression to the gospel message. For example, the entire group can plan and implement a fundraiser that benefits the poor.

✔ Ask the members to carry their bibles each day at school or wear a religious medal as a way of identifying themselves to others as followers of Christ.

Generally speaking, teens (as well as adults) will be more deeply invested when they have the opportunity to chart a course of action for themselves. Additionally, we must follow up during the faith sharing portion of the next meeting to see how each member fared with the application.

Application

The "Catechetical Planning Worksheet" on page 222 provides a format to record activities and resources for the message and application phases of a small faith community meeting along the movements of *grab, dab, gab, jab,* and *lab.*

Closing Prayer (10-20 minutes)—The closing prayer is generally focused on the personal needs of the members of the small faith community and is usually expressed through prayers of petition and intercession. It can be helpful for a group to share a mutual prayer list or journal. During this time, members can refer to their list to check on how each prayer need is progressing, and follow up accordingly. By sharing one another's prayer concerns, the group will become more deeply invested in one another's lives.

Additionally the closing prayer period can be used to address the prayer needs that surfaced during the faith sharing. A teen may have revealed a very difficult family situation that can use some prayer support. Or, this time can be used to pray for the integration of the meeting's message into the members' lives. The challenges faced in applying the message should also be prayed for.

Fellowship (5-20 minutes after the formal meeting)—Adolescents are always hungry—especially after a one-and-a-half to two hour meeting. Providing refreshments after the meeting will usually keep teens beyond the formal gathering time. It is during these informal times of interacting that we can build deeper relationships. This is an especially good time for leaders to check in with the introverts who are more comfortable sharing informally.

Characteristics of a Mature Small Faith Community

Over time, a small faith community that meets regularly is able to grow towards maturity. Group maturity is marked by several characteristics, including the following:

Mutual Commitment—Each member of a mature small faith community shares a common commitment to one another and to the group as a whole. Foundational to commitment is a sense of trust. Group members must come to the point where they care for one another and know others care for them. Developing this trust takes considerable time and intentional community formation on the part of the leadership. Many groups never get to this point.

Mutual commitment is lived out by some very practical expressions including:

- ✔ consistent attendance at meetings
- ✔ calling ahead of time if we are either missing or arriving late to a meeting
- ✔ actively listening to fellow group members when they are sharing
- ✔ checking on, interacting with, and praying for one another beyond meeting times
- ✔ willingness to say difficult words to one another when love requires it
- ✔ actively encouraging and ministering to one another.

These practical expressions of mutual commitment will not come without intentional effort on the part of the leadership. The following practical strategies can help assist a group in moving towards mutual commitment:

- ✔ drafting a covenant agreement that defines the nature and commitment of the group
- ✔ empowering the group to write, develop, and enforce the covenant agreement
- ✔ modeling and training group members in active listening skills, communication skills, pastoral skills, and any other skills necessary to live out the covenant agreement
- ✔ dividing the group into smaller prayer and support partners who check in with one another throughout the week.

Being part of a mutually committed and cohesive group is a great gift. It is not without its dangers, however. The flipside of cohesiveness can be exclusivity, or cliquishness. Group members' needs can be so well met that they can easily be detoured into a small-group narcissism—existing solely for themselves, and forgetting their mission to serve those outside of their community. In some cases, outsiders can be seen as threats to the group's unity, mutual relationships, and security, and therefore are driven away! Healthy community is always balanced by service to those outside the community. Our love for one another as a community is always invitational. Leaders must always keep the group focused on the mission of Christ.

Healthy community is always balanced by service to those outside the community.

Group Reciprocity—A maturing small faith community enjoys a healthy flow and balance of positive interaction, sharing, and prayer. Members mutually and reciprocally minister to one another. A sign of unhealthiness is when one or two members dominate the group with either their contributions or problems. Good reciprocity is achieved when everyone gives and receives, where members' gifts are mutually appreciated and utilized, and where members' struggles are jointly addressed.

There will certainly be seasons in teens' lives when they will be receiving more from the group than they are giving. For example, this would be the norm for a teen whose parents are going through a divorce. However, over the life of the group, there should be a general flow of giving and receiving that meets the needs of all members.

Some practical strategies a leader can implement to help develop a reciprocity among members include:

- ✔ carefully observing and monitoring the flow of interaction among members while factoring in personality types
- ✔ breaking the small faith community into dyads for discussion
- ✔ employing discussion techniques that give each member a chance to share
- ✔ encouraging quiet members to share in a one-to-one setting outside the group meeting
- ✔ positively addressing the member who has a dominating personality and helping him or her to become more comfortable with silence
- ✔ referring teens who may have emotional or psychological needs to the appropriate professional agencies.

Deepening Faith—The mature small faith community is an incubator for personal and spiritual growth in the young person. Deepening faith is characterized by growth in trusting, believing, and doing. Young people should grow to love the Lord with all their heart, mind, and strength.

First, their relationship with Jesus grows in trust and confidence. Second, teens grow in the cognitive dimension of faith by deepening their understanding of the teachings, traditions, and wisdom of the Catholic faith. Young people should leave the small faith community with a better understanding of the scriptures, doctrines, moral principles, sacramental practices, liturgical expressions, and history of our Catholic faith tradition. Third, the members of a small faith community grow in their faith by *doing*. Lives are transformed by the experience of small faith community as teens seek to integrate what they have learned into their daily lived experience.

Summary

Teens need a safe place to digest, unravel, and communicate what is really going on in their lives. The pressures they experience with friends and family, school, extracurricular activities, work schedules, and other responsibilities have molded them into "human doings" rather than "human beings," and as a result, a great percentage of teens regularly experience loneliness and detachment from meaningful relationships. Even the typical family has morphed from a place of refueling refuge to a microcosm of endless activities. Small faith communities can be those needed "safe places" that give teens a genuine opportunity to share life, deepen faith, and live out the mission of the church.

A small faith community should meet weekly to provide optimal continuity and momentum. At the very least, it should meet bi-monthly. The time span should be one-and-a-half to two hours. A workable group size could range from five to ten members. The group should be led by one or two adults who are appropriately trained, spiritually mature, and emotionally healthy. The community should ideally meet in the comfort and informality of one's home. The group should be bound together through some type of signed written agreement detailing their commitment to the group.

As a microcosm of the church, the most effective small faith community intentionally provides teens with an opportunity to experience all five of the church's dimensions through the meeting's format and structure. Vibrant small faith communities proclaim the good news of Jesus Christ (*kerygma*), set aside time to share life and faith in fellowship with one another (*koinonia*), teach the truths of the faith *(didache)*, pray and worship together (*lietourgia*), and commit to being the "hands" of Jesus to the surrounding world by applying the message learned with others (*diakonia*).

The small faith community that displays mutual commitment, group reciprocity, and deepening faith will provide teens with a chance to experience the Lord as "our refuge and our strength, an ever-present help in distress" (Psalm 46:1). A small faith community will also help teens to grow in their love for God and one another and in the desire to positively impact the world with the good news of Jesus Christ.

Catechetical Planning Worksheet

Movement	Possible Activities	Activity Type	Final Choice(s)	Resources Needed	Person Resp.
1. Grab					
2. Dab					
3. Gab					
4. Jab					
5. Lab					

Theme: ____________________ **Objectives:** 1. ____________________
2. ____________________
3. ____________________

12

Practical Skills to Help Foster Growth

One winter morning, I awoke to three inches of freshly fallen snow. Reluctantly, I threw on my coat, hat, and gloves and began to remove the uninvited tenant from my driveway. It was bitter cold outside, and I took no pleasure in leaving the comfort of my warm home.

I was ten minutes into my task, when I noticed my neighbor, Dave, making his way out of his garage with a snow shovel. We cordially exchanged greetings, whined about the weather, and then went about the business at hand.

I was about a quarter of the way down my driveway when he pushed his first pile to the side. BANG! The gun fired and the race began—at least in my mind. Every now and then I would pick up my head to see if I was holding my lead or pulling ahead. It seemed, to my utter surprise, he was gaining on me! "Work faster, push harder—I will not lose!" I determinedly muttered.

I entered the home stretch in a fury. "This race is mine," I confidently mused. I glanced over at Dave's lot to relish my gains and celebrate my soon-to-be-victory only to be stunned by the sight of Dave waving to me as he backed his car down his clean driveway.

My fury of physical movement slowed to a defeated pace. My energy was redirected to an ego-inspired interrogation.

How could I have lost? I had a head start, worked harder, and moved faster. In defeat, I hung my head, casually catching sight of my shovel. It was small, flat, and bent from years of use. Could it be? I searched Dave's driveway until I found his shovel leaning victoriously against his garage. It was modern, big, and deeply curved. My ego found solace. He had the better tool! His effort was multiplied by the use of an effective tool.

It's not so different in youth ministry. Utilizing the right tools can reduce frustration and multiply our effectiveness. This chapter will introduce some practical ministry tools and skills we can use to help foster growth in the teens of our parish. First, we will examine the role of the spiritual cultivator, comparing that role to that of the experienced farmer. In addition, we will examine several other "tools" for improving our youth programming: listening skills, principles for catechetical learning designs, catechetical lesson planning, and the "do's" and "don'ts" of question-making.

The Role of the Spiritual Cultivator

The process of growing teen disciples requires some skills related to those the experienced farmer uses to grow a bumper crop of grain, fruit, or vegetables. For example, the master cultivator walks among his crops, thoughtfully observing their condition and present state of need. This farmer keeps a watchful eye of concern, carefully considering what must be done to help the fields toward fruitfulness. The farmer also monitors the environmental conditions, the health of the growing leaves, the menacing threat of insects, the porousness of the soil, and the amount of moisture received. Let's look at how the role of the spiritual cultivator compares to the role of the farmer.

Watching

The spiritual cultivator also walks with those in his or her care, carefully observing how they are progressing in their faith. He or she asks:

> "What are the conditions surrounding their spiritual habitat?
>
> "Are they getting enough spiritual food to grow up healthy and strong?
>
> "What outside dangers threaten their growth?"

Watching is a positive and nurturing activity; it means attending with care and responding with love. It is not spying with suspicion and hounding with guilt. Watching means being personally interested in our teens. An alert leader is attentive to the situations, circumstances, vulnerabilities, and assets of those in his or her care. A watchful leader asks genuine questions motivated by sincere interest and love. He or she is able to assess the spiritual progress or lack thereof in teens, and then, in turn, address their particular needs.

Watering

Water is a critical dietary need for any budding vegetation. Likewise, the growing teen disciple needs suitable spiritual and personal nourishment to be healthy and sound. The effective spiritual cultivator helps provide teens with an appropriate spiritual diet.

We must feed our teens' faith if we want it to grow. A steady diet of spiritual junk food (activities that are very appealing and entertaining, but lack any spiritual nutritional value) will produce unhealthy, spiritually anemic disciples. Rather, the cultivator must provide a steady diet of solid, spiritual nutrition to the growing teen disciple. This includes providing experiences of prayer, scripture, sacraments, and Christian community. As a disciple begins to mature, the role of the cultivator shifts from provider to equipper; teens must be taught how to feed themselves by learning how to incorporate spiritual disciplines into their lives.

We must water our sprouting plants; too little moisture and they wither and weaken, but too much irrigating can drown a crop. The effective spiritual cultivator provides enough spiritual food to ensure growth, but not so much that a teen is left overwhelmed.

Weeding

One of the most significant dangers to a legitimate plant is the threat of being strangled by alien weeds. Thorns and thistles do not literally suffocate plants. Instead, they compete for space, nutrients, water, and sunlight. As weeds grow unchallenged, they take charge, plundering the competing plant of its nourishment and keeping it from growing to maturity and fruitfulness. The plot overrun with weeds is usually indicative of an inattentive gardener. Weeds are a fact of agriculture—and of our faith.

The spiritual cultivator is willing to address a weed. Weeds represent characteristics in the lives of teens that cause spiritual suffocation (for example, hanging around a group of friends who are a negative influence). Spiritual weeding requires speaking the truth in love (see Ephesians 4:15, NIV). It means addressing legitimate concerns in teen's lives that can threaten their personal or spiritual growth. It means caring enough to take the risk of saying something uncomfortable, difficult, or challenging.

Staking

Plants are staked for protection from wind, storms, and, if they are weak-stemmed or top-heavy, from their very selves. Stakes prevent young and insecure plants from bending, breaking, and eventually dying.

For many teens, the most memorable and significant faith experiences come not with dynamic deliveries or momentus meetings, but through compassionate adults who took the time to listen during particularly trying times in their lives.

Likewise, teens are in constant need of our support. Adolescence can be like a monsoon season in the journey of life with storm after storm sweeping over the horizon, threatening to smash a vulnerable teen in its path. If it is not an external storm advancing with rage, it is an inner one as the teen develops socially, intellectually, emotionally, physically, and spiritually. In any case, the spiritual cultivator is there to support, encourage, listen, and love. For many teens, the most memorable and significant faith experiences come not with dynamic deliveries or momentous meetings, but through compassionate adults who took the time to listen during particularly trying times in their lives. The weight of adolescent issues and crises can be heavy and jeopardize a teen's ability to stand stable on his or her own two feet. So, caring adults serve like stakes to protect them and hold them straight until the storm passes or they grow strong enough to stand on their own.

Fertilizing

Fertilization enhances a chemically depleted soil with the nutrients needed to nourish a crop effectively. Fertilization alone is useless. But add it to soil, seeds, water, and sunlight and a combination far more powerful than any of those elements standing alone is created. Fertilizing can provide that extra zip that makes all the difference in the world.

The spiritual cultivator fertilizes the spiritual acreage of another's heart by regular praying. Intercessory prayer enhances all other ministry activities. As we "watch," our first response should be prayer. The spiritual cultivator consistently intercedes on behalf of his or her teens.

Over the years, as youth ministry has continued to develop as a profession, we have become more "sophisticated" in our approach. We have more resources, conferences, programs, and activities to offer teens. Many of these are good. On the downside, however, as we have become more "competent," we have relied less on the power of God. Old-fashioned prayer and intercession has been squeezed out by endless activities. Many youth workers are so busy that they have very little time left over for prayer.

Conversion, growth, and fruitfulness are supernatural works. We need to invest our time in those activities that bring about a supernatural result. The effective spiritual cultivator recognizes the power and priority of prayer.

The Importance of Effective Listening Skills

Two men were talking with each other about life when one revealed, "I am pretty worried about my wife. Ever since our oldest became a teenager, my wife has been talking to herself a lot."

The second man replied, "I know what you mean. My wife talks to herself all the time, but she doesn't know it."

"What do you mean?" asked the first man with a puzzled face.

"Well, she thinks I am listening to her," replied the second man.

As a whole, our society does not listen very well. However, contrary to common understanding, listening is not a gift. We are not born with or without an ability to listen. Listening is a skill that can be learned. Once learned, it becomes a gift to those around us.

For those involved in youth ministry, it is especially worth the time invested to master the skills of good listening. Listening is a concrete expression of respect, care, and love. In essence, we say to teens, "You are so important to me that I will put away my own agendas, concerns, and issues to completely focus on what is important to you at this moment." Listening is an act of servanthood. We place the concerns of others above our own.

On the other hand, how do we feel when people fail to listen to us? Most often, we feel devalued, unimportant, boring to others, and basically not worth their time. When we fail to listen, we essentially communicate to others, "Don't bother me with the details of your life because I don't care." Instead of an emotionally elevating event, it becomes a demoting, denigrating experience.

Jeanette is a case in point. She is a young, married woman who enthusiastically serves on the youth ministry team of her parish. The energy and excitement she brings to the ministry is infectious. When asked why she volunteers for youth ministry, she responds with a moving story of her own youth:

> It was during my teenage years that I struggled with a number of issues, including my parents' break-up. My youth minister, Cathy, was always there to listen and understand what I was going through. She walked with me through a tough time, and I want to be there for other teens in the same way that Cathy was there for me.

The gift of listening made a lasting impact in Jeanette's life, and now Jeanette is multiplying its impact by serving other teens in her parish community.

Listening involves far more than our ears. It involves our whole body, mind, and emotions. *Listening is the whole body process of encouraging, interpreting, and understanding the essence of what another is communicating*. Effective listening can be broken down into these categories: connecting skills, encouragement skills, and reflection skills.

Connecting Skills

Connecting skills are nonverbal, physical gestures that communicate to the speaker that we are attentive and interested in what they are saying.

One connecting skill is making *eye contact*. We can say with our gaze, "I am with you, interested, and engaged." Or, just the opposite. Positive eye contact is the green light for a speaker to proceed; it assures a speaker we are interested and desire to listen. Positive eye contact includes the following characteristics:

- ✔ soft, warm eye contact with the speaker's face and eyes
- ✔ brief shifts in gaze to acknowledge and follow any gestures, such as hand movement.

Negative eye contact is, at best, a yellow light, forewarning a speaker to proceed with caution, or, at worst, a red light blaring, "Halt—stop where you are!" Negative eye contact includes cold or hard stares, eyes darting around the room, or looking away when being spoken to.

Positive eye contact must be accompanied by an *engaged posture*. Our body position should be inviting to a speaker, gently beckoning the other person to share more of herself or himself. This is best done when we express a "relaxed alertness." We want to be relaxed enough that the speaker feels at home and comfortable with us, but alert enough that we communicate active involvement in what they are saying.

An engaging posture includes the following characteristics:

- ✔ maintaining a comfortable distance from the speaker (In our culture, the distance tends to be three feet. Beyond or within three feet increases a speaker's level of anxiety.)
- ✔ being open (for example, arms and legs uncrossed)
- ✔ moving in response to the speaker (A general rule of thumb is that we match postures, gestures, and movements of the speaker. Matching involves imitating their energy level, mood, or posture.)

Encouragement Skills

Encouragement skills help the speaker to tell his or her story and the listener to follow the story. Whereas connection skills are nonverbal or physical expressions that assure teens that we are interested in what they are saying, encouragement skills are verbal expressions. For example, whether starting a conversation or stalled in the middle of one, there are times when we need gently to encourage our speaker to share. These non-forceful *invitations* give a teen an option to reveal more of what is on his or her heart. Often, the troubles of teens have a way of being tattooed on their faces. Be alert to body language. For instance, we might observe that Dee Preshen has been uncharacteristically quiet the last couple of times we saw her. We might respond by saying, "Dee, you seem down lately. Is everything okay?"

Or, maybe Valerie Dictorian appears to be nervous, short with others, and anxious. We might offer, "Valerie, you seem stressed."

Valerie might respond by saying, "I just got a B on a test in Advanced Aeronautical Engineering. I thought it would be a blow-off class." We might further "invite" her comments by responding with a brief phrase such as, "Really?" or "Tell me more." These short statements encourage a teen to continue. Sometimes we just need to let the speaker know we are with them by saying things like, "mm-hmm," or "yes," or "I see."

Often, teens exhibit hesitancy. They may be ambivalent and fearful of self-disclosure. We might respond by identifying with their feelings by saying, "I know it's tough to talk about."

Inviting questions, phrases, or brief words are meant to be just that—inviting. We cannot push ourselves on teens by forcing our way into their lives. Inviting questions or statements leave the choice of response in the hands of the speaker. Good listeners are always respectful of others.

Additionally, we need to be careful not to take off on the runway of listening only to give flight to our own ascending agendas. We must be cautious not to listen only long enough to diagnose. Then, once we've got the fix, we begin a long prescriptive discourse of advice-giving, judgment, minimizing, or reassurance. For example:

Advice-giving	"You need to toughen up and tell your teachers that they are demanding too much! And furthermore . . ."
Judgment	"You are a Christian. You shouldn't feel that way. The scriptures say . . ."
Minimizing	"Ten years from now this trivial matter will make no difference. You'll laugh that you even considered it a problem! When you're an adult you'll know what real problems are."

Reassurance "Don't worry, be happy. It will work out. It always does. When I was your age . . ."

There are some appropriate circumstances for positive reassurance and even advice-giving, but these opportunities usually take place after the person who is sharing feels thoroughly understood.

A proper use of *questioning* can be very helpful in clarifying content, feelings, nonverbals, and our interpretations. It is very important, however, that we asks questions for the good and purposes of the speaker, not the listener. Our own intentions, perspectives, agendas, and curiosities can lead us in a direction that is detrimental to true listening. Additionally, we need to be cautious not to ask too many questions, and therefore distract a teen from his or her flow and thought.

On the positive side, good questioning can clarify content. We can arrive at a better understanding of the facts and sequence of events. For instance, we might be foggy on who arrived and when, and ask Magnolia, "Who was there? What time did Mable and Morris arrive?"

Second, effective questioning clarifies feelings. We may know when Mable arrived, but we are unclear about how Magnolia felt about her being there, so we ask, "How did you feel when you saw her walk in the door with Morris?"

Positive questioning helps us clarify or check our interpretation of what we think a teen is communicating.

Third, good questioning clarifies nonverbals. When we asked Magnolia how she felt about Mable and Morris going to the party together, she verbally responded, "It was no big deal." But her sinister tone, repetitive pounding of her right clenched fist into her open-cupped left hand, and rabid facial expressions declared something very different! Sometimes a person's words say one thing and his or her body language says something else. We might respond by noting, "Magnolia, your body language seems to tell me you are bothered by the situation. Is that true?"

Also, positive questioning helps us clarify or check our interpretation of what we think a teen is communicating. Interpretive questions help us arrive at a deeper understanding of what the speaker is saying and often help the speaker better articulate or understand what he or she is thinking and feeling. For example, we might say to Magnolia, "Do I understand you correctly? You don't want to be bothered that Mable and Morris went to the party together, but inside it really hurts?"

Finally, we must be comfortable with enough *silence* to allow for our speaker to gather his or her thoughts and feelings. Though too much silence may make it seem that we have lost interest, too little silence can thwart the reflective process of a speaker. This will be especially true for teens who have a preference towards introversion. Typically, extroverted speakers do not know what they are thinking until they hear it come out their mouths. Introverts, on the other hand, will not usually say anything that is not well thought out. During these periods of silence we should continue connecting nonverbally through positive eye contact and an engaged position.

Reflection Skills

Reflection skills involve restating in our own words what we understand the speaker to mean. These statements help insure that we have correctly understood what a teen has tried to communicate. Reflecting should be nonjudgmental, concise, and accurate. Additionally, reflecting is not parroting or repeating a person's statements word for word. Often, reflection statements contain more than the words spoken, as we attempt to include the feelings and meanings behind the words. Reflection statements can be used to communicate what we understand to be the content of a speaker's words, the emotions behind the words, and a compilation of both.

Reflecting *content* provides the speaker with a concise response that states the essence of his or her content back in our own words. We rephrase what we understand him or her to be saying. Like *Dragnet's* Sergeant Friday, we focus on "just the facts." These statements help ensure we are progressing through the conversation with a clear understanding. Reflecting keeps the listener on target and assures the speaker that we are with him or her. For example:

Gomer: I would like to join that small-group community. I know I would grow spiritually, but I am afraid my grades will suffer. I have to maintain an A average.

Barney: You would like to be a part of that small group, but you fear your grades might slip.

Gomer: Yeah. That's right.

We reflect *feelings* to our speaker when we describe the emotions we understand him or her to be experiencing. For example, we describe emotions such as anger, joy, discouragement, excitement, hope, or sorrow. A young person may never describe their feelings about a situation with words. We often have to glean this information from a person's tone of voice and body language.

Gomer: School, school, school. That's all my parents think about. I am more than just an intellectual person. I am a spiritual person.

Barney: You feel frustrated.

Gomer: Yes. I want more in life than just good grades.

Summary statements are brief disclosures that summarize both the content and feelings a speaker shared. We are basically compiling the factual events and the speaker's emotional reaction to the situation. Summary statements get to the meaning of a speaker's words.

Gomer: I might earn great grades and get into any school I want. But, I am afraid I will go down my parents' path for my life and fail to know and do what God wants.

Barney: You are fearful that if you do not address your spiritual needs you will default into your parents' plan for your life.

Gomer: Yes. I really want to understand and follow God's will for my life. My parents just don't understand what I am feeling.

Barney: You are discouraged by your parents' inability to understand your spirituality.

Gomer: I just wish they understood how important God is in my life.

Application

The resource "Rate Your Listening Skills" allows youth ministry leaders individually to critique their skills as effective listeners.

We can utilize listening skills in many different youth ministry contexts. Whether it be in large groups, small groups, or interpersonal relationships, teens feel empowered, cared for, and loved when we take the time to listen.

Developing a Positive Catechetical Learning Experience

I transferred into a new college during my junior year. To make the transition easier, new students were assigned "transfer cousins." My transfer cousin was very kind, helpful, and hospitable. Her experience and knowledge of the college's procedures, locations, and expectations helped me immensely during those early weeks. It was during that time that she invited me over for dinner at her apartment. She unveiled the main entrée, a tuna casserole. Sounded great. I always liked tuna. That is, until I tasted hers! Let's just say cooking wasn't one of her better attributes. Being polite, I forced down every awful bite of that casserole. I soon exhausted my glass of water in an attempt to dilute its displeasing taste. Before I finished, swells of nausea were all I could feel.

Nevertheless, I survived the evening. However, I no longer eat tuna casserole. Today, I have an aversion to tuna casserole. When I see or smell it, I actually begin to feel nauseous again. I am reminded of that night and I lose my appetite.

Adolescent catechetical experiences can be similar. The gospel message might be a great raw ingredient, but if we don't prepare it well, it can end up poisoning our teens and turning them off to something that is spiritually nutritious.

Designing positive catechetical learning experiences can be challenging. A look at the root meaning of *catechesis* hints that catechetical training has always been a challenge. The Greek word catechesis means "to resound, to echo, to hand down." It was often used to describe the content and process of passing on the elementary teachings of the faith after the initial *kerygma.* But the real jewel is that the word was used in the early church times to describe the process of training a jackass to do tricks![35] Any resemblance to adolescent catechesis? Don't answer that!

Actually, catechesis is an important dimension of disciple-making. The *Catechism of the Catholic Church* describes catechesis this way:

> Quite early on, the name catechesis was given to the totality of the church's efforts to make disciples, to help people believe that Jesus is the Son of God, so that believing they might have life in his name, and to educate and instruct them in this life, thus building up the body of Christ.[36]

The following acronym will pull together some important learning design principles that can help "educate" adolescents in our faith:

E mphasize Interaction
D iversity of Learning Approaches
U tilize Life Experience
C ontent Moderation
A pplicable to Real Life
T hree-Fold Response
E nvironment of Concern

Let's look at each principle in greater detail.

Emphasize Interaction

I was once invited to give a short talk to a confirmation class at a nearby parish. I squeezed into a grade school desk in a cramped classroom with the rest of the sophomores until it was my turn to present. It didn't take me long to realize that the evening offered little opportunity for teens to interact with the material, the teacher, or one another. The teens' only involvement was to respond to their names when announced during role call.

As the evening pressed on, I could see the energy level of the teens rising like a swelling river with no bank left to guide its direction. What I watched next was rather amusing, but sad considering the lost potential. When the teacher turned his back to the board, the teens would mimic him and make unusual noises. Like a bursting dam, they were desperate to release their pent-up energy. Because there was no legitimate avenue to pursue, they resorted to their own creative forms of interaction. Their classroom contributions could have been channeled into something more constructive and meaningful, had interaction been incorporated in the program design.

Allowing for interaction by the teens actually communicates to them that we value their contributions. We say, in essence, your participation is important and helpful to *our* group. On the other hand, little interaction equals little learner investment. When a teen is not given the opportunity to interact and be a partner in learning, he or she concludes that the class does not belong to him or her in any way, shape, or form, but is solely possessed by the catechist. Teens respond to this discovery with passivity, or worse, passive aggression.

We can promote interaction by including plenty of opportunities for group involvement, such as discussions, role plays, case studies, simulations, games, and skits.

Diversity of Learning Approaches

Occasionally, I make dinner for the family. My cooking is certainly not the preferred choice of my children. The family dialogue is always the same:

Daniel: Where's Mom?

Dad: She is out for the evening.

Rebekah: Who's making dinner, then?

Dad: I am.

The kids in unison: OH NO! NOT PORK CHOPS!

Dad: Well, it could be worse. At least you're not getting tuna casserole!

I make good pork chops. The problem is, that's all I make. My predictability has become a sore spot with my children. They have eaten my pork chops so often that they don't like them anymore. The lessons are relevant for catechesis: good things begin to taste bad if we have them all the time. Additionally, what tastes good to me may not taste good to someone else. If I only serve what I like, those who don't share my dietary preferences end up starving.

Variety of activity is a boredom-buster. Employing a diversity of learning approaches ensures we keep interest alive. Teens learn differently. By utilizing a variety of different methods we increase our likelihood of satisfying a greater number of our participants. This means using diverse exercises and activities such as discussions, presentations, videos, journaling, reflections, problem-solving, readings, skits, and games throughout the meeting.

Utilize Life Experience

Every adolescent arrives at a session with relevant experiences. We need to capitalize on these experiences by helping draw a connection point from their life to the teachings of the church.

According to *Renewing the Vision: A Framework for Catholic Youth Ministry*, effective adolescent catechesis "utilizes the life experience of adolescents, fostering a shared dialogue between the life of the adolescent—with its joys, struggles, questions, concerns and hopes—and the wisdom of the Catholic faith."[37]

Content Moderation

An all-you-can-eat buffet looks good when our stomachs are growling. All too often, however, we eat far too much and waddle away with bloated bellies and sleepless nights of gastronomically-induced nightmares. Catechetical programs that pile on spiritual food to gluttonous heights usually only result in spiritual indigestion. Smaller meals tend to be healthier, better metabolized into energy, and better digested. Our program content should reflect the principle of moderation.

We must resist the temptation to cram many years of experience and knowledge into one two-hour meeting. A ten-cup coffee pot cannot fit twelve cups of water. Our minds are similar in that they are only capable of assimilating so much information before the container is filled to capacity. Once our minds exceed their limit, the content only spills over and is wasted. Our meetings should emphasize only one, two, or maybe three key points of content. We are on a lifelong faith journey. No one needs to know everything before their eighteenth birthday. Bite-sized content allows for better understanding, reflection, and application.

We are on a lifelong faith journey. No one needs to know everything before their eighteenth birthday.

Applicable to Real Life

When a young person describes a class or subject as "boring" or "a waste of time," what he or she often means is that "I will never have to use this information in real life." Subjects that appear to have "no real-life value" are considered by many a waste of time. This principle certainly applies to the manner in which we do catechesis.

Effective catechesis "provides for real life application of learning by helping adolescents apply their learning to living more faithfully as Catholic adolescents—considering the next steps that they will take and the obstacles that they will face."[38] Faith is a verb. It is an action word. We are meant to live it.

Three-Fold Response

Genuine faith involves a response of the whole person—mind, heart, and will. Effective catechesis helps foster faith growth in all three dimensions: trusting (heart), believing (mind), and doing (will).

We foster trusting faith when we help teens grow into a deeper relationship with Jesus and his community. We nurture believing faith when we facilitate a deeper understanding and knowledge of the core content of our Catholic faith. We promote growth in doing faith by providing adolescents with practical challenges and opportunities to live out their faith in the world surrounding them.

Environment of Concern

We may possess all of the ingredients necessary to make a cake. We may even be able to mix them all together. Still, we may not have a cake. The ingredients of a cake are dependent on the warm environment of an oven to make the transformation from mere batter to tasty cake.

Catechesis is similar. We may employ all of the above principles for effective adolescent catechesis, yet foster little or no growth. Without a warm, caring, and accepting environment, we possess only the "batter" for spiritual and faith growth. This batter is transformed into the real thing when "baked" in an atmosphere of genuine love. Catechetical leaders must help model and foster a climate of concern in the learning environment. Teens need a place where they can be themselves, question, search, and struggle—yet have the security of knowing they will be accepted, cared for, and loved.

Lesson-Planning Steps

The following six steps can be followed to develop a catechetical lesson plan for adolescents:

1. *Choose the Topic or Theme*—Our choice of theme should be developmentally appropriate, based on the needs, concerns, and interests of adolescents, and focused on the core teachings of the Catholic church.

2. *Specify Objectives*—Forty-two objectives will only overwhelm the catechist and frustrate the learner. Name two or three main objectives. Based on the theme or topic, ask: what essential points do we want the teens to walk away with? Our

objectives should address growth in the three dimensions of faith: trusting, believing, and doing.

3. *Gather Learning Activities*—Create or locate learning activities that help to achieve the thematic objectives. These learning activities can be custom-designed, borrowed from the creativity of our peers, or found in catechetical resource books or programs.

After compiling numerous options, choose those that will best fit the audience and the objectives.

4. *Sequence Activities*—Place the activities into an order that builds from one to another. Activity order should basically support a learning process that: (1) introduces the topic in a memorable way (grab); (2) draws on the teens' experiences with the topic (dab); (3) presents church teaching (gab); (4) allows for personal interaction with the teaching (jab); and (5) provides time to integrate or apply the message into their lives (lab). (See pages 215-217 for more information on this learning process.)

5. *Detail the Overall Process*—Pull the details together. How will we transition between activities? What supplies do we need? What must be done in advance? Who will do it?

6. *Evaluate*—What we do on paper does not always work out the same way in reality. Set time aside after the meeting to evaluate the content and process of the session. Were the objectives met? Were the activities appropriate for the theme and the age group? Were teens involved, invested, or engaged? If the session was not rated as excellent, what changes would increase its likelihood of being excellent? Implement any necessary changes.

Small-Group Discussion Do's and Don'ts

Small-group discussions are an important component of both large- and small-group meetings. This section examines some "do's" and "don'ts" of preparing for and leading small-group discussions.

Do prepare in advance. We should carefully plan our discussions. Focus on both the content of each question and the flow of the entire discussion. Questions should be sequenced to build one upon another. Begin with light, low-risk questions and move towards more difficult or thought-provoking questions. We should know where we are going and have a plan to arrive there.

Don't use yes or no questions. Do yes or no questions stimulate great thought or challenge? Do they provide the ingredients for a lively discussion? Do I need to say any more?

Questions are best posed as open-ended rather than as close-ended. For example, we can rephrase the question by asking, "What do you see as some of the major limitations of yes/no questions?" If we must use a yes or no question, it should be followed up with the addendum: "Please explain your answer."

Do make the questions interesting. Prepare questions that engage teens in a lively discussion, that don't lull them into a boredom-induced trance. Questions should be relevant and connected to teens' experience. Hypothetical situations, case studies, using the name of a member of the group as the main character of a question, controversial questions, and playing the devil's advocate as a leader are all useful methods to make a discussion interesting to the participants. Avoid simple and obvious questions.

Don't use questions with right or wrong answers. Why should we not employ questions that have only one right answer? (Please answer this question before reading the correct answer below.)

The primary reason we avoid this type of question is because it requires too much risk. To be told we answered a question wrong in front of a group of our peers can be rather embarrassing. Most teens are not willing to chance it. There are only winners and losers in this game. (Are you a winner or loser? Did you get it right—and therefore feel intelligent? Or, did you get it wrong and are now feeling like you have the intellectual capacity of a fruit fly?)

Do make use of content, feeling, and behavioral questions. Content questions are the *what* questions: "What did the scriptures say? What did John say?" Feeling questions ask: "*So what?* How do you feel about what John said?" Behavior questions ask, "*What now?* What are you going to do about what John said?"

Providing a good mix of content, feeling, and behavioral questions will make for a more productive discussion. They can be used to build upon one another.

Don't fish for the right answers. Fishing is great for rivers, lakes, and oceans, but is forbidden in discussions. Fishing looks like this:

Discussion leader:	Why do you think fishing for answers during a discussion should be avoided?
Sarah:	Because it's difficult to know what the discussion leader is looking for.
Discussion leader:	Yes, but what else?

Rebekah:	Because you try to answer what you think the discussion leader wants or is looking for, instead of what you think.
Discussion leader:	Okay. But, I need more.
Angela:	It's too risky!
Discussion leader:	We're still not quite there.
Deborah:	The problem with fishing for the "right" answer is that everyone who gives an answer or partial answer that is not quite right (like Sarah, Rebekah, and Angela) feels humiliated.
Discussion leader:	Exactly, Deborah! (Need I say more?)

Do answer questions with questions. When a teen asks a question, consider responding with a question. If we consistently provide the "right" or final answers on all the questions, the group will be under-challenged, and eventually become bored. We can help group members feel valued when we confidently turn questions over to them. Teens feel more deeply invested and positive about themselves if they are given opportunities to contribute in a significant manner.

Don't be afraid of silence. Silence can be a good thing. Teens with a preference towards introversion need more time to process questions than extroverted teens who tend to think out loud. Do not intervene immediately when a question is met by silence. The quality of response can rise if teens have a few moments to reflect on the question. If silence gets excessive, however, we might rephrase the question.

Do vary the approaches to questions. We should utilize different methods for discussion to avoid falling into a predictable rut. Creative approaches (for example, answering with body gestures like a "thumbs up" or "thumbs down," answering predefined multiple choice questions, or responding to open-ended questions) will reduce the potential for boredom.

Additionally, make sure to follow the energy of the group. Travel down paths that are life-giving. Even though we may have spent a considerable amount of time preparing, we should be ready to divert, especially if we see something positive and meaningful happening. Don't follow the book for the sake of the book.

On the other hand, do not follow roads that are frivolous and non-related to the topic at hand. Gossip, for instance, will energize a group, yet it is far from life-giving. Adapt intelligently.

Finally, we should read our questions to others before using them in a meeting to ensure they make sense. Ask one question at a time. Use language that is appropriate for the audience. Keep things simple and concrete and a productive small-group discussion will likely follow.

Summary

Fans of the popular television sitcom *Home Improvement* will agree that Tim "the Tool Man" Taylor always has the right tool for the job (although he often struggles with actually using that tool effectively). As disciplers or spiritual cultivators, we also need to have the tools or practical skills necessary to help foster faith maturity in teens. Unlike the Tool Man, however, we also need to be able to use such tools skillfully.

The spiritual cultivator's job description is similar to that of the farmer who cultivates his field. He must watch the crop with an attentive loving concern. He must provide the "water" (spiritual nourishment) that will foster further faith development. At times, weeding (caring enough to challenge gently our teens to remove the obstacles that keep them from experiencing the fullness of God's life) will be the cultivator's role. Staking (supporting teens through encouragement, love, and listening ears) and fertilizing (praying for the teen's growth through intercessory prayer) will also be required.

Listening is one of the most practical skills that can be learned. Listening impresses on the speaker that he or she is valued. Teens need to be affirmed in this way. It opens the doors of their hearts to the ministry we offer.

If teens are truly to grasp the truths of the faith and apply them in practical ways, we also need competently to design catechesis in a manner that is relevant to their lives. They must be given opportunities to enter into dialogue with their faith, rather than sit as passive observers during instructor-led monologues. We must offer teens a variety of activities and exercises and utilize their real-life experiences. Topics should be based on real needs and concerns of teens and on the core teachings of the Catholic church. Sessions should foster a faith response of the whole person: mind, heart, and will. The positive catechetical learning experience is one that is strategically and orderly planned and is clothed in a warm, caring, and accepting environment where teens are affirmed and loved.

Rate Your Listening Skills

Answer each question for yourself as you critique your skills as a good listener.

1. Do you politely interrupt a speaker to ask a question when you don't understand what was said?

2. Do you consciously make eye contact with the speaker?

3. Do you try to glean added information from the speaker through his or her body actions and inflections of speech?

4. Do you avoid the urge to think about what you are going to say when the speaker is finished rather than just concentrating on what is being said?

5. Do you avoid judging what is being said?

6. Do you make sure you are not trying to carry on two or more conversations at once?

7. Do you communicate your own care and compassion through your body language?

8. Do you indicate your interest by nodding or with verbal expressions like "Uh, huh" or "I see"?

9. Do you avoid pushing the speaker to share past the point that he or she is willing to?

10. Do you try to summarize what was said to you by repeating it back to the speaker in your own words?

Answering "no" to more than two questions should encourage you to develop your listening skills more. Look at your strengths as a listener and see how your development of them can enable you to improve in the other areas as well.

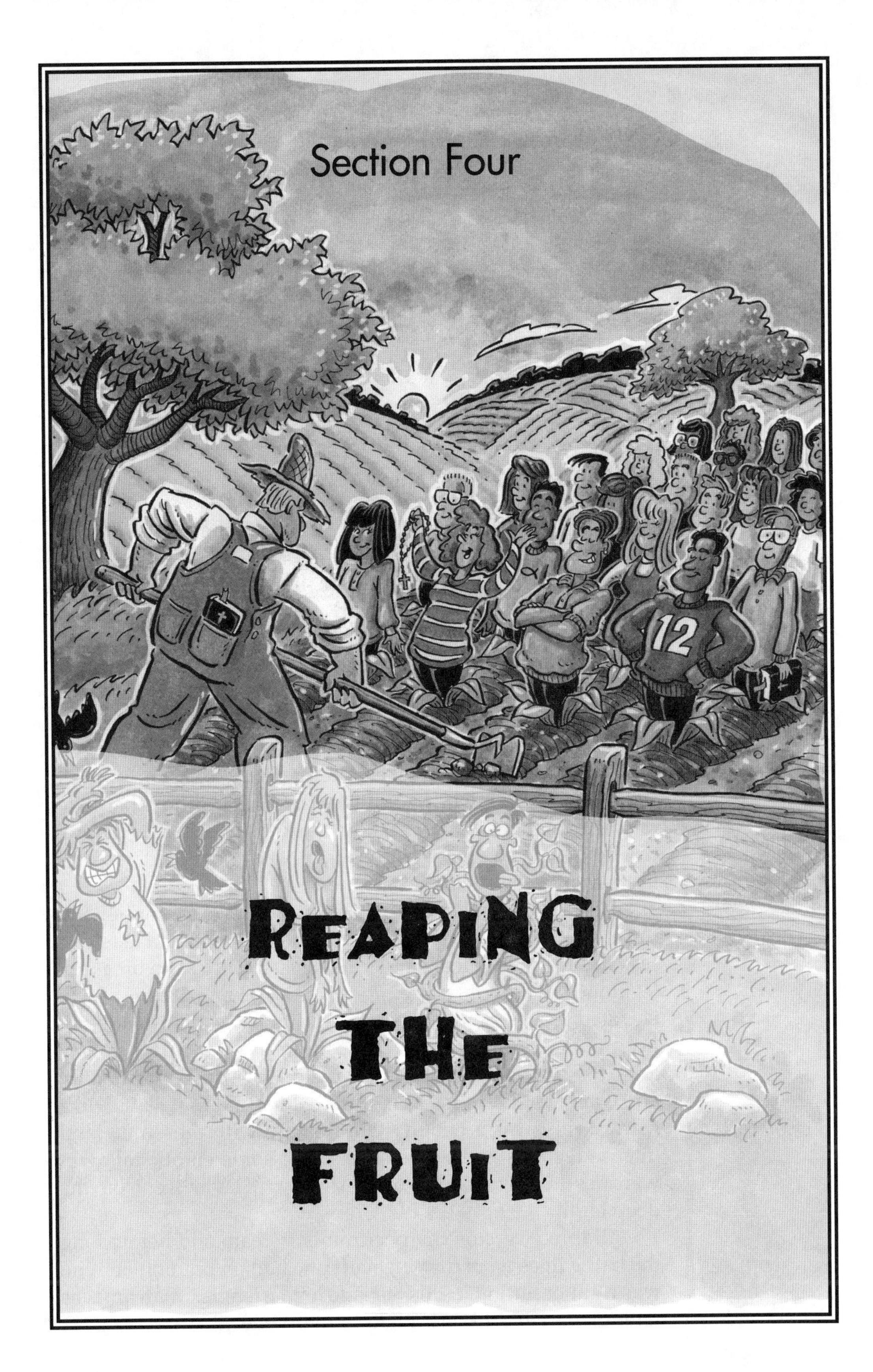
Section Four
12
REAPING
THE
FRUIT

13

MULTIPLYING THE HARVEST THROUGH TEEN LEADERSHIP

David, a popular member of our peer ministry team, was having a great junior year. Not only was David an "A" student, he was dating a very attractive senior peer minister named Nicole. However, David was not the only ministry team member interested in Nicole—so was Steven. As a matter of fact, Steven repeatedly badgered Nicole about her relationship with David. Steven didn't think David and Nicole were right for each other, and he didn't mind telling them so on numerous occasions.

David laughed off Steven's remarks as jokes and didn't seem threatened by him until the day Nicole suddenly broke off their relationship. To make matters worse, before the ink dried on David's "Dear John" letter, Nicole accepted Steven's invitation to the senior prom.

David didn't take this lightly. To say he was emotionally upset was, shall we say, a bit of an understatement. He felt he was in love with Nicole and was devastated by the breakup, let alone the thought of her going to the prom with his newly elevated "arch-enemy," Steven. Additionally, his friends noticed a change in David's disposition. David started to say and do things that were uncharacteristic of his personality and character. From my perspective, I figured that David, like many teens, was a neophyte in dealing with these new and intense feelings and was experiencing some emotional awkwardness. Others said it more simply: "David went off the deep end!"

All three were on my peer ministry team and before long the battle lines were drawn; everyone had an opinion on who was right or wrong in this teenage love triangle. My team was falling apart and I knew I had to intervene.

I gathered all three of them in my office in an attempt to facilitate some type of reconciliation and healing. The meeting began with Steven and David exchanging verbal blows while Nicole sat awkwardly, in obvious discomfort, being the object of their modern day chivalry. I mediated as best I could, repetitively going two steps forward and three back, as the boys would emotionally trigger one another into explosive exchanges. We steadily progressed until David asked to be excused for a moment to get something from his car. We needed a breather, so I readily consented.

While David was gone I started to wonder what he needed from his car. As my mind entertained all the possibilities, I kept trying to talk myself out of one crazy thought. David was obviously upset with Steven and emotionally devastated by the breakup. He was not acting like himself lately, and I wondered what was surging through his mind. I had read stories in the paper about similar incidents where people resorted to violent acts. Was David capable of this? I did not think so—he was one of my finest teens. But, on the other hand, he was pretty upset and was already doing things uncharacteristic of his personality. Good people do snap, I thought, as I was startled out of my daydream by David's shuffling behind my office door.

David stood at the entrance of my office facing Steven, Nicole, and me. He did not proceed back to his chair, but remained under the door frame with his hands behind his back. He was obviously concealing something! I swallowed heavily as a jolt of adrenaline surged through my body. "What *is* he hiding from us?" I anxiously wondered.

David then addressed Steven in a nervous and quivering voice with an introductory speech—the kind that precedes some type of momentous and memorable action—like the words one pronounces before giving out an award, or a wedding proposal, or even before an execution. "Steven, what you did to me was wrong and I feel betrayed by you. You hurt me deeply by your negative words over the year, and now you take my girlfriend," he said.

I craned my neck in a desperate attempt to catch a glimpse of what David had in his hands, but he intentionally positioned himself in a way that no one could see what he was holding. Steven and Nicole became visibly nervous as David continued. At this point, I resolved I could not take any chances. I mentally prepared for the worst—as if David had a knife or gun behind his back. I was the closest to David and as soon as I could identify a weapon in his hand, I was determined to pounce on him and save Steven from harm.

I will never forget what happened next. David was finishing his introductory speech and was about to initiate the action for which we were all waiting. His hands started to move forward from behind his back. I visually locked in on his hands and moved myself in position to tackle him. Sweat was dripping down my face as I was nearing my "life or death" cue. Then I caught sight of what David was concealing and my jaw dropped. In his hands was a small scrunched up hand towel. He proceeded to go out in the hallway and retrieve a container of water which he placed at Steven's feet. He said, "Steven, I forgive you and want to wash your feet as a gesture of my forgiveness and reconciliation." David proceeded to take off the shoes and socks of a stunned Steven. Then David washed Steven's feet. When David finished, he embraced Steven and reaffirmed his forgiveness and desire to be reconciled.

Steven, Nicole, and I sat utterly speechless. I was humbled by David's heroic actions. He was obviously applying the idealism that comes with adolescence to living out the gospel in the world around him. He read in the scriptures how Jesus, in utter humility, washed the feet of Judas—who he knew was about to betray him. David reasoned, "If that is what my Lord did, then that is what I will do."

The church needs young people like David. Developmentally, teens are in a unique place during adolescence. Their time of life is characterized by unbridled enthusiasm, energy, and idealism.

The goal of this phase is spiritual fruit—that is, reproducing the life of the Holy Spirit more deeply in the young people and those around them.

After a teen's faith is awakened (sowing) and maturing (growing), he or she enters the stage of fruit-bearing (reaping). It is during this stage that teens are trained, equipped, organized, mobilized, and supervised in service to others. The goal of this phase is spiritual fruit—that is, reproducing the life of the Holy Spirit more deeply in the young people and those around them. This phase presupposes conversion and a significant level of faith maturity. It does not, however, preclude the presence of an evangelistic, or a formational, dimension. Igniting and re-igniting the flames of faith and growing to deeper spiritual maturity will always be an important need throughout every disciple's journey. Once a person enters a new phase, the previous stage(s) must remain active and ongoing.

Jesus' first disciples entered the fruit-bearing phase when he sent them out to the villages to proclaim the kingdom of God (see Luke 9:1-6; 10:1-20). Paul taught this principle of multiplication when he exhorted Timothy to hand on the message he was given to those who could teach others (see 2 Timothy 2:2). This stage is marked by a change of focus. As

David did, the teen disciple is concerned with the needs of others and not merely his or her own needs. He or she begins to do the works of Jesus. This chapter provides some ways to draw young people into active ministry and discipleship.

Why Teens Should Be Active in Ministry

When I was growing up, my father hollered at me on more than one occasion for not taking care of his tools. Each time I left a wrench in the rain or a hammer on the sidewalk, Dad would yell: "Why don't you take care of my tools?"

I would respond profoundly: "Um . . . I don't know."

Today, the tables have turned and it's me yelling at my kids, "Why don't you take care of my tools?" And they can't give me any better answer than I once gave my dad.

However, I am a little wiser after viewing this situation from both vantage points. I now know why I did not take care of my father's tools years ago, and why my own children do not take care of my tools today. *We take better care of things we own.* Similarly, one of the reasons teens should be active in ministry is that they will come to own it, and thus take more pride and responsibility in their roles as active disciples.

Spectacular youth ministries challenge teens to go beyond spiritual spectating. Teenagers soon get bored with programs that seek only to entertain them spiritually. When we emphasize entertainment we produce spectators. Youth search for and need opportunities for meaningful involvement. When we provide these opportunities by equipping, organizing, and mobilizing teen leaders, we produce servants of Jesus Christ. As they invest themselves in the ministry, they become partners in the church's mission. This partnership leads to ownership. Ownership leads to greater excitement, responsibility, and participation. Young people will tenaciously support those things which they have worked for or created, just as anyone takes care of things that cost them something. That's what ownership is about. As the NCCB document *To Teach as Jesus Did* points out:

> Youth have a right and duty to be active participants in the work of the Church in the world. Obviously, however, they face certain obstacles because they are young and lack experience, organizational skills, and other necessary abilities. Adults engaged in youth ministry therefore should function mainly as guides and helpers by giving young people direction and support.[39]

Another reason youth should be involved in ministry is that it challenges the script of the "American Dream" for living.

I often ask teens what they would like to do for a living when they get older. I hear things like:

"I want to be a lawyer."

"I'd like to go into engineering."

"I am going into business."

I usually follow up with questions like, "Why do you want to go into that career?" If I press enough I typically hear something to the effect that "I'll make a lot of money. I'll be able to afford the things I want in life."

In other words, the "American Dream."

In the minds of many teens (and adults), the American Dream is an unchallenged assumption for living. It is the *de facto* philosophy of life for most people, and it is no wonder: its tenets are resoundingly trumpeted in every corner of life. At the heart of the American Dream is the pursuit of the "good life" in which we have lots of things, money, leisure, and comfort. And this in essence becomes the meaning of life.

As young people experience the joy of serving and ministering to others, many begin to question and challenge the assumptions of the dominant culture's American Dream. As young people serve, they begin to experience "God's Dream" for the world. The focus of God's Dream is not comfort for oneself or accumulated material riches and the status that comes with it, but love for the poor, the needy, the hungry. Serving and loving others can open one's eyes to this entirely different orientation to life. Seeing life through the eyes of the less fortunate opens the heart of a teen to answer the call to lay ministry, religious life, or priesthood.

Eric was one such young man. He was an exceptionally gifted baseball player. At the age of fourteen, he was a top-rated catcher in his state. Major league scouts were already watching him play. In high school, Eric was also a leader of his parish's peer ministry team. It was during that time that he experienced the joy of God using him to touch the lives of others. Later, in his first years in college, Eric combined his baseball skills and love for the Lord to share his faith in Latin America through some short-term missionary work.

By Eric's junior year in college, compelled by God's call on his life, Eric gave up baseball to devote all of his time to prepare for full-time youth ministry. In his mind, the chance to play professional baseball paled in comparison to the honor and adventure of serving the Lord through full-time ministry to youth.

Had Eric never experienced peer ministry and the joy of serving others while in high school and college, he may never have considered ministry as an option for his life. Positive experiences of ministry during one's high school years help young people question the American Dream for living and consider Jesus' call to "serve the needs of all" (see Matthew 20:26-28).

As mentioned previously, teens have the ability to ignite the church with their natural idealism, enthusiasm, and energy. These gifts have a tendency to evade us during adulthood. Like our childhood belief in Santa Claus, we often abandon idealism during our adult years, as we become conditioned by the cold and hard realities of life. Our idealism becomes tempered through experience. So, adults are often known to say things like:

"That'll never work."

"You can't live on love."

"It's not like that in the real world."

Adolescence gives birth to idealism because of a teenager's increased ability to use formal operational thought. This type of thinking allows teens to consider things beyond the "what is" to the "what can be." Ideals and perfection are conceptualized for the first time in a teen's mind. This is why adolescents are often so critical of their parents. They have a new ability to conceive of the "perfect parent" and they uncover daily evidence that their parents have fallen woefully short.

This same idealism is applied to living the gospel. Teens may see an injustice and say, "That's not right. Let's change it." Or, they may see a world in need of evangelization and say, "Let's go to the ends of the earth with the good news." Confronted with the same realities, adults might dismiss them with, "That's just the way the world is—we can't change it."

Great movements are very often started by young people who apply their natural idealism to addressing a pressing need or an important cause. Making a difference in the world today requires the undiluted vigor of adolescent idealism, the driving momentum of teenage enthusiasm, and the surging charge of youthful energy.

Teens need to be involved and the church needs them to be involved in active ministry. Every parish who wishes to build a disciple-making youth ministry must commit their energy, time, and resources to empowering teens for leadership and service. One of the most effective means to foster in young people a deeper and fuller participation in the life, mission, and work of the church is through the organization of teen ministries. These ministries include *peer ministry, justice and service teams, liturgical ministries, retreat teams, catechetical ministry, peer counseling*, and many more.

We have noted the important role teens play—or should play—in the mission of the church. We see that God has equipped young people with special gifts to offer. Let's consider the specific steps we as adult leaders need to take to empower teens to participate in ministry.

Identifying Potential Teen Leaders

The first step in stage three of the disciple-making process is to identify young people who are ready to move into positions of leadership in ministry. Effective ministry is directly related to the quality of leaders we develop. We must resist the temptation to recruit anyone who has a pulse. The church should never reject anyone, but leadership is not for everyone. Young people should be directed into ministries that are appropriate to their level of maturity. Youth who will *touch* other youth will possess certain qualities, as identified in the following acronym:

Application

A worksheet, "Identifying Potential Teen Leaders," using the TOUCH acronym can be found on page 258.

T eam player
O ther-centered
U sable by Christ
C ommitment
H unger to grow spiritually

T*eam player*—An effective teen minister is a young person who works well with others. This person does not seek to be the "new messiah" or "star" of the team or ministry. Instead, he or she should be willing to give freely his or her gifts in an unselfish manner, and encourage, appreciate, and support others in their particular gifts. Gift are never given for our own benefit, but for the good of others. A team player has the ability to work in a manner that is complementary to others, rather than competitive.

O*ther-centered*—An effective teen minister must be able to take the focus off of himself or herself and place it on others. Leadership in God's kingdom is synonymous with servanthood. A leader must have the ability and willingness to be a servant.

Other-centeredness must be expressed in a healthy manner. It cannot be primarily driven by co-dependency, the need to be needed. Some teens who are attracted to ministry may not be the best suited for leadership. They may be trying to meet their own real needs rather than serving the needs of others. In such cases, we need to redirect them lovingly to programming or resources that will help facilitate any growth or healing they need so that they can function in a truly healthy manner.

U*sable by Christ*—The potential teen minister must have a humble and teachable spirit. He or she must be willing to be formed, trained, and equipped. This is being usable, that is, being usable by Christ. Growth is only possible through a disposition of humility. We can never learn if we begin with the assumption that we already know it all.

C*ommitment*—An effective minister commits herself or himself to attending scheduled meetings, completing assigned tasks, and to living the lifestyle of a disciple of Jesus Christ. An uncommitted minister or ministry will make little positive impact on others.

H*unger to grow spiritually*—To be a fruitful disciple of Jesus Christ, we must have a desire to grow in our relationship with Jesus and his church. Teens in leadership positions should be those who faithfully attend to things of the heart: celebrating the sacraments, studying the scriptures, praying individually and communally. Ministry is not about doing good things for God; it's about God doing good things through us.

Remember, when looking for potential teen leaders for ministry, recruit those who are able to "touch" the hearts and souls of others.

Equipping Teens for Ministry

Once teen ministers are assembled, they must be equipped appropriately for their ministry. Adult leaders need to model, train, and supervise teens in effective ministry. The most effective method of teaching teens to minister is by example. Teens will emulate what they see in their adult leaders. If their adult leaders treat prayer as a perfunctory activity, so will they. If their adult leaders do not value people, neither will they. If their adult leaders are awkward and uncomfortable sharing their faith, they, too, will be hesitant. Teens will do what they observe the adults doing. Like the apostle Paul, we must be able to say to our teens, "Follow my example as I follow Christ's."

In addition to our example, we must help develop ministry skills in our youth leaders. Young people need to be trained in the particular skills needed for their specific ministry focus. For instance, a teen involved in leading a small group needs to be trained in group-facilitation skills, listening skills, and group dynamics. We can offer retreats, training days, and time blocks within regular team meetings to help nurture these ministerial skills.

We also need to supervise and observe the teen leaders as they are ministering to other teens. Afterwards, we should allow for corrective feedback. Over time, with some intentional effort, teens will begin to mature in their abilities to minister effectively to others. Effective ministry reproduces itself as younger teens are touched by older, more mature teen ministers. The manner of values, conduct, and style of the older teens will evolve into a teen-leadership tradition and culture that is passed down to successive generations of young people.

Formation of Teen Leaders

Leaders are not born, they are formed. Following are five suggestions for developing teen leadership. Each should be integrated into our overall approach to ministry training and development.

Be Relational!

Programs do not produce leaders. Leaders develop leaders.

First and foremost, relational ministry should expand far beyond the evangelistic door of entry. It is a foundational practice for all three phases of disciple-making. Programs do not produce leaders. Leaders develop leaders. In the same way we build relationships with all teens as a vehicle for sharing our faith, we must be willing personally to invest in our young leaders by spending time with them.

For example, every Thursday at 6 a.m. I met with the teen captains of my peer ministry team. This was my time to focus exclusively on them. My purpose for the meeting was to equip, support, encourage, and challenge them in their roles of leadership. I spent a lot of time caring for them individually as they navigated their way through the difficulties of being a Christian leader. The investment paid off immediately as I watched these young people grow in their abilities to lead their fellow peers. It was only over time, however, that I fully realized the long-term value of this investment as several of these teens became full-time youth ministers after college. Leadership is best cultivated through relationships with other leaders.

Encourage Potential!

Paul was a new convert in need of a lot of "encouragement" and a man who bore that very name arrived on the scene. Barnabas ("son of encouragement") befriended a friendless Paul after Paul returned to Jerusalem. The rest of the Jerusalem church welcomed Paul with the same enthusiasm one has for an IRS audit.

Barnabas, on the other hand, was a trusted and respected brother to the Jerusalem believers. He knew that Paul had been touched by the hand of God and had wonderful potential as a leader and missionary for the young church. Barnabas looked beyond Paul's soiled past and believed in him. Because of his position in the church he was able to sponsor

Paul's acceptance into the Jerusalem community. Barnabas lived up to his name.

Barnabas and Paul joined forces and traveled extensively throughout Asia Minor, sharing with others the gospel of Jesus Christ. While serving in this manner, a young man named Mark joined them in their missionary effort. Shortly afterward, Mark abandoned them, but had a change of heart and asked to join them again. Barnabas, seeing past Mark's youthful fickleness, generously laid down the welcome mat. Paul, on the other hand, saw Mark as unreliable and pulled up the mat. Their disagreement regarding Mark led to Barnabas and Paul separating. Barnabas left for Cyprus with Mark.

Once again, Barnabas was true to his character. He stood by a young and insecure Mark, choosing to focus not on his past inconsistencies, but his future potential. Barnabas saw something special in Mark in the same way he had in Paul. Mark did not disappoint Barnabas either, becoming a devoted disciple.

Like Paul and Mark, teens need people like Barnabas in their lives—people who believe in them more than they believe in themselves; friends who see past their inconsistencies, fickleness, and soiled past, to call them on to their true potential.

Mrs. Cairns was one such "Barnabas" in my life. She was a professor of Christian Education and taught the "Teaching the Bible" course during my undergraduate studies. She was a teacher who was able to see past my quiet demeanor. One day, after I did an oral presentation in class, she wrote to me: "I cannot say this very often, but I can say with a very high degree of certainty that you have the gift of teaching. I want to encourage you to use this gift to build up the body of Christ."

Prior to that moment I would have never believed what she said. But I trusted her opinion of me and confidence in me more than my own chorus of doubts. She inspired and encouraged me to do more than I ever dreamed. In the years since, I have tried to do for others what Mrs. Cairns did for me.

Challenge to Greatness!

The church is often guilty of under-challenging teens. We resign ourselves and with a deep sigh, settle for the minimal. We can be heard saying, "At least they are coming." Or "Let's just get them through confirmation." Our mediocre expectations are met with a mediocre response. We are often guilty of complaining about the spiritual apathy in teens, yet are completely unaware of how we actively contribute to the problem by not offering youth a worthy adventure in which to invest their lives.

Instead of conceding church involvement as just one more inconvenient activity in an already overstuffed life, why not challenge young people to greatness? Let's stop asking for their time and begin asking for their lives! Jesus did not moan or whine about the spiritual apathy surrounding him. Instead, he challenged his would-be followers to greatness with words like:

> "Come after me, and I will make you fishers of men" (Matthew 4:19).

> "And so I say to you, you are 'Peter,' and upon this rock I will build my church, and the gates of the netherworld shall not prevail against it" (Matthew 16:18).

> "I say to you, whoever believes in me will do the works that I do, and will do greater ones than these . . . " (John 14:12).

Today's teens crave to be challenged beyond the status quo of uneventful living to the greatness of God's kingdom. No one responds more enthusiastically to a worthy challenge than teenagers.

Nurture Gifts!

As represented by the following story, Dale Carnegie was a master at identifying people's gifts and then nurturing them:

> Once asked by a reporter how he had managed to hire forty-three millionaires, Carnegie responded that the men had not been millionaires when they started working for him. They had become millionaires as a result. The reporter next wanted to know how he had developed these men to become such valuable leaders. Carnegie replied, "Men are developed the same way gold is mined. Several tons of dirt must be moved to get an ounce of gold. But you don't go into the mine looking for dirt," he added. "You go in looking for the gold."[40]

Like Carnegie, we must place our focus on the gold we see in young people, like a teen I knew named Bill. Hidden within Bill's apparently average persona were the qualities of a strong leader. He was a sophomore in high school when I told him of the unearthed potential I saw in him. Bill was pleasantly stunned by my belief in him. In his own mind, he was just an average kind of guy with no special qualities. I could also see he really wanted to believe me and was even willing to act on what I was saying. Over the next two years I watched Bill evolve into a highly respected peer leader. He lived up to and even exceeded the potential I saw within him. Bill was not the same kid when he graduated. He had a new confidence and inner strength. He was a powerful influence on others, a true leader.

Producing teen leaders involves identifying both latent and obvious gifts in teens, affirming their gifts, and providing opportunities for them to both use and further develop their gifts. Young people need to know the valuable contribution they are either making or have the potential to make.

Supervise Appropriately

I was fired from one job in my life. The dreadful event occurred when I was at the tender age of twelve in a local bicycle shop. I was the third guy among my friends to land the job one week and get fired the next. My first day began with my boss dragging out a large box containing an unassembled bike. "Put it together," he barked.

No problem, I thought. I was experienced in fixing my own bike. I put together several bikes that week without any feedback from my boss. I thought I was doing great until I asked at the end of the week what days he wanted me to work the following week. His reply was simple and to the point: "None."

My boss wasn't into supervision and therefore, as far as he was concerned or could tell, I wasn't excelling in my job. Good leaders supervise those under their care. So must we when developing teen leaders.

The first step to supervising is simple modeling. They must first see me do what I expect of them. They should be able to watch me perform the entire task. In other words, I do, you watch.

Second, we begin to do it together. I still take the lead, but allow them to play an active role in the task. I can foster greater understanding as I not only demonstrate how, but explain why. Additionally, they learn by doing a limited portion of the task. In other words, I do, they help.

Third, we do it together, with them playing the lead role and me supporting. This time they are handling the bulk of the task and my role becomes one of encouragement. In other words, they do, I help.

Fourth, they do it on their own, without my involvement. It is during this time that the teen begins to exercise competency in the task.

If we do things right, we can supervise a teen into the final stage of "multiplication." This is when a fully trained teen begins the same process of supervision with a fellow teen. When our leadership enters this stage we stop growing through addition and begin growing by multiplication.

Summary

Teen involvement in ministry will foster in them feelings of ownership and investment. Relinquishing teens to the role of "pew potatoes" (if we are even blessed to get this much!) does them an incredible disservice. It screams loudly and clearly: "Your involvement is unnecessary; your contributions are unwanted!" When the "torch" is passed and shared, and teens are given the opportunity to make an investment in parish life, there will be great dividends and returns, and personal ownership will result. Teens will see the church as their own . . . as their home.

As leaders, we also need to challenge teens to look at what they are being told is the American Dream. Our culture states that happiness and significance come from things, money, leisure, and comfort. Essentially the attitude is, "The person who dies with the most toys wins." When teens become invested in their parish youth ministries they begin to see that God's Dream is countercultural. God's Dream is about serving, loving, and putting Jesus and others first.

Potential teen leaders need to be strategically identified. An injustice is done to the ministry when the assumption is that leadership is for everyone, and therefore everyone is given an opportunity to lead. This is not the case. The call to discipleship is all-inclusive, but the ability to develop leadership skills is a gift that not everyone possesses. Teens who have the ability to lead are not in the ministry solely for what they can gain for themselves, but for the team as a whole and the good of God's kingdom. They are other-centered, usable by God and their adult leaders, and exhibit sincere commitment to the team. An effective teen leader also displays a personal hunger to grow spiritually. He or she realizes that one cannot give what one does not have.

The most effective means of equipping teens to do ministry is for adults to model what this means. Through modeling, training in specific ministry skills, supervising, and providing positive feedback and affirmations, teen leaders will see firsthand what leadership is all about. Adult leaders who promote and practice relational ministry will have the opportunity to be like the apostle Barnabas ("son of encouragement") for teen leaders, encouraging their potential and nurturing their gifts. Not only does their potential need to be encouraged and their gifts need to be nurtured, but teens also need to be challenged to live a life of greatness. The gospel message is not one of laziness, spinelessness, and passivity. It is an active and incredibly demanding call on one's life.

The church will never be a complete "Body" until all of its members recognize and respond to their role within it. The church needs the unbridled enthusiasm, energy, and idealism of teens to bring it vitality and life. As youth workers, it is our responsibility to give teens the opportunity to be fruit-bearing by recognizing and affirming their unique contributions, and equipping, empowering, and providing meaningful opportunities for them to serve and minister in their parishes and beyond. If this can be accomplished, church as we know it today will look radically different in the years to come.

Exponential growth will occur in parish youth ministries when teen leaders rise up to Jesus' challenge to make disciples of all nations. St. Paul exhorted the young Timothy: "Don't let anyone look down on you because you are young, but set an example for the believers in speech, in life, in love, in faith and in purity" (1 Timothy 4:12, NIV). As youth workers, we must express a similar sentiment to our teen leaders if the harvest is to multiply.

Identifying Potential Teen Leaders

The first step in developing teen leadership is to identify potential teen leaders. The acronym TOUCH can help with this task. Brainstorm a list of names of teenagers for each category. Discuss and compare the names you have for each category with other adult leaders as a way to determine which teens you will invite to particular ministries.

T Who are **team** players? (Who are teens who work well with others?)

O Who are **other-centered?** (Which teens have the ability to take the focus off of themselves and place it on others?)

U Who are **usable** by Christ? (Who are teens with a humble and teachable spirit?)

C Who are **committed?** (Which teens are already committed to keeping on schedule, completing assigned tasks, and living the lifestyle of a disciple of Jesus Christ?)

H Who have a **hunger** to grow spiritually? (Who are teens who accomplish great things through God's working through them?)

14

Planting a Fruitful Peer Ministry Team

It was six in the morning on a cold, early spring, school day, and our parish center was packed with well over one hundred teenagers. Why would so many teens gather so early, when it was so cold?

Because they wanted to be on our peer ministry team.

Five years earlier I could hardly convince a handful of kids to consider such an option. The spiritual condition of our youth ministry at that time could have been likened to a group of teens tentatively wandering along the edge of an in-ground pool on a hot day. No one was willing to immerse themselves in the water because it seemed too chilly. Besides, no one wanted to be the first one in the pool. What if no one else joined them? So, they would figuratively walk around the rim and grimace while testing the water with their feet.

It was within this contextual image that my first peer ministry team of four emerged. They affectionately referred to themselves as "The Divers." They coined that term to distinguish themselves from those who were paralyzed in spiritual immobility because of hesitancy, indifference, and fear. They were willing to commit themselves fully by diving into the waters of spiritual commitment and leadership. As they boldly entered the pool of peer ministry, they provided other teens with the example, courage, and motivation to follow. They began meeting weekly at 6:00 a.m. as an indicator to others that being a part of this team required dedication. They committed themselves to daily prayer and active service, a lifestyle "worthy of the gospel." Their impact rippled through our parish and community. Five years later, our ranks were swelled with teens who were touched by these leaders and hoping to touch others in the same manner. Our youth ministry's impact was multiplied significantly through peer ministry.

What Is Peer Ministry?

Peer ministry is simply teens ministering to fellow teens. Teens are *very* effective in reaching their own. If they weren't, teens would not have such a problem with peer pressure. Peer ministry seeks to make a positive application to the influence teens have on one another. During adolescence, a teen's primary reference for approval shifts from parents to peers. Also, teens are more likely to seek out peers for advice than they are parents, teachers, or youth ministers. Besides, teens have greater access to other teens. They spend most of their time with their peers at school in such activities as sports, clubs, and parties.

Teens are *very* effective in reaching their own.

Peer ministry works. Many successful Catholic youth ministries are investing time, energy, and money into developing peer ministry teams.

Peer ministry teams are comprised of about six to twelve teens who contribute their gifts and work together to minister to their peers. A team should be made up of both male and female members and meet together at least once a week. They should have at least one adult youth worker, preferably two, facilitating the group. Additionally, each team ideally should have both a male and female teen captain to help lead the team. The captains should be juniors and seniors who are respected leaders and both spiritually and emotionally mature. In larger parishes, a peer ministry program may have two or more teams that meet separately for regular meetings, but come together for larger activities like a service project or retreat.

Why Peer Ministry?

During my first couple of years in youth ministry I designed the flyers, ran the games, gave the talks, and led the discussions. From set-up to take-down, I did it all, and I did it well.

Occasionally, I would allow a couple of teens to get involved in the meetings. I noticed that there was usually an increase in attendance, enthusiasm, and attentiveness on these occasions. The funny thing was that though I was the more skilled leader, the teens seemed to command a greater response among their peers than I did. Finally catching on, I gave more and more responsibilities to teen leaders, and I found our attendance doubling, our impact multiplying, and our teen leaders becoming more invested and skilled.

Youth listen to and are more likely to apply what they hear from their peers rather than the "archaic" information they hear from Geritol-ingesting adult leaders. The gospel message becomes credible to a young person when it is lived and proclaimed by a peer. Teens reason, "Adults need to start thinking about God and eternity. They're old and will probably be kicking off soon, anyway. They had best be prepared." However, when a fellow teen shares the same gospel message—because they are going through the same struggles, trials, and stresses of life—their words cannot be so easily dismissed. Besides, teenagers aren't motivated by the statistical probability of "kicking off" soon!

Why peer ministry? Simply because parish youth ministries will multiply their impact with the investment. Peer ministry makes the gospel message more credible and relevant to many, many teens.

Characteristics of an Effective Peer Ministry Team

A healthy and effective peer ministry team is known by several characteristics. First and foremost, the peer ministers must be *equipped to succeed*. It is important that we do not set young people up for failure by not preparing them adequately.

This characteristic was brought home to me a number of years ago when my twins were small. At that time we were involved in an organization that held an annual race called the "Pinewood Derby." I was inexperienced, but my kids confidently put their trust in me. They also put some rectangular pine blocks, axles, and wheels in my hands a couple of weeks before the race.

Not knowing what to expect, I called my good friend Jay, who was a veteran of the Pinewood Derby. He assured me that the event was all for fun—"no big deal"— and that the kids should really do most of the work on the cars. "Many of the cars never even make it down the track!" he laughed.

So we went to work. I cut the wood, but for the most part I encouraged my then eight-year-old twins to have fun with the project and not to worry about little things like perfectly straight axles, rough edges, or paint drips.

On race day we lined up our little cars on the judge's table before the competition. To our dismay, the other cars weren't exactly what we anticipated. Let's just say that most of the parents either had well-equipped workshops or consulted with an Indy team of engineers! My friend Jay's kid's car may have been the best of all—it looked as if it just came from the Ferrari showroom. So much for our chance at a trophy for design.

Well, I thought, all is not lost. Maybe we can make up for the mild humiliation with our blinding speed. "Speed over beauty," I reminded my embarrassed little twins. My daughter Sarah's first heat arrived and she lined up next to one of those polished beauties for a two-car race. She was not only beaten soundly, but her sad little car never made it to the finish line. It slid to a pathetic halt about two-thirds of the way down the track.

As our competitor proudly retrieved his car from the finish line, the room quieted to a hush. Necks craned as the entire room anxiously awaited a chance to get a glimpse of the loser who crafted that miserable car. I will never forget the look in Sarah's eyes from a few yards away. Without words, she was pleading, "Dad, you get the car." I looked at her just long enough to feel guilty, but turned away, essentially saying, "I'm not getting that thing. You're on your own, little girl." There was no way in the world I was going to get that car and identify myself with its dismal appearance and performance. The rest of the evening, if not my kids' cars, went downhill from there. It was the last time we were involved in a Pinewood Derby—and that organization for that matter. We were too humiliated to show our faces again.

Looking back, I see that it wasn't my finest fathering moment. I should have rescued poor Sarah—after all, it was my fault. (Or maybe it was my *ex*-friend Jay's fault!) But, on the bright side, the whole experience did drive home the lesson on preparation.

There is nothing worse than being thrown into a situation in which we are ill-prepared and do not know what is expected of us. To ensure that our peer ministers are equipped in their roles, we must make an assessment of what skills are needed to perform their ministry competently. If they are expected to evangelize, then they should be trained in how to share their faith. If they will be performing skits, they should be taught some basic drama skills. If they are expected to give talks, they should be given speaking preparation and delivery skills. Good preparation eases anxiety in new situations and fosters both competence and confidence.

Ministry training can be done in a variety of different ways. Teens can be prepared through training retreats or camps, day-long sessions, or in-service evenings. Or, training can be integrated into the normal format of regular meetings. A combination of the above is also effective. The important thing is that peer ministers are trained and prepared for their ministry.

A second characteristic of an effective peer ministry team is that it *operates as a Christian community.* Good ministry does not come out of an individual's isolated ventures. It comes from the mutual support and efforts of an entire team of teens. As Margaret Mead wisely stated, "Never doubt that a small group of thoughtful, committed citizens can change the world; indeed, it is the only thing that ever has."[41]

Community-building is essential during the early stages of a peer ministry team's development. A team that invests time into growing to love and trust one another will be better able to address the adversities that come in ministry. Without developing a cohesive group, a team stands vulnerable to attrition and conflict during tough times. Teams can succumb to in-fighting as a result of frustrations that are bound to occur in their ministry.

Oppositely, a team that functions as a Christian community finds support, solace, and strength within. This in turn equips and refreshes them to reach out.

When a team functions as a Christian community it becomes a place where members' gifts are discovered, practiced, and appreciated. It is also a place where members are taught to care enough about one another to challenge each other when needed. Put-downs, which are a common staple of normal teenage conversations, are cultural taboos within an effective peer ministry team. When put-downs are detected, some savvy teams require the perpetrator to give three "put-ups" as atonement. "Put-ups" are positive, up-building statements about another person. These kinds of practices ensure a profitable experience among members and help community life to be a "fill-up" for ministry as opposed to a drain.

Teens need to minister out of a full reservoir of God's love.

Jesus said his disciples would be recognized by their love for one another (see John 13:35). This distinguishing characteristic has to be constantly maintained and balanced. The flipside challenge of a group that operates well together is exclusiveness. A group can easily settle inward as members enjoy the support, security, and friendships of good community. When this happens a peer ministry team can exist for its own purposes and neglect the needs outside their group. Inreach must be held in constant tension by focused outreach. A peer ministry team will be very effective when it is balanced within these tensions.

Like adult youth workers, peer ministers must understand that ministry is intimately connected to spirituality. Teens need to minister out of a full reservoir of God's love. Adult leaders must model this in their own lives and integrate this priority through the organization of the peer ministry team's activities. Scheduling a peer ministry team with activity upon activity without the benefit of spiritual refueling provides a poor example of ministry and sets the group up for burnout.

Though teens may be serving others within the third phase of the discipling process, they must continue *to grow actively through spiritual and faith formation.*

A peer ministry team that ignores its need to walk in an intimate relationship with Jesus will always be in danger of making ministry a scripted set of lifeless lines and Spirit-absent activities. Adult leaders must help peer ministers value spiritual and faith formation, and practice it in their daily lives.

We can integrate time for spiritual growth in our regular meetings, retreats, days of reflection, or evening experiences. The important thing is to make these opportunities a regular occurrence. We cannot be spiritual binge eaters. Starving ourselves over long periods of time and then spiritually feasting can be unhealthy. Healthy spirituality is comprised of consistent spiritual nourishment.

Another characteristic of effective peer ministry is that it *allows for meaningful and appropriate service.* Anyone who has worked with teens for several years has heard requests similar to:

> Hey, we got da Big Bingo Blast going on Friday night and need some of those yutes to clean up afterwards. How many can we count on? Those free-loading rascals need to be pitching in to the efforts of this parish, too. When we were kids we cleaned up after every adult party and. . . .

Now, I am not opposed to teens supporting the parish by helping with clean-ups, set-ups, take downs, or any other menial tasks. I am, however, against teens being consistently *used* by adults as convenient janitorial crews for adult social events. Teenagers need to serve in a meaningful and dignified manner. No one should ever feel used after serving others in the church.

A positive outline for a peer ministry team's service, rather, should be geared to reaching out to their peers through evangelization. This can be done through one-on-one interaction, small-group and large-group meetings, retreats, overnights, social activities, and more. It is critical, however, to reach local teens. It is within this pool that our future peer ministers reside. Without attending to this group, a peer ministry team may have a short life-span.

Additionally, a peer ministry team can serve the parish through supporting grade school and middle school religious education efforts, justice and service programs, liturgical ministries, and retreat-planning teams.

Some peer ministries have individual teams devoted to different efforts. For instance, there may be a team that primarily concentrates on middle school religious ed. Another group may focus on helping to maintain the parish food bank, a third on supporting the parish school's afternoon day-care program.

Peer ministry teams can also be divided by the particular gifts of their members. For instance, there may be a skit peer ministry team, or a presentation peer ministry team, or a hospitality peer ministry team. Or peer ministry may do all of the above activities throughout the year. This gives them opportunities to discover new gifts and develop established ones as they experience the various ministries of the church.

The service peer ministers are engaged in should not only be meaningful, but it should be appropriate. Remember, teens should not be put into situations that are beyond their training, development, or age.

A fifth characteristic of peer ministry teams is that they should be *consistent in their prayerfulness.* The following incident relates the importance of this well:

> One evening we assembled one of our peer ministry teams for a night of video taping. They had put together a skit that had a major impact on the teens of our community. We thought it could be a strong contender in a national video production contest for youth groups. The night began in disaster as our young videographer could not figure out how to work our rented camera. Then the smoke machines for one of the scenes triggered the church's smoke alarm, at which point the city's fire department arrived in full force. Everything was going wrong!
>
> Finally, in desperation, one of our peer ministers yelled, "Why don't we pray?" I am embarrassed to say that I neglected this significant detail. While we were gathered in a circle praying, each of us could sense a wonderful peace coming over us. Our anxiety and edginess dissipated like a blinding fog burnt by the heat of the morning sun. While still in prayer, our videographer, who was still wrestling with the camera, yelled, "It's working! I figured it out!" The remainder of the evening went off without a hitch.

Prayer works that way. It's not magic, but it does give us what we need in every situation. We were meant to rely on this source of strength, guidance, and peace. It is our fuel for ministry. An effective peer ministry team understands the place and primacy of personal and communal prayer. As we get together as a team, intercession should be an important part of what we do. There should be a consistent attitude and practice of prayerfulness. Our decisions should be based in prayer, seeking God's wisdom for the situation. Our projects should be bathed in prayer, asking God's blessing upon each facet of a program or event. This kind of dependence on prayer does not come naturally to a team. It needs to be modeled by the adult leadership. Too often, as in this case, we wait until we are frustrated before we begin to pray.

Peer Ministry Team Meeting Format

There are many elements that make up a peer ministry team meeting or a series of meetings. The elements described in this section can be included sequentially in a single two-hour meeting, or divided over several different meetings. For example, a peer ministry team might focus on prayer, community-building, and faith formation at one meeting, and then on prayer, ministry training, and ministry preparation at the next meeting. The key is to ensure peer ministers are receiving a steady diet of all five elements throughout the year even if it means they are receiving some of these elements in programs separate from the peer ministry meetings.

Prayer is the pasta of spiritual gatherings. It should be a staple for every peer ministry meeting.

Prayer

I am from an Italian family. We grew up with pasta as a dietary staple. While other kids in the neighborhood were eating potatoes with their meals, we were eating spaghetti, rigatoni, and linguini. Pasta went with every gathered meal. Prayer is the pasta of spiritual gatherings. It should be a staple for every peer ministry meeting, though it may be served in different styles or forms (quiet reflection, petition, meditation, contemplation).

Meetings should always open or close with prayer, allowing for extended prayer at least one of those times. Personal concerns, ministry projects, and daily activities should all be a focus for prayer. We should also offer opportunities for worship, praise, thanksgiving, reflection, and intercession.

Community-Building

Community-building should be a major focus during the early stages of a new team's development. We can offer mixers, games, faith sharing, and other types of interactions that help facilitate sharing, openness, and trust. As a group grows as a community, this time will be spent sharing with one another the ways God is active in our lives. We may introduce it with, "What is God doing in your life?" Or, "How is everyone?" The key is to create a place where teens feel comfortable sharing their joys, concerns, and pains.

Faith Formation

Peer ministry without ongoing faith formation is like a football team without a generous supply of the latest sports drink. Eventually the team will collapse on the field for lack of physical energy. Peer ministers must be spiritually fed. The energy expended through active ministry must be replenished through ongoing faith and spiritual formation. They should be continually challenged to grow in their Catholic identity and their understanding of key disciplines like scripture, church history, spiritual disciplines, and sacramental life.

Ministry Training

Peer ministers must be equipped with essential ministry skills. This includes learning how to listen, facilitate discussions, give talks, lead prayer, and evangelize peers. Teens should have some time to process and reflect on the practice of such skills.

Ministry Preparation

Peer ministers need an appropriate amount of time to plan, organize, and develop their ministry activities. Before sending teens out, we need to make sure they are organized and prepared to do their tasks. Cutting short the time to be creative and prepare usually results in a lack of quality. When meetings appear to have been thrown together at the last minute, an audience usually feels devalued, as if they are not worth a team's time to do things well. This, in turn, devalues the gospel message. Skits and talks should be memorized, game directions rehearsed, discussion questions reflected on, and handouts completed. The time spent in preparation is well worth the investment. Team members feel better about doing an excellent job, and the participants feel better about coming.

Recruiting Potential Peer Ministers

As with recruiting adult leadership, recruitment of teens for peer ministry should be approached both broadly and selectively. The broad approach is an appeal to any teen in the community. This is principally done through bulletin articles, flyers, mailings, Mass announcements, meeting announcements, bulletin board advertisements, newsletters, and phone networking. The broad appeal invites everyone to consider applying.

The advantage to this approach is that everyone feels included. Young people won't feel like it is an elite society that is accessed only by the few. Another important advantage is that we do not miss any possibilities. We may not know all of the potential peer ministers in our parish, and therefore, miss some excellent candidates. This is especially true for quiet teens or teens who may have only recently moved to the area.

The broad appeal raises the awareness of more people than a selective approach. It does not, however, motivate more people towards involvement. On the other hand, the selective approach first identifies teens who have the qualities of potential peer ministers. Second, these teens are personally invited to apply for the team. Prospective peer ministers can be identified by taking recommendations and fathering lists from several sources, including:

- ✔ adult leaders in various programs
- ✔ current peer ministers
- ✔ the pastoral staff
- ✔ teen participants in various programs.

Once potential peer ministers are identified, they need to be contacted in some personal manner.

Once potential peer ministers are identified, they need to be contacted in some personal manner. They can be sent a handwritten letter stating that they have been identified as a person who has the qualities of a potential peer minister. If nothing else, at least they may walk away affirmed by the letter. Teens can also be telephoned and spoken to in person. The key to the selective approach is to make the contact personal.

Timing of peer ministry team recruitment is also critical. Summer is the worst time of the year to recruit because many teens may not be around due to vacations and the lack of ongoing parish youth programming. Scheduling a recruitment campaign after a major impact event sponsored by a peer ministry team (for example, a retreat), usually elicits interest from many motivated teens. Spring is usually the best time to recruit new peer ministry team members. Formation and training of the new team can begin during the summer months, while active ministry might start with the fall semester.

Combining both the broad and selective approach helps ensure we personally invite teens we have recognized as potential leaders, and not miss those hidden diamonds of whom we are unaware.

The Introduction Meeting

After inviting potential peer ministers, an introductory meeting is planned and held. This meeting has two primary objectives: (1) to communicate a clear understanding of what peer ministry is, and (2) to influence and motivate the teens to apply for the team.

Both teens and their parents should be invited to the introduction meeting. For parents to support their child, they will need a clear understanding of the ministry. Both parents and teens should walk away from the meeting with a firm grasp of:

- ✔ the vision and purpose of peer ministry
- ✔ the activities, programs, and ministries a peer ministry team may participate in
- ✔ the time commitment
- ✔ the application and selection process
- ✔ the expectations for involvement.

All of the above information should be communicated both verbally during the meeting and also through printed information sheets that can be taken home and read. Additionally, a question-and-answer time should be set aside at the meeting.

The second purpose of the introduction meeting is to motivate teens toward involvement. This is best done by communicating the vision of peer ministry, its outreach efforts, and the personal benefits of participation. A slide show, a video presentation, or a witness talk by a current peer minister may make up an important part of the meeting. There are plenty of activities competing for teens' time. It is essential that we do an excellent job in motivating them towards involvement.

Application

The resources on pages 273-282 provide several of the information and registration sheets needed for potential peer ministry team members. The resource on page 283 provides a sample outline of a peer ministry introduction meeting.

The Application Process

The application process for peer ministry sets the tone for the entire experience. A team with little or few requirements for participation may later suffocate under its own weight. Easy and carefree access to peer ministry usually results in easy and carefree exits.

On the other hand, our application requirements should be in line with the maturity of our youth ministry. As the peer ministry grows in quality of leadership, so can our expectations for involvement. First-time peer ministry programs will do well to avoid having an application process that exceeds that of Harvard or Yale.

Consider gleaning the following information as part of the application process:

1. Parental recommendation—Parents should be included in the peer ministry application process. It is critical that parents are informed about what their child wishes to join. Their initial understanding of the program will ensure their future support. Additionally, parents have insights into their sons or daughters that can be very helpful as we consider a teen's potential involvement. Some teens think they have time for everything that is appealing to them. Parents will often provide a more realistic perspective.

2. *Adult sponsor recommendation*—An adult sponsor can be a teacher, church leader, coach, neighbor, family friend, or mentor. The answers from this form provide another important perspective. Often, this person can give us insight into what it is like working with a particular teen, or how a teen relates to adults, or how a teen interacts with and functions with other peers and in other organizations. This can be a valuable perspective.

3. *A lifestyle covenant*—A lifestyle covenant is an agreement among team members on how they will live and witness as peer ministers. The agreement is stated as a covenant and not a contract because its tenets are written in the context of how the teens will relate to one another as peer ministers. Without a Christian lifestyle to which they are accountable, a team can quickly lose its credibility. Applicants should sign and date a covenant agreement in order to be considered for peer ministry.

4. *Teen application*—This application gives teens an opportunity to evaluate why they want to be involved in the peer ministry program. It consists of essay questions. A teen's answer to these questions can provide valuable insights into who they are, what motivates them towards involvement, what they feel they have to offer a peer ministry team, and their current spirituality.

5. *Personal interview*—A personal interview is a very helpful screening tool, especially in larger parishes where some teens may not be well known. Additionally, there is nothing like face-to-face interaction. Interview questions can be follow-ups to the written portions of the application process. We may read something of interest or an apparent contradiction in answers and ask a teen to elaborate on it. Or interview questions can be completely new.

The Selection Process

Long before we decide which individuals will comprise our teams, we must establish our criteria for membership. What do we expect from entry-level participants? For instance, must they be upper-class high school students? Should they have received the sacrament of confirmation? Should they exhibit a certain level of emotional and spiritual maturity? Also, should we expect certain skills, or moral positions, theological perspectives, or lifestyle behaviors? And, do we only have room for a certain number?

The answers to these questions depend on our parish context and the maturity level of our youth ministry. A very young youth ministry program cannot ask teens to demonstrate a faith maturity that exceeds the program's formational capabilities. On the other hand, a youth ministry that has a strong history and more applicants than they can put into service can ask much more from teens. The important thing is to establish some type of criteria based on the present situation.

Once common criteria are agreed upon, a selection team (usually comprised of the adult peer ministry leaders) must come together to prayerfully consider each teen application. A teen's application forms, recommendations, and personal interview (if applicable) should be discussed and considered. The adult leaders should individually and communally pray for each applicant and discern who is to be on the team. All decisions should be reached unanimously.

Some youth ministries are uncomfortable turning away a teen for any reason, yet its leaders know that peer ministry requires a certain level of maturity. To negotiate the tension, some have made their application process extensive enough to weed out those who are not fully ready. The process is designed in such a way that most teens discover their own level of readiness and either proceed forward or discontinue.

Once a team is chosen, a congratulatory letter or personal phone call should be sent out to each new peer minister. Personal meetings—held before the new peer ministers are informed of their acceptance—should be set up with teens who did not get selected to explain why in a sensitive manner. Additionally, those who did not make a peer ministry team should be given some other appropriate options for involvement. This should always be handled with the utmost care. We should leave a teen with viable options for involvement, and a sense of hope and encouragement towards peer ministry participation in the future.

Summary

Peer ministry (teens ministering to fellow teens) is perhaps the most effective means of spreading the gospel among this age group. Peer ministry is a positive form of peer pressure. Teens actually listen to one another better than they listen to adult leaders. Teens recognize one another as credible and have greater access to each other. Because of such realities, one can logically and practically deduce that peer ministry is a critical piece of a thriving parish youth ministry. Truth be known, successful Catholic youth ministries develop teen ministers.

The effective peer ministry team is one that equips its members to do impacting ministry. A vibrant peer ministry team operates as a micro-Christian community, building one another up, loving one another, and avoiding an attitude of exclusivity. Its members see themselves as the "body of Christ," not a bunch of renegade, rugged individualists on a "mission from God." Members are nurtured, grow in the faith, and are assigned meaningful and appropriate responsibilities. Most importantly, the effective peer ministry team finds its source of power and strength through a consistent attitude and practice of prayerfulness.

A typical peer ministry team meeting format includes prayer, community-building, faith formation, ministry training, and ministry preparation. Recruiting potential peer ministers includes such pieces as broad and selective recruitment approaches, a peer ministry introduction meeting, an application process, and a period of prayerful reflection on potential members.

When McDonald's began to market chicken sandwiches, it became the world's largest distributor of chicken. When it decided to promote Matchbox cars and include the little hot rods in its Happy Meals, it also became the largest supplier of Matchbox cars in the world. Essentially, when McDonald's decides to distribute most any product, it literally corners the market. Why? Because of the tens of thousands of restaurants it has around the globe. Who can compete with such an entity? When the church, with tens of thousands of "branches" around the world, promotes peer ministry as a part of its overall youth ministry structure, it will actually see its call to "make disciples of all the nations" come to fruition.

Peer Ministry Information Form

The ______________________________ Peer Ministry Team involves high school teens in grades 10 through 12 in serving, leading, and supporting their peers as they develop a deeper experience of God's love.

Through skits, talks, games, prayer, retreats, and personal example of Christian living, the peer ministry team will help foster in their fellow teens a life-changing encounter with Jesus Christ.

Team members should: have a personal understanding of Christ and an openness to growing in faith, have a desire and willingness to share that understanding with others, be spiritually and emotionally healthy, be free of serious wrong-doing in their life, and be enrolled in high school.

Applicants need to know and understand that this commitment to the peer ministry team involves a deep responsibility in time and challenge. Consistent attendance, a commitment to daily prayer, and the willingness to serve peers is essential. Warning:

Your involvement in peer ministry could change your life.

A member of the peer ministry team will experience hard work, the support and encouragement of a faith community, a sense of fulfillment and accomplishment, spiritual challenge and growth, the satisfaction of serving others, and lots of fun.

ADDITIONAL INFORMATION

Commitment is from ________________________ to ____________________ .

Team members are required to attend (weekly or bi-monthly) team meetings.

Team members are required to prepare for peer ministry by attending

____.

Step-by-Step Peer Ministry Application Process

Please read the following procedures for applying for peer ministry. Please note that the applications must be submitted on or before the due date listed in Step 7.

STEP 1

Attend the Informational Meeting on ____________________ or make arrangements to find out information presented that night.

STEP 2

Read the information and prayerfully consider your call to serve on the Peer Ministry Team.

STEP 3

Discuss this commitment with your parents. Have them fill out and sign the parental information/release form.

STEP 4

Fill out the teen application form as completely as possible.

STEP 5

Carefully read the Covenant/Lifestyle Agreement. Sign it if you are willing to adhere to it.

STEP 6

Ask an adult who knows you well and is not your parent to fill out the Adult Recommendation form.

STEP 7

Return the completed forms by ____.

STEP 8

Once your Application packet is received, a personal interview will be scheduled.

Peer Ministry Team

PARENTAL INFORMATION/RELEASE FORM

Teen's Name:________________________________ Phone:________________

Address:__________________________________ City:________________

State:____________________________________ Zip:________________

Church:___________________________________ Grad. Date:________________

School:____________________________________ Birthday:________________

We (I) give permission for our (my) child to attend and participate in the Peer Ministry Team events sponsored by____________Church during the year beginning __________________________ and ending __________________________.

In case of an accident, we (I) authorize an adult, in whose care the minor has been entrusted, to consent to any x-ray examination, anesthetic, medical, surgical, or dental diagnosis or treatment, and hospital care, to be rendered to the minor under the general or special supervision and on the advice of any physician or dentist licensed under the provisions of the Medical Practice Act on the medical staff of a licensed hospital, whether such diagnosis or treatment is rendered at the office of said physician or at said hospital.

We (I) will be liable and agree to pay all costs and expenses incurred in connection with such medical and dental services rendered to our (my) child pursuant to this authorization.

Father____________________________________ Date________________

Mother____________________________________ Date________________

Guardian__________________________________ Date________________

Insurance Co._____________________________ Policy #________________

PARENTAL INFORMATION/RELEASE FORM (CONTINUED)

Please briefly answer the following questions. These questions will help us in getting to know your son or daughter. Thank you for taking the time.

1. Why do you feel your son/daughter would like to be a part of the Peer Ministry Team?

2. Please list and briefly describe two strengths and one area for improvement for your son/daughter.

3. How could you support your son/daughter in his/her participation on a peer ministry team?

Additional Comments:

Peer Ministry Team

TEEN APPLICATION

Name:____________________________Phone:________________Gr/Yr:____

Address:__________________________________City:___________________

State:____________________________________Zip:___________________

School:______________________________Birthdate:___________________

Please complete the following questions as completely and thoroughly as possible. Please type or print legibly.

1. Why do you want to be a part of the Peer Ministry Team?

2. Please describe your relationship with God.

3. Please list and briefly describe two strengths or gifts you would bring to the team.

4. In what ways does your faith typically influence your daily life?

5. What activities do you plan on participating in during the next year?

6. Why do you feel that you will be able to participate fully as a member of the Peer Ministry Team in addition to the activities previously listed?

Additional Comments:

Signature:____

Covenant/Lifestyle Agreement

Jesus, in his life and ministry, showed us how to live in the world while remaining dedicated to God. The _______________ Peer Ministry Team has chosen to use Jesus and his disciples as the team model which they will attempt to follow.

- I will commit myself to respect and follow our adult team leaders and to serve on the team in the manner they request of me.
- I will help build our community by being consistent in attendance and by treating the other members as I would like to be treated.
- I desire to follow Jesus. Therefore, I will commit myself to serving others, remembering that what I do should bring glory to God and not to myself.
- I will do my best to share the good news of Jesus Christ through my words and prayers, and especially by my actions.
- I will choose to follow the teachings of the church, and to observe carefully the rules the church has established.
- I will commit myself to a lifestyle that will be a model to my peers. I will avoid the use of drugs, alcohol, sex, profanity, negative talk, and gossip.
- I will commit myself to pray on a daily basis for myself and for the members of my team, and will seek guidance from the Holy Spirit.

Signature of Student____ Date ____________

Peer Ministry Team

ADULT RECOMMENDATION FORM

Name of Teen Applying:____

The above teen is applying to be on the____________________ Peer Ministry Team for the _____ - ____ school year. The____________________________ Peer Ministry Team is an organized group of high-school-age youth who are committed to share with peers their Catholic Christian faith through their lifestyle, example, creativity, and words.

Because of the seriousness of this commitment, each applicant is considered carefully. Your honest response to the questions below would greatly help in our discernment process. Thank you for your cooperation.

Your Name: ____

1. How long have you known the applicant and in what capacity?

2. Please comment on what you know of the applicant's relationship with God and/or Christian lifestyle.

3. What are some of the applicant's personal qualities, gifts, or skills that would serve a Peer Ministry Team?

4. What is an area in which you feel the applicant is in need of further growth?

5. Please describe the applicant's relational skills, especially in regard to working in a team environment.

6. In your judgment, should the applicant be accepted to a Peer Ministry Team?

Additional Comments:

Your Signature: ____

Address: ______________________________ Phone: __________________

City: ___________________________ State: ______________ Zip: ______

Personal Interview Questions

- Clarify any questions from the teen application, parent recommendation, or adult recommendation forms.

- Who is a committed disciple of Jesus Christ who has impacted your life? What qualities characterize this person's life? How has this person impacted your life?

- If you were accused of being a Christian in a court of law would there be enough evidence to convict you? Explain.

- What are some of the leadership qualities you would bring to the team?

- What are some practical ways you practice your faith?

- When have you witnessed your faith to another? How did you do it?

- Describe the ideal peer ministry team. What would it take of the members to practically achieve your description? How would you contribute to the making of this ideal team?

Peer Ministry
Introduction Meeting

OUTLINE

1. Opening Prayer
2. Opening Mixer
3. Introductions (name, school, grade, and "why you came tonight")
4. Introduction to Peer Ministry (Talk by Peer Ministry Director)
   - Parish history of peer ministry
   - What is peer ministry?
   - Why is peer ministry effective?
   - What do we do as peer ministers?
   - What is the cost/commitment of being on the team?
   - What are the benefits? (could include a peer minister's witness)
5. Witness Talk by Current or Former Peer Minister
6. Application Process Explanation
   - Explain each form
   - Set due dates
7. Questions and Answers
8. Discernment Prayer
9. Refreshments

15

Cultivating a Lifestyle of Justice and Service

Robin enthusiastically rose to her feet to give the final announcement for the night. Her job was to inform her peers about an upcoming meeting for anyone interested in the parish's annual Appalachian service trip. She began with the basics: the meeting date, place and time, and what would be discussed. She paused for a moment, and almost as an afterthought, offered her personal experience of the trip that past summer.

Robin's energy and enthusiasm was infectious as she described the details of her journey. Her voice cracked, however, when she began to speak of a family she met in Appalachia. As she told of the impoverished conditions in which this family lived, she began to cry. It was a reality so different from her own. For the first time in her life, poverty wore a face. Her tears were not from pity, however. She did not see herself as the rescuer, but the recipient. The joy, simplicity, and love of that poor family touched her heart in an unforgettable way. She received more from the poor than she gave.

Robin's experience is typical of those who live the church's mission of service to those in need. As teens embrace a lifestyle of active servanthood, they take on the mission and work of the church, thus completing the disciple-making cycle.

The reaping phase of the disciple-making process prepares, organizes, and mobilizes young people to bear fruit in the kingdom of God. This stage involves training, equipping, and sending forth disciples to build up the church, serve the poor, and transform the world. In other words, it is the "Go!" stage for teens. This phase is characterized by the process of becoming like Jesus in an other-focused lifestyle. It targets those who have been evangelized, who are growing in faith, and who are now ready to become workers in the kingdom through proclamation, justice, and service. This is the "give it away" phase.

Jesus clearly intended for his disciples to be fruitful (see John 15:5-8). The scriptures generally refer to fruit as the positive result of God working through us. There are several types of spiritual fruit. This chapter will focus on the fruits of justice and service.

The fruits of justice and service foster in teens a deeper sense of compassion, empathy, and understanding of others as they identify and connect with the experience of the poor and oppressed. Our human nature seeks to isolate ourselves from the needs and pain of others. It is easy, if not preferable, to hide our faces from the injustice around us. We reason, "If I cannot see it, it does not exist." When we are exposed to those needs and serve in those situations, we find, as Robin did, that service offers more than it takes. However any personal benefits should not be our primary motivation for service.

Two Types of Service: Direct Action and Social Change

Direct action tends to be the type of service with which we are most familiar. With direct action, we serve by addressing the immediate difficulties of those in need. Direct action often deals with the consequences or results of injustices. For example, a group of teens might provide a helping hand at a local soup kitchen or homeless shelter. A benefit of direct service is that teens directly interact with those in need. Teens enjoy the interpersonal relationships and the action-oriented nature of direct service.

The following are some examples of direct service:

- ✔ visiting or serving the elderly in nursing homes
- ✔ building or rehabilitating homes for the poor
- ✔ collecting toys for children during Christmas
- ✔ stocking or distributing food for a food pantry
- ✔ raising money through hunger retreats or walks
- ✔ teaching or tutoring in a literacy program
- ✔ baby-sitting for mothers of low-income families while they work or attend school
- ✔ helping people with disabilities in various ways.

Social change focuses on the root causes of the effects that are addressed through direct service. Social change examines the structures and systems that cause and perpetuate the problems, and seeks to change these structures through such activities as political advocacy or change groups. Social change requires a knowledge of how systems or structures work.

Examples of social change include:

- ✔ volunteering or financially supporting organizations that seek social change
- ✔ writing congressional representatives or officials of offending corporations
- ✔ helping with voter registration drives
- ✔ attending public meetings where policies are decided.

The best service opportunities combine both direct service and social change.

Direct service alone is not enough because it does not address the root causes of a problem. Social change alone does nothing to address the immediate needs of those experiencing injustice. The best service opportunities combine both direct service and social change. For example, besides handing out blankets and serving food at the local homeless shelter, teens attend a community advocacy meeting for the homeless and learn what long-term solutions are proposed to combat this issue.

Service Experiences

There are many possibilities for justice and service programming in a parish. Some examples are described in this section.

Awareness Experiences

Before an injustice can be addressed, we must identify with the need and feel connected to the issue. Awareness of an injustice can be derived through educational opportunities. However, an even greater impact is usually provided from hands-on experience rather than conventional methods of learning. For example, rather than reading about hunger, a planned fast can help teens experience what it is like to be hungry first-hand.

Single Events

Single events are things like clothing and canned food drives or nursing home and hospital visitations. The commitment is not long-term, and therefore allows teens to evaluate whether or not they would like to pursue service to others in a greater capacity. Because they are not as time-consuming and demanding, single events also provide typically busy teens with the opportunity to serve in at least some small way.

Ongoing Projects and Programs

Ongoing projects and programs give the teens a chance to get involved with a designated or chosen cause on a regular basis. For example, one group may staff a local homeless shelter on the first Friday of every month. Another group may assist with bingo at a nearby nursing home every Wednesday. Ongoing service projects promote a real investment and ownership for those involved.

Immersion Experiences

Immersion experiences are extended service opportunities—like a work camp—which last at least a week and often longer. They allow participants to experience daily living in a given setting and help them to understand the history and causes of certain injustices. A deep awareness that enables one to "walk in someone else's shoes" is fostered.

Immersion experiences can be very expensive and require a tremendous amount of time to plan. However, benefits for both the "givers" and "receivers" are great.

There is also a valuable evangelistic component in immersion experiences When teens get involved in serving and doing the things that Jesus did, they are actually drawn into a deeper relationship with Jesus Christ. For many people, a new or deeper conversion results. Service to others, by its very nature, can be a great experience of evangelization, for the doer is taking an active role in the mission of the church.

Immersion experiences foster deep compassion, and often provide the impetus for teens to question the direction they are choosing for their lives. Immersion experiences encourage teens to consider other career and vocational choices that may be more in line with serving and giving their lives for the benefit of others.

Service Contexts

Justice and service activities, like all of youth ministry, can be a carried out in a variety of different ways. For example, teens need to be given the opportunity to link arms and work side by side with their peers in an effort to make an impact in the world. With their youthful energy and enthusiasm, teens can literally feed off of one another's ideas and dreams.

Depending on the maturity level and experience of our group, it may be valuable for teens to be involved in the initial planning and preparation for the chosen service activity, as well as participating in the actual event. This is another way to demonstrate to them that they have the capacity to make an incredible difference in the lives of others. In a practical sense, it gives them a chance to see and fulfill all the "nuts and bolts" that go into planning a service project.

With their youthful energy and enthusiasm, teens can literally feed off of one another's ideas and dreams.

Besides "just for teens" projects, *family activities* are also a necessary component of service. We have heard such phrases as "the family that plays together, stays together," or, "the family that prays together, stays together." Clichés they may be, but there is great truth in the idea that family satisfaction and closeness comes when families do something positive and meaningful together. Encouraging teens to participate in projects with their families like a CROP walk or serving a meal together at a soup kitchen helps to strengthen the family unit and, in turn, the larger church community.

Likewise, *parish activities* bring the entire faith community together. Gathering together for parish-wide outreach helps people feel connected and united to one another in a meaningful way. Teens can and should participate in these outreach events.

Some parishes do Thanksgiving and Christmas baskets for the poor and underprivileged people in the community. Through giving, organizing, and delivering, parishioners of all ages can help with this project. Parishes may also maintain a food pantry, adopt a sister parish to whom they can tithe and support, sponsor and send out lay missionaries into third-world countries, or create an escort service that will enable the elderly who cannot drive to attend Sunday Mass.

Connecting with other churches, in an ecumenical effort, is a great start at committing to *larger community efforts*. By focusing on our common beliefs, we will multiply our service and justice efforts exponentially. Community-wide events like baby-sitting co-ops for poor mothers, or pro-life activities, typically involve people from many different denominations. When churches come together to serve the needs of the poor and the oppressed in their community, teens get an invaluable experience of participating in the larger "body of Christ."

Steps to Planning a Service Event

Seven primary steps are involved in the planning of a service event. A description of each step follows.

1. Assess the Need—Assessing the need is really a two-fold activity. Both the needs of those "doing" the service and those "receiving" the service must be assessed.

When assessing the needs of those who will receive the service, ask and answer a number of questions: What are the perceived needs? What are the unperceived needs? Who or what will be targeted? What resources are needed to accomplish the task(s), and are they available? What is the deadline for meeting this need? Has any other group attempted to address the need?

Talk with pastors, civic and community leaders, and anyone who may have an "ear" to the "pulse" of society. Their feedback is very important.

It is also critical that we assess the needs of those "doing" the service, in this case the teens. We must ask and respond to questions like: Where are they developmentally? What types of events will work with them? Are they mature enough to handle a chosen project? What things will help them to grow spiritually? What skills must they have?

It is important that we make prayerful and Spirit-led project choices. If not, then even our good intentions can be accomplished in vain.

2. Choose Projects—Based on the assessed needs of the community and the teens, choose appropriate projects. If we really want to motivate teens to take some action in the world, present them with a number of possible options and allow them to choose for themselves. Allowing teens to choose ensures their future investment. Again, choices should be made prayerfully.

3. Prepare the Teens—First, prepare the teens spiritually. Connect the service they have chosen to Jesus' very ministry.

Second, teens need to be educated about the issues at hand. Help them to understand the injustice(s) that they will be addressing, including some of the structures and policies that have helped to create the situation. Take education to a deeper level by helping them to see why the need exists.

Finally, adequately train and teach the teens in the skills they will need when they get to the service site. If listening skills are required, take some time to review or teach those skills (see page 226). If they will be doing some construction at a work camp, give them an overview of what is going on and what they will be doing. In order for teens to have the best possible service experience, they must be fully prepared in every way.

4. Plan the Project—For an immersion or work camp project, the planning will be extensive; for some other events, it will be fairly simple. We must be sure to address every last detail. Questions to ask and answer are:

- ✔ What will we be doing?
- ✔ Do we have appropriate permission?
- ✔ What will we need to do to accomplish this?
- ✔ Where will we be doing it?
- ✔ How will we get there?
- ✔ To whom and how will we promote the event?
- ✔ Who will be participating?

✔ Who will the adult chaperones be?
✔ Do the participants have a detailed description and itinerary of the event?
✔ Who will be supervising the project?
✔ Will the project require a budget? If so, how much?
✔ If money is required, how much will each participant have to contribute?
✔ Do I have a release form for each participant?
✔ If overnight stay is require, where will we stay?
✔ What food provisions will be necessary?

5. Implement the Project—Even at the time of the project's implementation, we need to take time to pray as a group for its success and in thanksgiving for the willingness of the participants to adopt Christ's mission. They may be exhorted with the words of St. Paul: "Whatever you do, do from the heart, as for the Lord and not for others…." (Colossians 3:23).

As the project is being fulfilled, we need to stay attentive to those involved, being sensitive to their needs. If someone is working alone and could use a partner, we should find one for her or him. If someone needs a break, we should allow it. It is our responsibility to do whatever is necessary and realistic to make the experience the best it can be. A project of this kind should also be fun.

6. Reflect and De-brief With Teens—Giving teens time to talk about, discuss, and prayerfully reflect on the opportunity is a critical part of the overall experience. Oftentimes, there are really significant issues with which teens can grapple after encountering people in need. We can approach sharing from a variety of different levels. Some of these questions can be addressed:

✔ Regarding the senses, what smells, sights, tastes, feelings, and sounds did they experience?
✔ What were they thinking?
✔ Did they learn something about the people they were serving?
✔ Did they learn something about themselves?
✔ Did God speak to them at any point during the project?
✔ Would they do it again if they had the opportunity?
✔ What would have made the experience better?

Participants need ample time to process the experience. Keeping an ongoing journal during the experience is often helpful. It is also important to place reflection periods at appropriate intervals. For example, a brief time for discussion at the end of a day-long event might be ample, whereas a week-long experience might require more than one segment of processing. Our role is to discern how much time and what type of process is needed.

7. *Evaluate*—Evaluation of the overall experience is as critical as any step. When evaluating the experience, we should be sure to factor in the reflections of the teens during the debriefing. We need to evaluate not only the outcome, but also the entire process from start to finish. Questions to ponder are:

- ✔ Were there any suggestions for improvements or changes that could be made?
- ✔ What could be done differently?
- ✔ Were the participants given the opportunity and able to connect the action to their faith?

Continual evaluation of ongoing service opportunities will allow for changes to be made that will inevitably make the experience better, more efficient, and more effective.

Application

A list of seven "Do's and Don'ts for Service" is included in the resource on page 292.

Summary

As the planted seeds of faith germinate and grow to full maturity, they, by their very nature, cannot be contained, but rather expend their energy, producing all sorts of fruit. Similarly, the reaping stage of the disciple-making process involves the organization, preparation, and mobilization of teens. Following the Lord's command, teens must now be sent out to transform the world and bear much fruit. Justice and service issues come to the forefront in the growing disciples' lives.

Teens can address justice and service needs in the world through direct action experiences and social change. Awareness experiences, single events, ongoing projects and programs, and immersion experiences are some of the ways in which teens can serve their communities and surrounding world. Such experiences can be carried out in the settings of teen-with-teen, family, parish, or community.

As a service event is planned, the coordinator must assess the needs of those "doing" and those "receiving" the service and choose appropriate projects based on that needs assessment. The coordinator must also thoroughly prepare the teens for their venture, carefully plan the event in great detail from beginning to end, implement the project, provide an opportunity for the participants to reflect on the experience during and after its fulfillment, and evaluate the total experience based on a follow-up strategy that is in place.

Do's and Don'ts for Service

1. DO connect service and spirituality in a meaningful way.

The spiritual significance of serving others must be embedded within the experience. Teens must see that their service opportunities are a reflection of the conversion that is taking place in their lives.

2. DO NOT mandate service hours.

Service ought to be something that teens want to do. Mandating young people to serve others propagates the sentiment among teens that "This is just another thing the church is trying to cram down my throat."

3. DO provide interesting and challenging opportunities.

Teens will grow in faith and return for "seconds" if they are interested in what they are doing and feel challenged by the experience.

4. DO NOT neglect appropriate preparation and follow-up.

Preparation includes examining the "big picture" of the event as well as focusing on its ordinary details. Follow-up should focus on two audiences. First, we should follow-up with the teens via a letter, phone call, reunion event, Mass recognition, and the like, attempting to keep the experience alive and fresh in their minds. Second, we should follow-up with the people and/or agency we served to let them know how the teens were benefited by the experience.

5. DO offer up the service in prayer.

Make sure prayerfully to discern that the event will be safe and age-appropriate for our group.

6. DO NOT overwhelm teens with the magnitude of large-scale problems.

There are large-scale injustices that can overwhelm a teen's idealistic heart. When looking at world problems, it becomes very easy for doubt and pessimism to overshadow hope and optimism. Provide a sense of hope as teens nibble away at the oppressive societal foundations that keep people from experiencing life to the full.

7. DO provide meaningful, bite-sized activities while addressing large-scale injustice.

Encourage a mentality among teens that says "Little by little, bit by bit, change can and will occur."

16

THE MATURING FULL-CYCLE YOUTH MINISTRY

It was late June. De and I had just purchased our first home. She was close to seven months pregnant with our first child. We had two months to get our new home in order and prepare the nursery for our new arrival. While cleaning and painting, we were startled by a loud banging at our side door. We had our first visitor.

Welcoming us to the block was our new four-year-old neighbor, Ben. His first question was, "Do you have any kids in the house?"

Ben was the only child on the block at the time and was desperately hoping for a new playmate or two. Pointing to De's stomach, I told Ben, "In about two months, we will have a kid in the house." Ben seemed quite satisfied with my answer and skipped his way home.

Within a couple of days, De went into early labor and had twins. After five weeks in the hospital, we brought Michael and Sarah home. Phil, Ben's dad, told him the good news. Ben was pretty excited about having not one, but two kids to play with.

A few days after the twins came home, Ben was once again pounding on our door. His eyes disappeared in a smile wider than his face, as he anxiously anticipated an opportunity to meet his new playmates. He enthusiastically bounded up the stairs as we led him to the twins' room. When his eyes caught sight of the two little blobs in their one bassinet, his face sank with obvious disappointment. He said nothing, but his expression clearly stated, "What's this? These kids can't play. They just lay there and do nothing!"

Ben hung his head and dishearteningly meandered out the door. The disappointment was too much for him. He had had no idea that it would take some time before those babies would be able to walk, talk, and ride a Big Wheel with him.

Over the years, I've met some youth workers who were not all that much unlike Ben. Because their expectations were unrealistic, they experienced disappointment and disillusionment. As a matter of fact, I was one of them. I thought a solid, mature youth ministry could be raised overnight—and I was just the guy who would do it. But, I have come to realize that there are no youth ministry overnight sensations, just as there are no magical, twenty-four hour harvests. Fruitfulness comes in due season. Mature, disciple-making youth ministries take a lot of time and a considerable amount of effort to develop. We must work patiently, doing all the tasks necessary and in their proper order—laboring towards the future harvest.

How do we build and maintain a comprehensive, disciple-making youth ministry that is evangelistic, formative, and service-oriented? How do we sequentially link our programmatic efforts into a purposeful movement that leads teens towards greater spiritual maturity and discipleship? What are some important youth ministry principles that we must keep in the forefront of our praxis? This final chapter summarizes the important principles of cultivating an effective parish youth ministry.

Starting From Scratch

We must have a clear understanding of our starting point if we are successfully to navigate to our destination. Therefore, if we are beginning a youth ministry from scratch, it is best to start by establishing a team of adult youth workers. We should recruit adult leaders, form them into a community, and foster a passionate vision and plan for creating an impacting youth ministry. Additionally, youth workers should have an opportunity for spiritual formation and renewal, as well as skill training in specific youth ministry aptitudes.

After our team is formed and has established a plan, sowing (or evangelization), the first phase of the disciple-making process, should be a priority. Before we can build a peer ministry team of leaders who are doing effective ministry, we must ignite the faith of these future leaders. By emphasizing evangelistic activities such as retreats, large-group evangelization, and relational evangelization we help foster conversion in young people's lives.

Conversion, or an experience of an "aha moment," creates a hunger for more faith. When teens begin to respond to an evangelistic message and crave more, we can start to emphasize the growth-oriented programs and activities in our strategic plan. For example, we may begin in the fall with a monthly large-group evangelistic program where the gospel is communicated in a culturally relevant manner. Adult leaders may also begin to develop relationships with teens who are attending.

In the winter we may build on these experiences by sponsoring an evangelistic retreat that touches on personally encountering Jesus Christ. After such a significant experience, teens are often interested in following it up with ongoing programming that helps sustain and build on that experience. Therefore, a weekly small faith community opportunity for any interested teens may be the next step. Now we have both sowing and growing programming established; one naturally building off of the other.

At this point, instead of offering a catechetical program that looks great on paper (that no one is really interested in attending), we have designed a sequential process that actually creates the need for catechesis and faith formation by preceding it with evangelization. This movement is not unlike the RCIA (Rite of Christian Initiation of Adults) process that begins with inquiry and leads to catechesis. At this point, the youth ministry program is growing in a step-by-step manner.

As this happens, many teens will want to exercise their faith by taking part in active ministry. This natural desire will give birth to the third phase of the discipling process—reaping. Reaping activities include peer ministry, justice and service, and liturgical ministries. Also, teens who joined a small faith community and feel they want to get involved in ministry may apply to be on a peer ministry team that meets twice a month. This team might now become the leaders and ministers for the retreat and large-group evangelistic programs previously started, or they may begin new efforts. We now have all three phases of the discipling process integrated and linked together in a teleological expression. As the youth ministry continues to grow, we might add new activities, programs, and events in any of the three phases. Examples might include:

"Sowing" Programming/Activities

✔ Evangelistic youth rallies
✔ Social events (pre-evangelistic)
✔ Contacting/relational ministry
✔ Coffeehouse
✔ National, regional, ecumenical youth conferences

"Growing" Programming/Activities

✔ Catechetical retreats
✔ Small faith communities
✔ Religious education classes
✔ Family retreats
✔ Mentoring/spiritual directing programs
✔ Youth liturgies
✔ Confirmation preparation programming

"Reaping" Programming/Activities

✔ Justice and service ministry team
✔ Catechetical ministries
✔ Peer counseling programs
✔ Retreat ministries
✔ Liturgical ministries
✔ Annual work camps/service projects

Although we are categorizing each of the above programs or events into only one of the three phases of the discipling process, it is important to note that no program or event is ever singularly pure in its expression of one discipling phase. There is always overlap. For example, an evangelistic program can have some catechetical elements in it, as a catechetical program can be evangelistic. The key, however, is to develop programs and activities that have as their *primary* purpose one of the discipling phases. We must provide a balance of the three phases, with each purposefully sequenced to build upon the previous, resulting in a full-cycle process. Without each activity being focused on a primary phase of the discipling process, programs and events often digress into a programmatic mush that resembles the old youth-group model—where only the spiritual needs of a few are being met.

Both teen and adult leaders should have a good comprehension of how the phases of the cycle work. Leaders should understand their own particular ministerial role, and how it fits into the whole discipling cycle. If, for instance, we are involved in evangelistic programming, we should exercise our role through sharing our faith; but we should also be able to direct a teen to the next level of programming as we see him or her growing spiritually.

Too often, youth ministry leaders lack a common vision of where the ministry is heading and an understanding of how all the different programs work together to arrive at the desired destination. Many leaders only understand their own particular role and therefore work in isolation. That is why the formation of a well-trained leadership team and the communication of a common vision is the first priority for a youth ministry starting from ground zero.

Beginning From Existing Ministry

However, most readers will not be starting from scratch, but will be working within an already-established system of youth ministry. The first step, in such a case, is to evaluate the programming in light of the three discipling phases (see page 23: "Youth Program Assessment"). Are all three phases represented? Is there a balance in their representation, or is one phase dominating? Is the programming linked in a purposeful manner? Does the leadership understand the vision? Are leaders working together to nurture teens toward greater faith maturity?

Once we assess our present situation and programming, we should establish specific goals and action plans in order to develop a more comprehensive, disciple-making youth ministry. On one hand, this process of assessment and development may affirm what we are already doing and simply involve a little tinkering here and there. On the other hand, our action plan may entail some foundational re-working. Any change should be approached with sensitivity and caution. A wrecking ball mentality often results in crumbled relationships and a sabotaged future. A complete re-working of a youth ministry works best when everyone agrees that it is time to make some major changes.

Some Final Considerations

Finally, I would like to discuss some important factors that have not received much attention due to the nature of our focus, yet are critical issues that merit serious attention from anyone involved in parish youth ministry.

Family Ministry

I believe youth ministry needs to become more family focused. The most effective discipling of teens occurs in their very homes. Because of the developmental nature of adolescence, there will always be a place for extra-familial programmatic expressions. Teens are moving away from their parent's identity en route to establishing their own. Their reference point for approval shifts from their parents to their peers. Teens want to be with their friends. Therefore, we have a unique opportunity and serious responsibility as members of the church to provide a place where young people can gather with their peers and encounter a Risen Lord who longs to give them abundant life. Still, we cannot replace the primary role that parents have in passing the faith on to their children; nor do we want to.

Adolescents want and need the stability and security of their parents' active involvement in their lives. Many teens—especially those ages thirteen to fifteen—will concede that they are thankful for the boundaries their parents provide them (as long as they are not insensitively suffocating). Appropriate parental restrictions can provide teens with a sense of security and protection. In attempting to maintain esteem with their peers, teens will often scapegoat their parents for the unpopular choices they are exhorted to make. They might say to their friends, "I can't do that. My parents won't let me. They suck." Underneath the party line might be a "Thank God! I feel pretty uncomfortable with that, but I don't want my friends to know. My parents can take the rap."

Our efforts should help draw teens and parents together. Family programming can be designed to primarily address one of three phases of discipleship. For instance, we can offer a family rally that is evangelistic in nature or a family-based service project that gives parents and their children an opportunity to minister together. Additionally, we should offer opportunities for parents to get together for support and direction on how to effectively relate with and pass on the faith to adolescents. In other words, one of our goals should be to support and partner with parents, not compete with or judge them.

Integrating Teens Into the Life of the Parish

It is also very important that young people are integrated into the life of the entire parish. Teens should be walking, working, and worshipping alongside the adult members of our faith communities. Youth ministry must be expressed beyond youth-only programming. Teens should be evangelized, grow in faith, and serve within the larger parish community. Again, we should be offering sow, grow, and reap programming options that are intergenerational and situated within the larger life of the parish community. We must foster in teens a connection to the entire faith community, not just the youth ministry. We must foster in the adult faith community an appreciation and love for our teens and assure that they reach out and welcome teens in the life of the parish.

Promoting Personal Growth

Some youth ministries might be described as being "so heavenly minded that they are no earthly good." We must be concerned with the whole person, not simply the spiritual life. Effective Catholic youth ministry should address adolescent developmental growth issues. We must help promote healthy growth in a young person's self-identity, sexuality, autonomy, responsibility, decision-making, social relationships, and so on. Effective youth ministry facilitates spiritual growth within the context of a teen's whole life.

Multicultural Emphasis

The United States is less perceived today as a melting pot, and more adequately viewed as a multi-colored tapestry of people from diverse ethnic backgrounds, cultures, and races. Catholic youth ministry practices should reflect this shift by recognizing, respecting, and valuing these diverse ethnic and cultural expressions among the teens in our communities. We must develop ministries that address the distinct needs and expressions of the cultures of adolescents in our communities, and promote positive multicultural awareness among all teens. Teens should have the opportunity to understand and appreciate the background and practices of those who are different from themselves. Instilling a respect for others is an important task for the church today.

Conclusion

Fruitful Catholic youth ministry is about making disciples of Jesus Christ. If we are to make disciples, we must be purposeful and intentional in our efforts. Everything we do must be understood in light of how it contributes to the disciple-making process. All of our programs, activities, and events should work together towards this end. Effective youth ministry is not measured by numbers, but by fruitfulness. We are unable to *produce* fruit—that is God's job. Our role is simply to provide the right conditions for growth, fertilize through prayer, and trust in the Lord of the harvest.

May our Lord richly bless your efforts as you "Go, therefore, and make disciples of all nations" (Matthew 28:19).

Application

The resource "Cultivation Strategy" provides a visual summary of the phases of disciple-making youth ministry.

Cultivation Strategy

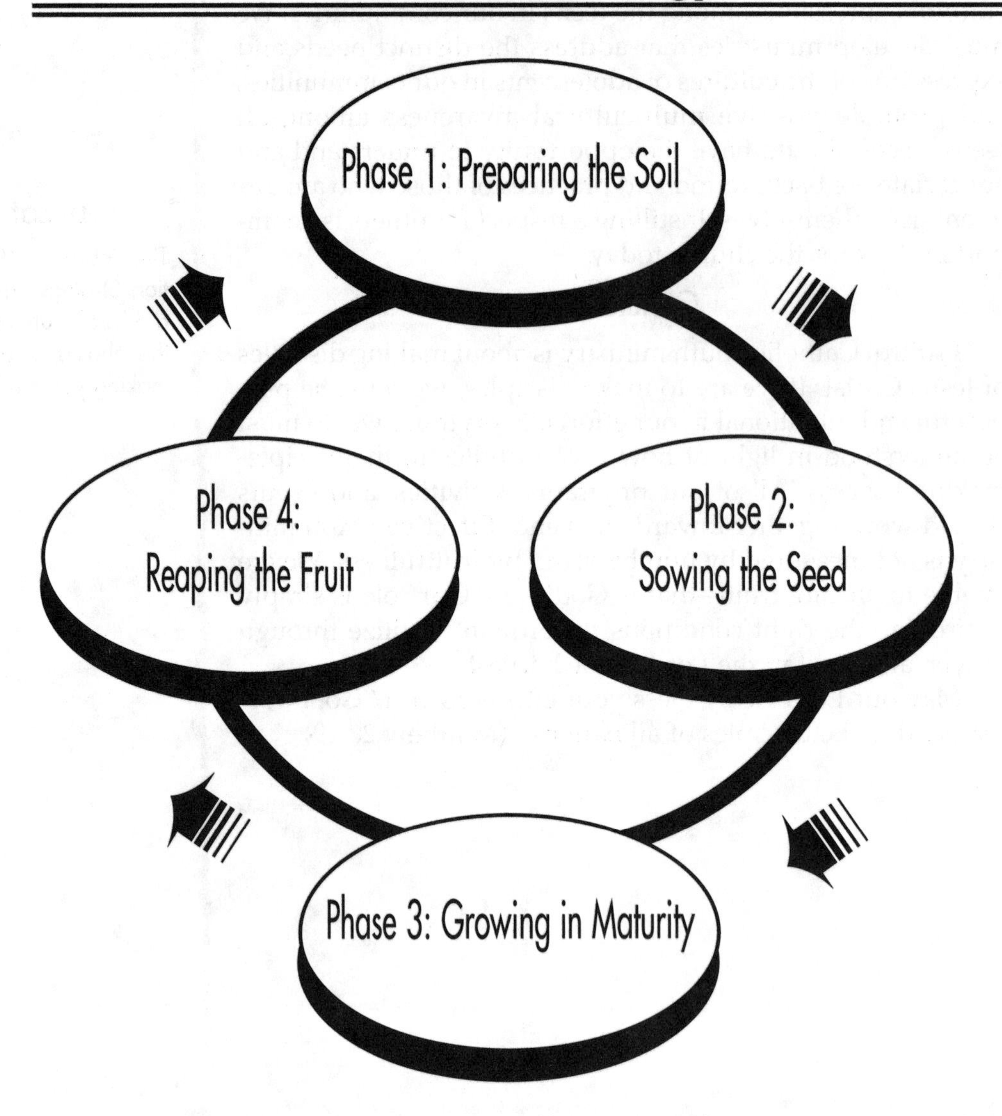

For more information on Cultivation Ministries contact:

CULTIVATION MINISTRIES
P.O. Box 662, St. Charles, IL 60174
Phone: (630) 513-8222
Fax: (630) 512-8233
E-mail: cultivation@earthlink.net
Web site: http://www.ymnetwork.net/cultivation

NOTES

1. Hispanic culture views youth differently from the dominant Anglo culture. Hispanic youth are categorized by life roles. Youth can include unmarried people ranging from twelve to their late twenties.
2. The term disciple is used 27 times in the *Documents of Vatican II.* Avery Dulles, "Discipleship" in *The Encyclopedia of Religion,* ed. Mircea Eliade, Vol. 4:361 (New York: Macmillan, 1987).
3. Michael J. Wilkens. *Following the Master* (Grand Rapids: Zondervan Publishing House, 1992).
4. Dulles, "Discipleship," 361.
5. The singular form of disciple is used only 28 times in the New Testament. The plural form is used 241 times.
6. Paul Borthwick. *Leading the Way* (Colorado Springs: NavPress, 1989), quoting Paul Lee Tan, *Encyclopedia of 7700 Illustrations* (Garland, TX: Assurance, 1984), 735.
7. Austin Flannery, O.P. *Vatican Council II,* Dogmatic Constitution of the Church (Northport, N.Y.: Costellos Publishing, Co., 1981), 50.
8. Ibid., Pastoral Constitution on the Church in the Modern World, 45.
9. *A Vision of Youth Ministry United States Catholic Conference,* Washington, D.C.: 1986.
10. Walter Wink. *Engaging the Powers*. (Minneapolis: Fortress Press, 1992), 298.
11. Peter C. Wagner. *Churches That Pray* (Ventura, CA: Regal Books, 1993), 36-37.
12. Basil Pennington quoted in Tobin, Eamon. *Prayer: A Handbook for Today's Catholic* (Ligouri, MO: Ligouri Publications, 1989), 72.
13. Wink, 299.
14. Anthony de Mello quoted in Tobin, Eamon. *Prayer: A Handbook for Today's Catholic* (Ligouri, MO: Ligouri Publications, 1989), 71.
15. UPI story from the Chicago Tribune, Nov. 13, 1986, pp. 1, 2.
16. Taken from *Coordinator Leadership Resource Binder, Cultivation Ministries* © 1995. Used with permission.

17. Pope Paul IV. *On Evangelization in the Modern World (Evangelii Nuntiandi)* (Washington D.C.: United States Catholic Conference, 1975).
18. *The Challenge of Youth Evangelization*, National Federation for Catholic Youth Ministry, Inc. (New Rochelle: Don Bosco Multimedia, 1993).
19. Pope Paul IV. *On Evangelization in the Modern World,* #21.
20. Ibid., #22.
21. Johannes Hofinger, S.J. *Evangelization & Catechesis,* (New York: Paulist Press, 1976), p. 33.
22. An often quoted saying first coined by Jim Rayburn, the founder of *Young Life.*
23. Rick Lawrence,"What Really Impacts Kids' Spiritual Growth," *Group* Feb. 95, 19.
24. Lawrence, 19-20.
25. James S. Hewett. *Illustrations Unlimited,* (Wheaton, IL: Tyndale House, 1988), 318.
26. Adapted from Wayne Rice, *Up Close & Personal,* Youth Specialties, Inc. (Grand Rapids, MI: Zondervan Publishing House, 1989), 14.
27. Adapted from Anthony Campolo, *You Can Make a Difference* (Dallas, TX: Word Publishing, 1984) 100-101.
28. *Renewing the Vision: A Framework for Catholic Youth Ministry,* (Washington D.C.: United States Catholic Conference, 1997).
29. *The Challenge of Adolescent Catechesis: Maturing in Faith* (Washington D.C.: National Federation For Catholic Youth Ministry, 1986).
30. Dallas Willard. *The Spirit of the Disciplines,* (San Francisco: HarperCollins, 1988), 160-62.
31. Based on surveys *Cultivation Ministries* administered to over 500 youth in Michigan and Illinois.
32. H. Steven Glenn and Jane Nelsen Prima. *Raising Self-Reliant Children in a Self-Indulgent World* (Publishing & Communications, P.O. Box 1260SR, Rocklin, CA 95677 916-624-5718,1988), 24.
33. Ibid., 30-31.
34. Thomas H. Groome. *Christian Religious Education.* (San Francisco: Harper & Row, 1980), 184-231.
35. *Theological Dictionary of the New Testament*, Vol. III, ed. Gerhard Kittel (Grand Rapids, MI: Wm. B. Eerdmans Publishing Co., 1965), 638.

36. *Catechism of the Catholic Church* (Ligouri, MO: Ligouri Publications, 1994), 8.
37. *Renewing the Vision: A Framework for Catholic Youth Ministry* (Washington D.C.: United States Catholic Conference, 1997).
38. Ibid.
39. National Conference of Catholic Bishops. *To Teach as Jesus Did* (Washington, D.C.: United States Catholic Conference, 1972).
40. John Thomas, C. Maxwell. *Developing the Leaders Around You* (Nashville, TN: Nelson Publishers, 1995), 37.
41. Daniel A. Tagaliere. *How to Meet, Think, and Work to Consensus* (San Diego: Pfeiffer & Company, 1992), 2.

20. [illegible] Burning [illegible] (Chicago?: [illegible] Mary [illegible] Publications, [illegible]).

21. *Remembering Who We Are* [illegible] (Washington, D.C.: United States Catholic Conference, [illegible]).

22. Ibid.

23. National Conference of Catholic Bishops, [illegible] (Washington, D.C.: United States Catholic Conference, 19[illegible]).

24. [illegible] Thomas [illegible] [illegible] (Nottingham?: [illegible] Press, [illegible]).

25. Daniel [illegible] [illegible] Notre Dame, [illegible]).